SLAVERY IN THE BRITISH EMPIRE
AND ITS LEGACY
IN THE MODERN WORLD

# Slavery in the British Empire and Its Legacy in the Modern World

Steve Cushion

MONTHLY REVIEW PRESS
*New York*

Copyright © 2025 by Steve Cushion
All Rights Reserved

Library of Congress Cataloging-in-Publication Data
available from the publisher

ISBN 978-1-68590-100-4 paperback
ISBN 978-1-68590-101-1 cloth

Typeset in Minion Pro

MONTHLY REVIEW PRESS, NEW YORK
monthlyreview.org

5 4 3 2 1

# Contents

Acknowledgments | 7
Foreword by Luke Daniels | 9
Preface | 13
Introduction: The Political Economy of Enslavement
    in the British Empire | 18
    The Calculation of the Modern Equivalent
        of the Value of Money | 26
    Terminology | 27

CHAPTER 1: THE EARLY DAYS | 28
    Divide and Rule | 30
    Sir Robert Geffrye (1613–1703) | 34
    Royal African Company | 35
    East India Company | 37
    Charity | 38

CHAPTER 2: THE BRITISH ATLANTIC EMPIRE | 41
    New England and the West Indies | 42
    Trafficking in Enslaved Africans | 44
    Indigenous Slavery and Genocide | 47

CHAPTER 3: PLANTATION MANAGEMENT | 53
    Soil Depletion | 54
    Scientific Management | 56
    Christian Slavery | 59

CHAPTER 4: LAW AND ORDER | 66
    The South Sea Company | 67
    Enclosures | 70
    The Black Act | 78
    West India Dock and the River Police | 80

CHAPTER 5: FINANCE AND INDUSTRY | 88
    Sugar and Health | 90
    Origins of Industrial Capitalism | 91

Guns, Steam, and Steel | 93
Financing the Business of Slavery | 100

CHAPTER 6: AMELIORATION, RESISTANCE,
   AND EMANCIPATION | 104
   A Different Kind of State | 107
   Radical Abolitionists | 110
   Breaking Their Own Chains | 113
   Amelioration | 116
   Demarara Rebellion | 117
   Enslaved Women | 121
   The Baptist War, Jamaica, 1831 | 127
   Compensation and Compromise | 130

CHAPTER 7: THE ORGANIZED WORKING CLASS | 139
   Cotton Production | 140
   British Responses to the U.S. Civil War | 143
   Marxism and the Political Economy of Slavery | 150
   Morant Bay | 164

CHAPTER 8: IMPERIAL RECONFIGURATION | 167
   Free Labor, Free Trade | 168
   Reorganization of Labor | 170
   Resistance | 174
   The Riot Is the Ballot Box of the Poor | 175
   Race and Class | 177

Conclusion | 181
Further Reading | 194
Selected Bibliography | 200
Notes | 205
Index | 234

# Acknowledgments

I would like to thank: Kate Quinn, Gad Heuman, Leonie Jordan, Mary Turner, Merilyn Moos, Michael Yates, Susie Day, Erin Clermont, Ian Birchall, Danny Reilly, Dylan Vernon, Emily Morris, Jean Stubbs, Carrie Gibson, Daniel Palacios Gonzalez, Kesewa John, Luke Daniels, Cauline Brathwaite, Ayodele Martin, Rafael Andrews, Chris Powell, Frank Murray, Laura Miller, Marsha Hinds Myrie, Nadine Finch, Ozzi Warwick, Paul Ward, Omar Leon, Bibi Elberse, Kwabena Dennot Nyack, Constance Bartholomew, Margaret Busby, David Horsley, Jane Bassett, Mike Simons, Soraya Adejare, Gareth Jenkins, Sasha Simic, Christian Høgsbjerg, Leah Levane, Les Kennedy, Glenroy watson, Judy Richards, Mark Anthony Bastiani, Darren Lewis, Graeme Atkinson, Alan Scott, Noreen Scott, Jean Tate, Phil Marfleet, Candy Udwin, Lynne Hubbard, David Denny, Pat Gordon-Smith, Mandy Banton, Jean Besson, Lesley Catchpowle, Deborah Lavin, Francis King, David Morgan, Greta Sykes, Duncan Bowie, Leila Kelly, Fabienne Viala, Pat Noxolo, Ken Fuller, Jenny Golden, Pete Green, Katie Donnington, Richard Kirkwood, Jenny Bulstrode, Mike Barton, Sybil Cock, Tony Conway, Roger McKenzie, Angelina Rojas Blaquier, Jorge Renato Ibarra Guitart, Jorge Ibarra Cuesta, René González Barrios, Belkis Quesada, Yoel Cordoví Núñez, Elvis Rodríguez Rodríguez, and Servando Valdés Sánchez for their advice, encouragement, and assistance.

*This book is dedicated to the
staff of the University College Hospital Macmillan
Cancer Centre and Holly House Hospital*

# Foreword
by Luke Daniels

The movement for reparations has picked up momentum and is steadily growing. Two of the key demands by Caribbean governments are for an apology and reparations to be paid for the heinous crime of enslavement of Africans in the Americas. Their demands fell on the deaf ears of the last Tony Blair Labour Government and the four consecutive Conservative prime ministers. All responded with a version of too long ago, time to move on, looking to the future, albeit with lots of regrets and sorrow, but steadfastly no apologies. How long the British establishment can withstand the pressure for an apology and reparations is anybody's guess, but time is not on their side, as other European enslaver governments are beginning to apologize and make some limited attempts at reparations, or at least show they are prepared to consider the issue seriously. The Church of England, apologizing for slavery and putting aside £100 million, seemingly to help young Black people in the UK to become entrepreneurs, does not go far enough. Stipulating that the sum be spent in the UK ignores the millions of descendants of enslavement living in poverty, ill-health, lack of opportunity, and with the legacies of enslavement in the Caribbean. The Church is studiously not calling the pot of money reparations, although it is a fraction of the sum they were awarded for the loss of their enslaved. The British government paid the enslavers £20 million in 1834 for the loss of their "property." Thanks to the excellent work of Catherine Hall, Richard Draper, and others at UCL (University College London), we know exactly who received what. That many of the "heirs" of slavery are also apologizing and making some reparations can only add to the pressure on the British government to at least have the conversation the Caribbean governments have been calling for.

The idea of reparations is not a new one as the trafficked Africans received not a penny at emancipation. Many no doubt took what reparations they could lay their hands on, as they departed the crime scene of their enslavement. There are recorded instances of demands for reparations going back centuries. Prince Hall, a black lawyer born in Barbados, was ignored when he lobbied Massachusetts legislators in 1777 for reparations. Some Jamaican enslaved even wrote to Queen Victoria demanding they be given land, also ignored. More recently Audley Moore, aka Queen Mother Moore, collected one million signatures in 1963 to lobby President Kennedy for compensation. Met with silence. Here in the UK, one of the first Black MPs, Bernie Grant, tabled a motion in the House of Commons in 1993 calling for reparations. Lord Anthony Gifford in 1996 also raised a motion in the House of Lords for reparations. Today groups in Britain fighting for reparations are making international links around the world to strengthen the movement. African and Caribbean governments are also working closer to raise their demands for reparations.

The cold-blooded murder by police of George Floyd saw Black and White people the world over take to the streets demanding justice and an end to racism. But it is not only in the United States that African heritage people are victimized and often killed by the police. Wherever Black people find themselves they are confronted with discrimination—a legacy of the ideology of racism developed to justify the enslavement of Africans for over four hundred years. We are here in the "mother country" because of the legacy of enslavement and colonialism. The mistreatment meted out to the Windrush generation who were separated from children and loved ones for generations is reminiscent of the dehumanizing practices of enslavement.

In 1944, when Dr. Eric Williams wrote *Capitalism and Slavery* arguing that the enslavement of Africans was crucial to the development of the Industrial Revolution no one in the UK would publish it for twenty years. Ignoring and denying the role enslavement played in making Britain one of the richest countries in the world continues in the elite class. Burying heads in sand will bring no results as the issue of reparations will not go away. Much has been written about enslavement in the Americas, but Steve Cushion's book draws attention to the spoils of enslavement. This is the tool the reparation activists have been waiting for. Cushion goes after the money—he has brought together history and economics in a compelling argument for the paying of reparations. The book goes to the heart of the issue with facts and figures to make it one of the best tools available for all those fighting for reparations for the enslavement of Africans. No stone is left unturned as he unearths the crimes committed against my African ancestors. He calculates the astronomical sums made from this heinous crime and leaves one in no doubt as to who should pay for the crime. He exposes the deep flaws of capitalism with its greed that would see humans treated as mere machines for producing quick profits—with its cold calculations of what a human life was worth—whether to kill with overwork in seven years or to sustain a miserable life for a bit longer with no hope of escape.

We applaud all those who have come forward to apologize for their ancestors' crimes that allowed them the possibility to not only dream but often to realize those dreams. It is right that they join with the descendants of the enslaved in the fight for justice. A fight that can only help them redeem themselves. This book not only provides the tools for activists fighting for justice for their ancestors it offers the government an opportunity to correct a heinous crime committed against humanity. Sorrow and regrets with the insulting "time to move on" statements are no longer acceptable. It is left to see how many more prime ministers will go down that cul-de-sac. It is time for European governments to put up their hands, own up to their crimes, make apology, and pay reparations.

—LUKE DANIELS
PRESIDENT, CARIBBEAN LABOUR SOLIDARITY

# Preface

Every nation-state has a series of myths, legends, and assumptions legitimating its existence. The United States has the *Mayflower* and the Constitution. The United Kingdom relies on the Dunkirk Spirit and the Abolition of Slavery. These, of course, conceal the uncomfortable historical reality that the growth of the United States was based on slavery, land grabbing, and genocide, while the Battle of Dunkirk was the worst defeat that the British Army ever suffered.

Surely, however, we can all be proud that Britain was the first to abolish slavery and the slave trade. The British Establishment has boasted of its freedom-loving generosity ever since, probably believing its own propaganda. Unfortunately for mythology, Denmark outlawed its citizens' involvement in the trade in 1792 and Mexico abolished slavery in 1829. Meanwhile, it took the British Empire until 1807 to stop the trafficking of enslaved Africans and 1838 to finally abolish legalized chattel slavery. In any case, desisting from a crime against humanity, while welcome, should surely be a cause for remorse and apology rather than rejoicing.

But the history of slavery in the British Empire concerns much more than the United Kingdom and the Caribbean nation-states that are the successors of the British West Indies. Very few parts of the world were untouched by the British Empire or remain unaffected by its legacy today. The Empire started with, and got its financial power from, the business of slavery. The profits from trafficking and enslavement were significant in financing the Industrial Revolution in Britain, and many of today's capitalist corporations can be traced back directly to enterprises that had their first growth through their participation in the West Indian trade. Atlantic slavery was inextricably interwoven with the markets, commodification, capital growth, credit, and raw materials that were required for the expansion of capitalism in Europe and North America.

The original thirteen British North American colonies, which would become the United States of America, were part of the British Empire for over 150 years before 1776. These colonies were based heavily in the business of slavery, not just those directly employing enslaved labor such as Virginia or the Carolinas, but also the more northerly colonies such as Massachusetts or Rhode Island whose economies were based on shipbuilding and rum production for the slave trade, as well as direct trafficking of enslaved Africans. And all thirteen colonies were also based on the ethnic cleansing and genocide of the Indigenous nations, a process that started under the British Empire and continued as the new nation expanded to annex much of the North American continent from "sea to shining sea." The racial discrimination experienced every day by African Americans can be traced back directly to the introduction of the enslavement of Africans by British imperialism, as can so much of the institutional racism in British public life.

Taxation on the profits from the sugar trade provided a sound financial base for the emerging British capitalist state, in particular the Royal Navy, which ensured British domination of trafficking in enslaved Africans and defended the Caribbean colonies from rival imperialist powers. The Royal Navy then went on to become a highly effective military machine for enforcing the will of the British Empire on Africa, India, China, and the Americas.

The business of slavery took place in a context of other means of exploitation and expropriation. West Indian plantation slavery, East Indian and African colonization, landed property in Britain, and land-grabbing in the White settler colonies are normally treated as separate phenomena. However, closer examination shows that they were interconnected, with many individuals profiting from more than one of these income streams. In the 1830s over three hundred British subjects who owned enslaved Africans in the West Indies also had close financial connections to the East India Company.

The loss of the North American colonies caused the British Empire to look to Africa and Asia for new sources of plunder. Cotton textiles from India were originally used as trade goods for the slave trade, but, as steam-powered mechanization overcame the higher cost of labor in Britain, the British Empire deliberately undermined textile production in India, ruining the economy of Bengal. India went from being the world's major exporter of cotton fabric to importing its textiles from Britain, and its economy moved to cash crop production, principally tea and opium.

The British taxpayer funded the emancipation of the enslaved Africans to the tune of 20 million pounds paid to the enslavers. This enabled a reorganization of the British Empire, with some of that compensation used to finance the expansion of the White supremacist settler colonies, which led to Indigenous genocide in Australia and apartheid in South Africa. Many businessmen, who made their initial fortunes in the business of slavery, moved their investments and compensation money to trading with India.

The British government may have abolished slavery in 1838, but the British bourgeoisie continued to profit from cotton produced by enslaved labor in the United States. The British ruling class favored the Confederacy during the U.S. Civil War (1861–1865). It was only the resistance of workers in Britain that prevented the British government recognizing and supporting the slaveholders' rebellion. British capital continued to invest in, and profit from, slave-grown products in Cuba and Brazil right up to the final abolition of slavery in 1888.

Meanwhile, Africa was devastated by the slave trade. It is true that some African rulers collaborated with the European traffickers. There is no oppression without collaboration. However, the increasing demand for enslaved Africans, the selective sales of armaments to friendly rulers, and the direct meddling in African politics so weakened the previously strong African kingdoms that European imperialism was able to quickly colonize the continent. The underdevelopment that Africa continues to suffer can be traced back to 1563, when the ship *Jesus of Lübeck* was chartered by Queen Elizabeth I to a group of merchants involved in the Atlantic slave trade. Today, the exploitation of Africa concentrates on the extraction of natural resources, of both the fossil fuel responsible for global warming and the rare minerals required for the batteries purported to be a solution to the dangers of climate change.

The legacy of slavery in the British Empire lives on. Global warming, which is a threat to the existence of humanity in general and the populations of the Caribbean islands in particular, has its origins in the fossil fuel–driven, steam-powered Industrial Revolution, which, in turn, obtained much of the finance necessary for the launch of new industries from the profits made in the West Indian trade and cheap cotton grown in the United States by enslaved labor.

There are other, less obvious, legacies of slavery. Workers all over the world are subject to practices now known as "scientific management." There is a direct connection between the management techniques developed on the slave plantation and modern human resource management practices. White supremacist racism underpinned the creation of the managerial identity.

Sugar, the major product of slavery in the British West Indies, has become central to the modern diet, in processed and preprepared food as well as fizzy drinks. As a result, there is a worldwide epidemic of obesity. The World Health Organization estimates that two billion people are overweight, with 600 million classified as obese. This has devastating implications for their health.

However, while many of the problems facing the world today

have their origins in slavery in the British Empire, this has not gone unchallenged. The people of the Caribbean and the African Caribbean diaspora are campaigning for reparations for African enslavement. This is a social justice issue that deserves the support of working people everywhere, especially workers in Britain. By exposing the origins of so many of the challenges facing the world today we may make progress toward finding a solution and, hopefully, a better tomorrow for us all.

INTRODUCTION

# The Political Economy of Enslavement in the British Empire

In the four hundred years of the Atlantic slave trade between twelve and fifteen million Africans were enslaved and transported by force to the Americas in conditions that were so inhumane that between one and two million died in the crossing, while millions more people also died in Africa as a result of slave raids, wars, and on the way to the coast for sale to European slave traffickers. British enslavers were responsible for around three million of this total.

Once in the Americas, these enslaved laborers were forced to work in labor camps, where the conditions were so harsh that the accumulation of fatigue, whipping, and hunger resulted in an average life expectancy of seven years, with between 25 and 30 percent dying in the first two years.[1] Edward Littleton, a seventeenth-century Barbados plantation owner who enslaved approximately 160 people, reported that one-fifth to one-quarter of his workforce died every year. To give an example of the rate of attrition, between 1708 and 1735, the island's slaveholders purchased 85,000 Africans, yet during that period the total enslaved population of Barbados only rose by about 4,000.[2]

# THE POLITICAL ECONOMY OF ENSLAVEMENT

By 1807, when the British transatlantic slave trade was abolished, there were, of the millions who had been sent to the British West Indies, only 775,000 survivors, whose numbers would decline still further in 1833 to 665,000. Any attempt on the part of the enslaved to build a normal social life in the few hours of personal time that remained to them was frequently and brutally disrupted, for at any moment they could be sold to different estates and permanently separated from family and friends.

Enslaved women were subject to the same brutal regime as the men, whom they worked alongside in backbreaking field labor. But they were further subjected to the additional oppression of sexual abuse by the managers and owners. Moreover, enslaved women were exploited for their reproductive as well as their productive work. Pregnant women were made to work nearly to their time of childbirth, and were expected to return to work soon after.[3] Historian Barbara Bush quotes Dr. Collins, a "professional planter" and author of the 1803 "Practical Rules for the Management and Medical Treatment of Negro Slaves in the Sugar Colonies":

> The life of an enslaved mother was "upheld by no consolation, animated by no hope ... her troubled pregnancy ending in the birth of a child doomed like herself to the rigors of eternal servitude."[4]

We can therefore add denial of the right to family life to the charge sheet against the business of slavery.[5]

Enslaved workers were paid nothing for their labor power. The island of Jamaica, for example, was a British colony with a slave-based economy for 179 years, from 1655 to 1834, with an average population of 150,000 enslaved workers. Given that, in 1780, a British agricultural laborer was paid around 25 pounds a year, a quick calculation leaves an unpaid-wages bill of £671,250,000, worth about £600 billion in today's money. And this is just for Jamaica. The absence of salaries made the business of slavery one of the biggest businesses of its day.

There is a tendency among many historians to see national

economies as if they were a single entity. This approach neglects the division of nations into classes and interest groups. For example, policies that help the financial services industry may be a disaster for industrial manufacturing. Profit and loss take place at the level of individual enterprises. A single businessman making an exceptional profit can be significant in promoting capitalist development, but his role is obscured if only average figures and global statistics are considered. Quantitative economics as currently practiced has a tendency to insulate the investor from the reality of the exploitation involved in the production of the profit it quantifies. This is particularly true in any discussion of the business of slavery, based as it was on kidnapping, murder, rape, child abuse, and torture. It is more appropriate when discussing the business of slavery, to adopt an older approach referred to as *political economy*, which sets economic factors in their social and political context.[6]

Using the term *prosperity* to describe a total increase in national wealth can also be confusing if the distribution of that wealth is not considered. It is particularly inappropriate to discuss national income in the historical context of the business of slavery, when the overwhelming majority of the population of the British West Indies received no wage income at all.[7] Similarly, to suggest that employers and workers have common interests has more to do with ideology than material reality.

This leads to the question of who is responsible for the actions of the government of a nation-state. To what extent were the employed workers in Britain implicated in these crimes? There is an assumption in many official pronouncements on slavery that citizens and subjects of a nation-state are automatically implicated in, and may be held responsible for, the actions of the government, military, and ruling class of that nation.

There is no way that the government of England or of Great Britain, during the years of legal enslavement, can be seen to have represented anyone other than the landed aristocracy, the enslavers, and slave traffickers, along with merchant capital from the

## THE POLITICAL ECONOMY OF ENSLAVEMENT 21

City of London. The first glimpse of representative government came with the Reform Act of 1832, which was followed almost immediately by the abolition of slavery in the British West Indies. However, much of the debate has so far been conducted in terms of whether Britain, as a nation, profited or not. The term "national interest" is normally used to justify or discredit the policy of the government of the day. During the debate about the abolition of slavery, variants of the term were bandied about, mainly to provide cover for selfish, sectional interest.

The exploitation of enslaved labor in the various slave-based economies of the Americas stimulated Western European and North American capitalist development. The devastating material, economic, social, and cultural damages—in particular for African, Caribbean, and South American societies—continue to haunt the present. European and North American governments and businesses have never properly addressed their role within slavery, neither the historical injustices committed in the various regions nor the ongoing legacies of historically rooted global inequalities.

The wealth gained by looting, enslavement, land grabbing, and murder in Africa, Asia, and the Americas flowed back to Europe and was turned into capital there.[8] The business of slavery led to increasing investment in the Empire, as well as in building maritime and transportation infrastructure. Return on this investment in turn increased the income of British capitalists. At the same time, the re-export of sugar to Europe brought enormous profits.[9] Exports played a leading role in the industrialization process in England between 1688 and 1800, and almost 50 percent of the non-agricultural workforce in England and Wales was employed in production for export, with the increases in overseas sales accounting for much of the growth in manufacturing output.[10]

Sections of the petite bourgeoisie, such as lawyers, clergy, military officers, and government officials, also profited. Whether the working class can be considered to have benefited is more contentious. It might be argued that workers gained employment on the back of the profits made by the enslavers. This argument assumes that employment is beneficial to a worker. But this ignores the exploitation at the root of the relationship between capital and labor. Employers only employ workers in order to make a profit from their labor power, leaving the worker with no say in what is produced once they have sold that labor power to the employer. The only means of survival for the propertyless is to sell their labor power.

The organized working class in Britain has, from its earliest days, expressed its opposition to the enslavement of Africans. The first genuine, independent organizations of workers in Britain, the London Corresponding Society and the Sheffield Cutlers, were resolutely and publicly opposed to slavery.[11] The solidarity of the Lancashire textile workers with the Union in the U.S. Civil War is justly celebrated.

Nevertheless, racism has proved an effective weapon of the ruling class in the class struggle. There has always been a struggle inside the working class between nationalism and internationalism, as there is between class collaboration and anti-capitalism. The campaign for reparations for African enslavement and the fight against the institutional racism of the capitalist state are important fronts in the class struggle.

There is more to the business of slavery than trade and politics. The enslavers needed ideological justification, both as a method of control and to deflect criticism. Business does not take place in a social vacuum; capital requires labor in order to accumulate more capital. Labor can be either enslaved or employed, but in both cases the laborers also have their own interests and the agency to pursue those interests in conflict with the owners of capital. Although the capitalist class has the armed forces of the state as its final defense, it requires ideological justification, both for its own self-respect and to convince its employed and enslaved laborers that there is no alternative to the existing hierarchical organization of society.[12]

Philanthropy and charity were useful ways to disguise the

shabby origins of so much wealth but, to be effective, this apparent generosity has to be public. Thus the proliferation of statues and other memorials to these ruthless businessmen, which play a role in sweeping this history under the carpet. But they are also part of a cumulative ideological construction that extols the great and the good: pub signs, street names, buildings, and schools, all named after ruling-class worthies. This cultural absorption of capitalist memorabilia has become part of a proxy war for control of the dominant narrative of how history is told.[13] When right-wing politicians speak of "taking back our culture," they are referring to a culture of nativism and nationalism.

In the past, this ideological offensive was far from universally successful, as demonstrated by the resistance of both the enslaved workers in the Caribbean and the employed workers in Britain. Thus, this book will examine the political economy of slavery from both sides of the class divide, as well as the different interest groups within the ruling elites. There were differences of economic and political interest between manufacturing capital, on the one hand, and the landowning gentry and their allies, who included the plantation owners, on the other, and both groups needed to control the state for their own ends. The Industrial Revolution required a strong state: a navy to force market access on reluctant overseas populations; the regulation and standardization of trade to enable large-scale, long-distance exchange between businessmen who did not know each other; and courts, soldiers, and police to enforce contracts and property rights, as well as repressing workers' ability to defend their standard of living and conditions of employment.

The abolitionist campaign served the industrialists as a useful stick with which to beat their opponents and produced popular support for parliamentary reform, which eventually gave manufacturing capital control of the House of Commons.[14]

But the contribution of the enslaved Africans to their own emancipation is no less important than political developments in Britain.[15] When looking at resistance to slavery, we also need to consider mass movements such as the various rebellions of the enslaved, the post-emancipation struggle against colonialism, the radical working-class abolitionists in Britain, and the movement of solidarity with the fight against slavery in the Unites States.

The business of slavery took place within a context of other systems of exploitation and expropriation. West Indian plantation slavery, East Indian and African colonization, and land-grabbing in the white settler colonies are normally treated as separate phenomena. However, closer examination shows that they were interconnected, with many individuals profiting from more than one of these income streams.[16] The development of capitalist agriculture was deeply entwined with the business of slavery, as funds from the business of slavery were also important in financing the mass privatization of agricultural land in the eighteenth and nineteenth centuries, a period known as the Enclosures in England and the Highland Clearances in Scotland.[17]

There is a tendency for many studies of slavery to finish in 1838, with the end of chattel slavery in the British West Indies. But British capital continued to profit for another generation from cotton from the United States and coffee from Brazil, as well as copper and sugar from Cuba, all produced by enslaved African labor. Meanwhile, after formal emancipation, the plantation oligarchy in the British West Indies continued to find extra-economic means to extract the maximum profit from the labor force by legal actions such as vagrancy acts or master and servant acts, threatening to evict tenants from their homes and provision grounds, preventing the emancipated laborers from obtaining land for subsistence farming, and, if these measures failed, using police and soldiers to repress any sign of resistance. However, the emancipated workers of the West Indies did not accept such coercion without a fight.[18]

There are also ongoing environmental consequences of the legacy of slavery. James Watt, the inventor of the steam engine, drew much of his early finance from the business of slavery.[19] The fossil fuel–driven steam engine started industrial capitalism onto the path that leads to the present crisis of global warming and climate change.[20] But climate change is not the only environmental legacy of slavery. Intensive monocrop production, begun during the slavery era, has deforested much of the Caribbean and depleted the soil of the islands.[21]

There is a continuation of many business practices, developed during the era of enslavement, which are in operation today. Perhaps this is one reason why business-friendly politicians and conservative historians have reacted so fiercely against the removal of statues and memorials to enslavers.[22]

The damaging effect of the legacy of enslavement on the descendants of enslaved Africans has given rise to the demand for reparations. For these reasons, this study continues up to the present.[23] In 2001, the United Nations finally condemned the transatlantic trade and slavery as a Crime Against Humanity and called on the former European colonizing countries to fight structural marginalization and racial discrimination still affecting the lives of Africans and people of African descent. There are now serious calls from representatives of the African diaspora for reparations for African enslavement. There are also increasing demands for climate reparations, as well as for the criminalization of the continued failure to act to prevent further climate change.[24] An aim of this book is to situate the past crime of enslavement and the modern-day dangers of climate change within the business practices that place profit before people.

The government of the Republic of Barbados is campaigning for the payment of reparations from former colonial powers and institutions that profited from slavery, including some of their present-day individual descendants, families, and companies, whose histories are discussed in this book. Both the government of Barbados and the Caribbean Community (CARICOM), of which Barbados is a member, have set up formal bodies to pursue the claim for Reparations. David Comissiong, vice-chair of the Barbados National Task Force on Reparations, part of the CARICOM Reparations Commission, said:

> The process has only just begun and we trust that we will be

able to negotiate. If that doesn't work, there are other methods, including litigation. It is now a matter that is before the government of Barbados. It is being dealt with at the highest level. This reparations journey has begun. The matter is now for the cabinet of Barbados. It is in motion. It is being dealt with.[25]

## The Calculation of the Modern Equivalent of the Value of Money

The calculation used in this book to relate monetary values of the past to today's equivalent is the *relative income measure,* which measures an amount of income or wealth relative to per capita gross domestic product (GDP). When compared to other incomes or wealth, it shows the economic status or relative prestige value the owners of this income or wealth have because of their rank in the income distribution. More details are obtainable from the MeasuringWorth Foundation.[26]

Today's values calculated in this manner will be placed in brackets after the original figure. For example, the annual rate of inflation between 1657 and 1704 averaged 1.5 percent, making £100 in 1657 the equivalent of £177 in 1704. This accounts for the same original figure being calculated differently, depending on the year. This figure can only be approximate, but it gives some idea of what a particular transaction would be worth today.

Other measures are available. To take an example, of the £20 million used to compensate the enslavers for their loss at the time of emancipation within the British Empire, the relative value of £20,000,000 in 1838 ranges from £1,916,000,000 or $14,953,209,660 to £85,730,000,000 or $107,581,291,050 in 2021. Within this range, there are four choices. In 2021 the relative

- real wage or real wealth value is £1,916,000,000
- labor earnings is £18,260,000,000
- relative income value is £24,770,000,000
- relative output is £85,730,000,000

The equivalent in U.S. dollars to these modern values is also given at the exchange rate current at the time of going to press.

Readers who wish to pursue the matter further may be interested in an article on the MeasuringWorth Foundation site titled "Defining Measures of Worth Most Are Better than the CPI" by Samuel H. Williamson and Louis Cain, emeriti professors of economics at Miami University and Loyola University Chicago, respectively.[27]

## Terminology

The National Archives website contains the following recommendation, which I followed:

> Enslaved person is the preferred term for an individual. Enslaved persons and enslaved people are preferred terms to refer to groups of people. Enslaved can be used as a modifier instead of slave before a person's name, role, or profession, or the modifier slave can be removed and not replaced in that instance, especially if the description elsewhere provides context related to enslaved people or slavery.
>
> Do not remove all uses of slave; the term should be retained when used as a modifier related to economic systems.[28]

The term "working class in Britain" is more useful than "British working class," as it recognizes the importance of immigrant workers in the workforce and as activists in organized labor, including considerable numbers of the descendants of enslaved Africans as well as other victims of British imperialism.

The use of the pronouns "we" and "our," unless used to describe a group of people physically present, presumes a common identity that may not have any validity. At best it can cause confusion, and at worst, can deliberately be used to draw the reader/listener into a presumed grouping, such as race or nation, in an inappropriate manner.

CHAPTER 1

# The Early Days

By the time English settlers established the colony of Barbados in 1627, Spanish and Portuguese colonists had been operating an economy based on enslaved labor for over one hundred years. Despite this late start, English colonists in the Caribbean quickly caught up. One of the first colonists was James Drax, the son of a Warwickshire Anglican vicar, who not only pioneered the use of enslaved Africans on his plantation, but was instrumental in introducing legislation that institutionalized the white supremacy that became a model for the business of slavery in the British Empire in the Americas.[1]

Back in London, Sir Robert Geffrye was a leading light in the trafficking of Africans to the Caribbean via the Royal African Company, a public/private partnership that held the monopoly of the English slave trade. As well as being a trafficker in kidnapped Africans, Geffrye traded as an ironmonger, invested in the East India trade, and was a successful London politician and a philanthropist. He is, therefore, a good example of the interconnections between London finance, English politics, and the early period of the British overseas empire.

But before considering the trafficking of enslaved Africans, the effects of the arrival of European colonists on the Indigenous population of the Americas and the Caribbean in particular must be addressed. The people of the region suffered a demographic collapse, whereby three-quarters of the population were killed by epidemics of smallpox, measles, typhus, and the like, brought from Europe and Africa by the colonists. This was made worse by the violence of the conquest, overwork in mines and on plantations, the breakdown of Indigenous trade networks, loss of land for subsistence farming and resulting malnutrition, as well as massacres and enslavement.[2] Historian Paul Kelton argues: "English-inspired commerce in Native slaves was the element of colonialism most responsible for making indigenous peoples across the region vulnerable to newly introduced diseases."[3]

One suggested effect of this demographic collapse is the phenomenon known as the Little Ice Age, starting around 1650, a period of regional cooling, particularly pronounced in the North Atlantic, when average temperatures dropped by as much as two degrees Celsius. A major contribution to this climate change was the mass deaths of the original population of the Americas, which caused Indigenous farmland to be abandoned. This allowed for extensive reforestation of the Americas, which in turn absorbed carbon dioxide leading to global cooling, colder summers, and more severe winters, worldwide.[4]

The settlers from Europe introduced cattle, pigs, and goats into the Caribbean, clearing much Indigenous vegetation. In contrast to the reforestation on mainland South America, the islands of the West Indies were stripped of their forest cover to make way for cash-crop agriculture. This led to the extinction of many native plants and animals. The colonists had little idea how Indigenous people had managed the landscape, nor were they greatly concerned to find out, as they turned the natural world to commodity production.

The death of such a high proportion of the Indigenous population left the newly arrived settlers in the Caribbean without a labor force. Early attempts by the landowners to use convict labor or political prisoners from Europe did not provide anywhere near the required labor force, so they turned to kidnapping people from Africa.

By 1641, James Drax owned over four hundred acres, making him one of the biggest landowners on Barbados. He was the first to enslave a significant number of Africans—twenty-two—on his plantations. In 1644 he purchased another thirty-four, and by the early 1650s, his plantation, Drax Hall Estate, was worked by over two hundred enslaved laborers. Drax was the first of the English settlers to successfully cultivate sugarcane on a large scale, having learned the techniques of sugar production and refinement from the Dutch, who in turn had acquired their knowledge in Brazil, part of which they had taken from Portuguese control in 1630. The Dutch colonists in Brazil had developed an industry based on enslaved labor that exported thousands of tons of sugar to Europe. Sensing an economic opportunity, Drax and other settlers began cultivating sugar around 1640, with the first Barbados sugar arriving in London by 1643.[5]

By 1654 James Drax presided over a plantation of over seven hundred acres and had ordered the construction of the island's first great house, Drax Hall. Now the richest landowner in Barbados, Drax was not content with purchasing kidnapped Africans from traffickers from England. In 1654 he helped finance two slave-trafficking voyages of the *Hope* and the *Samuel*, ships he jointly owned with two other Barbadian slaveholders.[6] But Drax and the other settlers needed an ideological justification for their activities.

## Divide and Rule

There was nothing scientific or natural about the discrimination experienced the world over on a daily basis by people of African heritage; it was a direct result of the plantation-owners' need for an ideological justification for their use of enslaved labor. Sugar and cotton production are still probably the hardest, most backbreaking jobs in the world; nobody would do such work willingly. Creating the myth that people in Africa were somehow primitive,

# THE EARLY DAYS

ignorant savages who were naturally inferior to Europeans, provided a useful justification for their enslavement.

Initially, the labor force in Barbados was made up of indentured laborers from Britain, poor farmers who had been driven from the land by the enclosures, along with vagrants and convicted criminals, who were working within a system of unfree labor that caused them to be bound by a contract to work for a particular master for a fixed time period. But the largest numbers came as a result of the English Civil War between the Royalists and the Parliamentarians, primarily a power struggle between Parliament and King Charles I. It ended in June 1646 with Royalist defeat and the king in custody, soon to be executed for treason.

Eight thousand Royalists were sent to Barbados between 1645 and 1650. Royalist prisoners of war were sold as servants in Barbados, and thus the government rid itself of potential enemies and made a profit at the same time. Next came the English invasion of Ireland by a parliamentary army led by Oliver Cromwell. After the English victory over the Catholic, Indigenous, Irish army at the Battle of Drogheda in 1649, Oliver Cromwell wrote: "When they submitted, these officers were knocked on the head, and every tenth man of the soldiers killed, and the rest shipped for Barbados."[7]

However, after the end of the Civil War and the successful colonization of Ireland, the supply of indentured laborers dried up. European indentured laborers were unsatisfactory from the landowners' point of view for a number of reasons: their period of indenture was limited; there was a limit to the whipping and torture that could be used to extract greater productivity; and word of the ill treatment they received got back to England and deterred further recruiting. Besides, one of the reasons people from Britain accepted the consequences of indentured labor in the first place was the hope of acquiring some land after their term expired, but they soon found that all the land had already been taken by the first colonists. As the supply of indentured labor from Britain and Ireland started to dry up, the landowners turned to purchasing kidnapped Africans. Faced with an increasing shortage of labor, the landowners discovered an alternative: the Dutch planters in Brazil had found that African enslaved laborers were a considerably more economical proposition, especially when Brazil's move to sugar monocrop production dramatically increased the demand for laborers as well as the intensity of their labor. This, then, accelerated the move from indentured to enslaved workers.[8]

However, in 1649, a conspiracy was discovered in Barbados for a joint rebellion of English and Irish indentured laborers in alliance with enslaved Africans.[9] This was the plantation owners' worst nightmare, and they did their best to disrupt any such workers' unity by giving small privileges to the poor Europeans. A militia became necessary to keep control of the enslaved Africans who, by 1660, greatly outnumbered the European population. European men were given the right to hold public office, to sit on juries, to vote if they held sufficient property, to carry arms, to move freely, and to engage in economic activity.

In contrast, enslaved Africans were kept subjugated by arbitrary and tyrannical punishments, always supported by the full force of the colonial state.[10] This chronic subjugation was first inscribed in the 1661 Barbados Slave Code, *An Act for Better Ordering and Governing of Negroes*, which established that enslaved Africans could be bought and sold. This act, which Drax had a large hand in drafting, instituted a system of legally sanctioned racial discrimination and violence:

> If any Negro or slave whatsoever shall offer any violence to any Christian by striking or the like, such Negro or slave shall for his or her first offense be severely whipped by the Constable. For his second offense of that nature he shall be severely whipped, his nose slit, and be burned in some part of his face with a hot iron. . . . And it is further enacted and ordained that if any Negro or other slave under punishment by his master unfortunately shall suffer in life or member, which seldom happens, no person whatsoever shall be liable to any fine therefore.

The Barbados Slave Code was adopted in Jamaica and other British colonies in the Caribbean, then was brought to the South Carolina colony as the legal basis for the treatment of enslaved workers in the British North American colonies.

The term "White," as applied to people of European heritage, starts to become common in the English language after Bacon's Rebellion of 1675 to 1676 in the English colony of Virginia, an armed rebellion by settlers. It was led by Nathaniel Bacon against colonial governor William Berkeley, after he refused the settlers' demands to seize the land of the Indigenous people. This rebellion sparked an alliance between European indentured laborers and African enslaved workers that frightened the colonial upper class. Colonial rulers responded by hardening the racial nature of slavery, culminating in the Virginia Slave Code of 1705.[11]

Key figures in the development of White supremacy were the Enlightenment philosophers John Locke and David Hume, both of whom worked in the British colonial administration. Locke helped draft the Virginia Slave Code.[12]

Allowing some inexpensive privileges to the poorer European settlers linked the white underclass with their white superiors, which gave race an importance it never previously had and began the institutionalization of White supremacy. If race is a social construct, then *White* is a construct of capitalism.

Privileges are granted and can be taken away. Rights are fought for and are more secure if they are universal. Those who feel they are entitled to privilege feel threatened by the unprivileged and grateful to the elite who granted them their minor privileges. This gratitude can develop into a belief among poor Whites that, because they share a skin color with their rulers, they have a common interest. This belief gives the poor White a feeling of having a stake in the status quo, obscuring the class privilege that goes with wealth.

Theodore Allen, author of *Class Struggle and the Origin of Racial Slavery: The Invention of the White Race*, writes:

First, racial slavery and white supremacy in this country was a ruling-class response to a problem of labor solidarity. Second, a system of racial privileges for white workers was deliberately instituted in order to define and establish the "white race" as a social control formation. Third, the consequence was not only ruinous to the interests of the Afro-American workers but was also disastrous for the white worker.[13]

## Sir Robert Geffrye (1613–1703)

There is a statue of a trafficker in enslaved Africans called Sir Robert Geffrye outside the Museum of the Home in Hackney, East London. The debate over this statue has opened a window onto the slave trade and its role in the creation of modern Britain. Geffrye's life, as a successful London businessman and politician, well illustrates the early development of capitalism in England, along with the relationship between the City of London and the origins of imperialism—particularly the importance of all aspects of the business of slavery.[14]

Geffrye came to London in 1630 from Landrake in rural Cornwall, where his family owned a farm. The family was connected to several influential members of the Ironmongers Company in the City of London, and this secured him an apprenticeship with Richard Peate, a trading ironmonger. He graduated from his apprenticeship in 1637 and was admitted as a Freeman of the Ironmongers Company and a Liveryman in 1646.[15] The London livery companies had started out as guilds to control specific trades, but by the seventeenth century had become cabals of rich businessmen who conspired to restrict profits to themselves and exclude others. Then, as now, the wealthy covered their tracks by engaging in charitable activities, although these charities were normally restricted to their own members and retainers who had fallen on hard times. The livery companies were more than just trading consortia; they also controlled the politics of the City of London, electing the Lord Mayor and Aldermen. They appointed magistrates who sat in judgment, managed policing, and even had their own militias, the Honourable Artillery Company and the Trained Bands. Finally, the livery companies served as dining clubs, enabling their members to do business over copious dinners and vast quantities of wine—a function they still perform today.[16]

Robert Geffrye did not restrict himself to the ironmongery trade. He was an investor in and officer of the Royal African Company, the East India Company, the Levant Company, The Honourable The Irish Society (Society of the Governor and Assistants, London, of the New Plantation in Ulster, within the Realm of Ireland), as well as the part owner of a slaving ship, the *China Merchant*, that was active in both the East India and West Indian trades. He was a colonel in the city militia and a substantial trader in tobacco, then entirely produced by enslaved labor.[17] On Robert Geffrye's coat of arms, when he was knighted, were placed five iron bars, which were a commodity in the slave trade.[18]

Colonial trade emerged as the most dynamic sector of the European capitalist economy in the seventeenth century, and it was the basis of British economic expansion in the eighteenth century.[19] At the heart of this Atlantic economy lay the slave trade and the plantation economy based on enslaved labor.

## Royal African Company

Originally set up in 1660 as the Company of Royal Adventurers Trading into Africa, the enterprise was relaunched in 1672 as the Royal African Company, with James, Duke of York, soon to be King James II, as its governor until 1688 and its largest shareholder.[20] The Royal African Company transported about five thousand enslaved people a year across the Atlantic and "shipped more enslaved African women, men and children to the Americas than any other single institution during the entire period of the transatlantic slave trade."[21] Between 1672 and 1713, the company's five hundred ships exported £1,500,000 [£45 billion, $56 billion][22] worth of goods to West Africa; transported 170,000 enslaved

Africans across the Atlantic, and returned with thirty thousand tons of sugar and enough gold to make half a million Guinea coins.²³

The Royal African Company owned several forts and slave trading posts, known as factories, on the West African Coast, which were staffed by permanent agents, providing fixed bases to organize what developed into a triangular mode of trade. On the first leg of the triangular journey, the Royal African Company exported English manufactured goods, East Indian textiles, and European iron and copper, all of which were traded in West Africa for ivory, gold, dyewoods, palm oil, other African raw materials, and in addition its primary concern, enslaved Africans. The enslaved Africans were then transported on the Middle Passage, as the leg of the slave trafficking triangle between West Africa and the Caribbean was known, to provide labor for the sugar plantations of the West Indies. The final leg of the journey transported Caribbean products, mainly sugar, to be sold in England or re-exported to Europe, as well as the bills of exchange by which the plantation owners arranged their credit and settled their debts.²⁴

The Royal African Company acted as a means for the Stuart royal family, Charles II and James II, to finance their dictatorial rule without parliamentary sanction, while personally enriching themselves and their associates and backers from the City of London. Denying other City of London businessmen, as well as traders based in other cities, access to this profitable trade was one of the reasons the increasingly powerful capitalist class in England turned against Catholic King James II. It led to their support, in 1688, for the invasion from the Netherlands, led by Protestant William of Orange and James's daughter Mary Stuart, which resulted in the coup d'état known as the Glorious Revolution. Opposition to the monopoly of the Royal African Company also came from the owners of the plantations in the West Indies, whose increased wealth, produced by enslaved labor, enabled them to buy growing influence in the British Parliament.

The Royal African Company could not supply enough enslaved

laborers to meet the West Indian landowners' requirements for the growing slavery-based economy. At the same time, restricting the numbers shipped by the company enabled it to exploit its monopoly to force up the price of enslaved Africans. But there were also financial difficulties. Because of the long-term nature of the capital investment, resulting from the long round trips at sea, the Company found it increasingly difficult to purchase the £100,000 [£315,800,000, $400,000,000] worth of goods required for annual export to Africa. So the company began to borrow money to pay dividends and, by 1688, interest payments reached £6,000 [£18,950,000, $24,000,000] per year. Because much of this debt had been raised from among the shareholders themselves, they were in effect receiving interest on payments they were making to themselves. Such a financial pyramid scheme could not last forever.

The investors in the Royal African Company tried to cling on to their legal privileges, as when Edward Colston (the slave trader whose Bristol statue was pulled down by antiracists in June 2020) sold the new King William III a large shareholding in the company. But pressure from businessmen excluded from the trade, as well as the demands of the West Indian plantation owners for ever-increasing supplies of enslaved labor, forced Parliament to pass the Trade with Africa Act 1697. This opened the slave trade to all English merchants who paid a 10 percent levy to the company.[25]

The loss of monopoly precipitated the decline of the Royal African Company.

## East India Company

In the seventeenth century, most legal foreign trade was carried out through cartels known as companies. At this time, the English East India Company was not yet primarily engaged in colonization but was still mainly a trading company using its armed forces to fight the Dutch East India Company (Vereenigde Oost Indische Compagnie), rather than to directly conquer territory in India.

That would come later. However, it was already an important player in the English imperial network.[26] In particular, the trade in calico, a cotton textile, formed an important part of the trade with India. As well as selling this cloth at a profit in London, East India merchants supplied calico for re-export to West Africa, where it was used as trade goods to purchase enslaved Africans.[27]

Most histories of the period treat the East India and the African trades separately, but in fact they were deeply entwined, with ship owners operating in both, depending upon which offered the best immediate profits. It was not just cotton textiles from India that were used as trade goods for the slave trade. The East India Company also traded in glass beads and cowrie shells, which were used as currency in West Africa. Moreover, while the company was not directly involved in the West African trade, it did enslave people in Madagascar and traffic them to the Caribbean from as early as 1621.[28] Given the overlapping directorships between the Royal African Company and the East India Company, it is difficult to untangle the extent of involvement, but it is clear that the City of London business community was deeply embedded in the business of slavery at this time.

The Royal Navy was also vitally important to the success of the slave trade. Without the power of its warships, foreign powers and pirates would have wreaked havoc with the trade. At the very least, the enslavers would have had to provide their own naval protection at considerable expense. Far better for them that the English state take charge of their protection and, at the same time, provide business opportunities in shipbuilding and refitting at public expense. The symbol of this connection was James, Duke of York, King Charles's brother, who was both Governor of the Royal African Company and High Admiral.

### Charity

A minority cannot rule a majority by force alone. It must convince the lower classes to submit or confuse them into paralysis. To

# THE EARLY DAYS

accomplish this, the capitalist class presents itself as the benefactor of mankind. Philanthropy is the key to this sleight of hand. Charitable giving also has the advantage of allowing the rich to determine social policy as they wish.[29] As Frederick Engels wrote:

> The English capitalist class is charitable out of self-interest; it gives nothing outright, but regards its gifts as a business matter, makes a bargain with the poor, saying, "If I spend this much upon benevolent institutions, I thereby purchase the right not to be troubled any further, and you are bound thereby to stay in your dusky holes and not to irritate my tender nerves by exposing your misery. You shall despair as before, but you shall despair unseen . . . this I purchase with my subscription of twenty pounds for the infirmary!"
>
> It is infamous, this charity of a Christian capitalist! As though they rendered the workers a service in first sucking out their very life-blood and then placing themselves before the world as mighty benefactors of humanity when they give back to the plundered victims the hundredth part of what belongs to them![30]

When Geffrye died in 1704, he left around £13,000 [£29,900,000, $37,538,400], which was split roughly equally between surviving friends and relatives on the one hand, and charitable donations on the other.[31] Nothing was left to ameliorate the conditions of enslaved workers in the West Indies. The major charitable bequest was to pay for the building of the almshouses that were eventually to become the Geffrye Museum, recently renamed the Museum of the Home.

The establishment of almshouses was one of the favorite forms of charitable giving in this period. There were eighteen in Shoreditch alone. They were frequently managed by one of the City livery companies, and members and supporters of the company concerned received precedence in the allocation of accommodation. This meant that, though presented as charitable institutions, they were as much a form of insurance for those freemen of the city who had fallen on hard times. They provided accommodation to a very limited number of people who were otherwise homeless but gave the founder a public edifice to boast of their generosity. In case there was any doubt as to who the benefactor was, most had statues prominently displayed.

The contentious statue of Geffrye, outside the Museum of the Home, is a good example of such glorification. Honor and reputation were very important to the ruling class of the seventeenth and eighteenth centuries, so whitewashing the public memory of a slave trader would have been considered money well spent.

CHAPTER 2

# The British Atlantic Empire

The British North American colonies, including the West Indian Islands, were part of a larger British Empire economy that was globally interdependent, but with internal rivalries. Different colonies had different economic and political interests but, at least until 1776, many colonies were mutually dependent, although not all parts of the empire carried equal weight. Of course, the colonies were subordinate to the perceived political, diplomatic, and economic interests of the imperial center based in London.

In particular, there was a close economic relationship between the New England colonies and the West Indian slave-based sugar economy. The Caribbean islands found it more profitable to devote all of their land to sugar production and import foodstuffs and other staples, whereas the New England colonies needed an export market so that they could purchase manufactured goods from England.[1] The foundation of Plymouth Colony in 1620 and the arrival of one thousand or so Puritan settlers in Massachusetts Bay in 1630, under Governor John Winthrop with a charter obtained from King Charles I, can be seen as part of a wider British imperialist expansion into North America.

The initial economy of the North American colonies was heavily dependent on the fur trade. The colonists supplied guns to some of the Indigenous population for hunting, which quickly led to the extinction of most fur-bearing animals in the region. These guns were then used by some Native American nations to seize new hunting grounds from their neighbors in a series of wars that rapidly reduced the population levels. This internecine violence and destabilization was made worse by the supplies of alcohol that were a substantial part of the goods that the New Englanders traded for the furs. Once the fur trade was exhausted and the Native American nations became sufficiently weakened by war and alcohol, the settlers moved in to seize their land. This led to the Pequot War of 1636–1638 in New England, which was a decisive defeat for the Pequot nation. About seven hundred Pequots were killed or taken into captivity and sold into slavery, to the West Indian plantation oligarchy. Metacom's War of 1675–1676, named for the intertribal leader of an Indigenous alliance including the Wampanoag and the Narragansett, also known as King Phillip's War, marked the last major effort by the Native Americans of southern New England to resist the English settlers. By 1694 the New England authorities were offering a bounty for killing "Hostile Indians," requiring their scalps as evidence.[2] The Puritans interpreted their victories as a sign of God's favor, but the Native Americans who survived faced disease, cultural devastation, and the expropriation of their lands.[3]

However, the colonists were aware of the dangers of using enslaved Native Americans in their localities of origin, as their friends and relatives could more easily assist their escape. The English settlers preferred to exchange Indigenous prisoners for enslaved Africans.

## New England and the West Indies

The first reliable reference to African enslavement within New England is in 1638, when the governor, John Winthrop, writes of the return to Boston of Captain William Pierce on the Salem ship *Desire*, which had sailed to Providence Island in the Caribbean with a cargo including Pequot people captured in the Pequot War who were sold into slavery there. The *Desire* returned with a cargo of "salt, cotton, tobacco and Negroes."[4]

Although there was a shortage of labor in New England, the land was not generally suitable for the kind of cash-crop agriculture to which slavery is most suited. One exception was the Narragansett area of Rhode Island, which developed its own plantation system, using enslaved labor on estates dedicated to raising horses, cattle, and dairy cows. There were at least ten plantations in Narragansett that ranged in size from one thousand to five thousand acres, each employing between ten and twenty enslaved laborers.[5] But plantations were not the norm, and slavery in New England was a predominantly small-scale, urban institution. The first census of New England's population in 1715 recorded 158,000 Europeans to 4,150 Africans.[6] Some of this European population were indentured laborers. Slavery and other forms of unfree labor were to disappear in New England, not because of any exalted moral objection to the holding of human beings as chattel, but because it did not pay.

Ulrich Phillips, a U.S. historian of slavery, wrote:

> An early realization that the price of Negroes also was greater than the worth of their labor under ordinary circumstances in New England led the Yankee participants in the African trade to market their slave cargoes in the plantation colonies instead of bringing them home.[7]

A division of labor developed among the Puritans in the British American colonies, with those who went to the Caribbean specializing in cash-crop plantations and those in New England supplying, servicing, and trading with them. Slavery in the West Indies became essential to the economy of the North American colonies. Once the fur trade had been exhausted by overhunting, New England had nothing to trade for manufactured goods that could not be produced cheaper in England. However, they were able to find a market for their horses, timber, candle oil, flour, dried fish, and barrels in the West Indies. Despite the dangers of the coastal sea routes beset by storms and piracy, by 1647 there was a regular trade between Barbados and the northern mainland colonies, which found in the sugar islands a market for their surplus agricultural production. This was also to the advantage of the plantation owners since, while New England produce was expensive, it was still cheaper and more reliable than imports from Europe. This trade expanded to the extent that, in the late 1660s, between thirty-five and sixty-five vessels a year from Boston, Salem, and Newport arrived in Bridgetown, Barbados.

### Trafficking in Enslaved Africans

The West Indian trade, aided by coreligionist and family contacts, led Boston and the nearby town of Salem, along with Newport on Rhode Island, to embark on an ambitious program of shipbuilding. A three-hundred-ton ship was built in Salem as early as 1641. By 1700 Boston and nearby towns were turning out seventy ships a year, the most in number and tonnage in the Western Hemisphere.

In his book *The Middle Passage,* Herbert Klein writes:

> American-built ships not only dominated the West Indian and Coastwise trades, where they accounted respectively for 96 percent and 93 percent of the ships, but were even important in the shipping coming directly from Africa. On this route, they accounted for 44 percent of the ships, with English-built ships making up the rest.[8]

Of course the "shipping coming directly from Africa" was full of enslaved Africans.

Trade with the colonies in North America was an important market for British manufactured goods while, in turn, the New England economy evolved so that these purchases of British manufactured products were financed by the trade with the West Indies. The early triangular trade, as pioneered by the Royal African Company, became more sophisticated in the mid-eighteenth century; the shipping of enslaved laborers between Africa and the Caribbean and the transport of sugar and other cash crops back across the Atlantic took place in different specialized vessels, with bills of exchange used to complete the financial transaction, but the principle was the same.[9]

There were other triangles, for example fish caught in Newfoundland were dried and processed there then taken to the West Indies, where the cheap cuts were sold as protein to feed the enslaved laborers and the choice cuts were taken to Spain and Portugal, where they were considered a delicacy.[10] Another important triangle went from New England to West Africa with rum, which could be traded for captives in Africa, who in turn could be exchanged for molasses in the West Indies to supply the rum distilling industry in New England. An enslaved person, who could be purchased in Africa for an amount of rum that cost £3 [£14,110, $17,750] to produce in North America, could be sold for £30 [£141,100, $177,500] in Barbados or the southern mainland colonies.[11] These enormous quantities of alcohol had the added advantage from the slave traders' point of view of setting in train a destabilizing epidemic of alcoholism in Africa that vastly increased levels of violence and broke down traditional relationships, thereby facilitating slave-taking. As Boston, Salem, and Nantucket became the preeminent slaving ports in the region, the distillation of millions of gallons of rum for the slave trade made this the largest manufacturing industry in New England. By the eighteenth century, Rhode Island had thirty distilleries and Massachusetts had sixty-three, producing five million gallons of rum a year.[12]

The first slave-trading vessel from New England to Barbados landed in 1643, and the eighteenth century saw the rise of the New England colonies as slave-carriers rather than direct exploiters of enslaved labor. As Lorenzo Greene of the Association for the Study of Negro Life and History wrote:

Quick to see the unprofitableness of the Negro slave as a laborer in such an environment, when the price of the slave was greater than the labor returned, the ingenious Yankee soon found a market in the West Indies for slaves, exchanged for rum, sugar and molasses on the Guinea Coast. Massachusetts early assumed a commanding position in this trade. The ports of Boston and Salem prospered especially. Their merchants carried on a "brisk trade to Guinea" for many years, marketing most of their slaves in the West Indies.[13]

Subsequently the slave traffic of Rhode Island outstripped that of Massachusetts. This not only played a vital role in maintaining and enabling the expansion of the slavery-based plantation system in the British Caribbean, but also underpinned the creation of a New England mercantile oligarchy through the fortunes that this commerce generated.

The reliance on the slave trade and the West Indian slavery economy persisted up to the struggle for independence by the thirteen colonies in the latter part of the eighteenth century. As Lorenzo Green wrote:

> The effects of this slave trade were manifold. On the eve of the American Revolution it formed the very basis of the economic life of New England; about it revolved, and on it depended, most of her industries. The vast sugar, molasses and rum trade, shipbuilding, the distilleries, a great many of the fisheries, the employment of artisans and seamen, even agriculture—all were dependent on the slave traffic.[14]

Indeed, one of the many reasons for the Declaration of Independence by the thirteen North American colonies was the way in which the proposed duties on molasses and sugar in the Sugar Act of 1764, passed by the British Parliament, would "ruin fisheries, cause the destruction of the rum distilleries and destroy the slave trade." The Massachusetts merchants asserted that the "destruction of the Negro commerce would throw 5,000 seamen out of employment and would cause 700 ships to rot in idleness on their wharves."[15] The Rhode Island merchants made similar claims. Even allowing for exaggeration, this demonstrates the importance of slavery to the New England economy at the time of the War of Independence.[16]

Another of the grievances expressed by the rebel settlers was the Royal Proclamation of 1763, which forbade Anglo-American settlement west of the Appalachian Mountains.[17] Intended as a money-saving measure to reduce the need for troops to defend the colonies from war with the Indigenous nations of the region, it infuriated the settlers who wanted to expand their landholdings westward and were prepared to exterminate the Native peoples to do it. A lesser known part of that process is the widespread trafficking in enslaved Indigenous people, sent to join the enslaved Africans in the British West Indies.

### Indigenous Slavery and Genocide

King Charles II issued a new charter for a colony of Carolina to eight Lords Proprietors in 1663 as a reward for financial and political aid in regaining the throne of England in 1660 after the end of the period of parliamentary rule that followed the English Civil War. The first settlers in 1670 mainly came from Barbados, bringing enslaved Africans to clear the land and produce timber products, beef, and corn to supply the British West Indian sugar colonies. Thus, Carolina has been described as a "colony of a colony."[18]

The settlers soon began cash-crop agriculture, principally rice, initially using enslaved African labor because the opportunities for enslaving Natives were limited given that the English were vastly outnumbered by the Indigenous population. The settlers supplied trade goods such as axes, brass and copper objects, steel knives, blades, fish hooks, iron hoes, beads, bells, pots and pans, clothing, and, importantly, firearms and rum to some allied Indigenous groups. They encouraged these Native allies to make war on rival Native nations and purchased the resulting prisoners of war as enslaved workers.[19] This had the double advantage of providing enslaved laborers who could be sold to the West Indies or other mainland colonies for a profit, while at the same time dividing the potential Native opposition to the colonization process. The addiction to rum destabilized traditional culture, increased levels of violence, and weakened Indigenous society while, in a manner similar to its effects in West Africa, further accelerating slaving activity.

Some fifty thousand enslaved Native Americans were sold away from Carolina, more than the number of Africans trafficked into British North America during the same period. Historian Alan Gallay writes, "The trade in Indian slaves was at the center of the English empire's development in the American South. The trade in Indian slaves was the most important factor affecting the South in the period 1670 to 1715," and financed much of the early development of Carolina.[20]

Also present in the region were colonies settled by Spain and France, and each of these imperialist nations formed alliances with different Indigenous nations. This enabled a war between the rival empires to be fought by Indigenous proxies, which also provided a considerable number of prisoners of war who could be trafficked into enslavement.

The English settlers in Carolina, joined by a fair number of Scots and Germans, initially allied with a slave-trading Indigenous nation, the Westo, but when this alliance had served its purpose, they switched to the enemies of the Westo, the Savannah, and later to the Yamasee, each time making war on their previous allies. As the area of European settlement expanded, the colonists encroached on Indigenous land, their different style of agriculture and extensive land clearances alienating those Indigenous nations with whom they had previously been in alliance, resulting in further war.

Early attempts by settlers to apply European military methods against Indigenous warriors had proved unsuccessful because the

Natives possessed greater local knowledge of the land and used guerrilla tactics, making it difficult for the settlers to come to grips with them. Rather than a futile hunt for elusive enemies, then, the settlers adopted a policy of destroying the towns, villages and, most important, the cornfields and livestock of the Indigenous people with whom they were at war. They formed companies of "rangers," gangs of murderous thugs who devastated Native settlements, who were paid for taking scalps and allowed to sell their captives into enslavement.[21]

A typical example is the 1711 war that the Carolina colony waged against the Tuscaroras who were resisting the steady encroachment by English settlers on their lands. A mixed force of rangers and auxiliaries, recruited from the traditional Indigenous enemies of the Tuscaroras, swept through the country, laying siege to villages, massacring women and children, and burning fields. The commander of this force, John Barnwell, wrote that the English ferocity shocked his Yamasee and Catawba allies: "It was Terror to our own heathen friend to behold us." The Tuscarora death toll is not recorded, but certainly numbered several thousand, while between fifteen hundred and two thousand were enslaved, producing a handsome reward for the rangers when combined with the bounty paid for the scalps they had taken. One attack, on the village of No-ho-ro-co, resulted in 360 Tuscarora dead and 192 scalps, attracting a bounty of £10 each and 392 prisoners to be trafficked to the Caribbean.[22]

Inter-imperialist wars became an excuse for ranging expeditions against the Indigenous allies of the European enemy. During Queen Anne's War (1702–1713), James Moore, governor of South Carolina, led fifty rangers and one thousand Indigenous auxiliaries to "go a'slave hunting" in Spanish Florida, returning with over four thousand enslaved Apalachees.[23]

While the rangers fought for plunder, slaves, and the bounty on the scalps of those they had slain, the killing and forced removal of the Indigenous inhabitants released land for settlers to colonize. Many rangers doubled as land-speculators, selling the land they had ethnically cleansed to newly arrived immigrants from Europe.[24]

During the course of the eighteenth century, the priority of the colonial governments moved from slave-taking of Indigenous people to their extermination. The bounty offered for an "Indian" scalp approached the same amount for which an enslaved Indigenous captive could be sold, thus encouraging rangers to kill rather than take prisoners. In any case, the depopulation resulting from disease, slaving, and massacres exhausted the main sources of potential captives and undermined economic relations between the settlers and their Indigenous allies, leading to the Yamasee War of 1715–1717, which signaled the end of the traffic in enslaved Native Americans and made the Carolinas[25] the most powerful military force in the region.[26]

This process of massacre and land grabbing, which started in the eastern colonies, moved westward across the continent and accelerated after the formation of the United States following the War of Independence. A similar story emerges in the British West Indies.

Barbados may have been uninhabited when the English started to colonize the Caribbean region, but the other small islands of the Lesser Antilles certainly were not. The native inhabitants of those islands, stretching from Guadeloupe to Tobago, were known as the Kalinago and their maritime civilization resisted European colonization, slowly retreating to their heartland in Saint Vincent and Dominica. But, in a combination of diplomacy and military action, they were able to seriously delay the development of the plantation economy on their islands.[27]

British and French settlers, normally hostile to each other, nevertheless allied in 1626 to massacre the Kalinago inhabitants of Saint Kitts, thereafter dividing the island between themselves. Having driven the Kalinago from Martinique in 1658, the French colonists were unable to advance further and, in 1660, a treaty between French, English, and Kalinago representatives formally recognized Kalinago control of the islands of Dominica and Saint

Vincent. Grenada was not covered by the treaty and constant skirmishing severely restricted French development of a plantation economy there. Using the prevailing winds, enslaved Africans frequently escaped from Barbados in stolen boats and arrived in Saint Vincent. Initially, the Kalinago handed such escapees back to the British authorities or sold them to French settlers on Martinique but, as relations deteriorated with the colonists, many of these Africans were integrated into Kalinago communities. This enabled the colonizers to change the narrative and start calling these new communities Black Caribs, using the story of a shipwrecked slave ship to justify taking the lands previously guaranteed to the Kalinago by treaty.

Over the next century, and despite treaties, the constant expansion of the plantation system increasingly encroached on the remaining Kalinago territory. However, by skillfully playing on the rivalry in the region between the British and French empires, the Kalinago people were able to maintain a measure of independence.

The turning point was the Seven Years' War between Britain and France. The Treaty of Paris in 1763 gave Dominica, Saint Vincent, Grenada, and Tobago to Britain, while France gained Saint Lucia and maintained control of Guadeloupe and Martinique. This apparently definitive division of the Lesser Antilles encouraged both empires to expand sugar production on their islands, a process that encroached on Kalinago land and led to the Carib War of 1772–1773. On Saint Vincent, using the presence of Africans, who had joined the Kalinago, to recast them all as a Maroon community of escaped Africans who had formerly been enslaved, rather than the Indigenous population, the settlers sought to remove them from the island and seize their lands. Despite the overwhelming military force of the British, Kalinago guerrillas, who managed to obtain supplies of firearms from neighboring French islands, fought the British army to a standstill. A treaty in 1773 granted the Kalinago people the eastern side of the island.

The French military captured Saint Vincent in 1779 during the American War of Independence, but it was restored to British rule by the Treaty of Paris 1783.[28] Hostilities broke out again in 1795, during the war between Britain and Revolutionary France, when Kalinago forces, aided by French irregulars, managed to seize most of Saint Vincent except the capital, Kingstown. A major British military expedition eventually suppressed the Kalinago/French opposition in 1797. The surviving Kalinago were deported from Saint Vincent to the island of Roatán, off the coast of present-day Honduras, where they became known as the Garifuna people. The main centers of Garifuna population today are Honduras, Belize, and New York City.

The demographic collapse that resulted in the widespread depopulation of the Americas is commonly blamed on epidemics unwittingly brought from Europe and Africa.[29] These diseases certainly played a large part in the population decline in the sixteenth and seventeenth centuries, but rangers and scalp hunters, land grabbers, and enslavers must also be held responsible for the deliberate genocide of the Indigenous populations of North America and the Caribbean.[30]

CHAPTER 3

## Plantation Management

By the end of the seventeenth century, the slave owners in the British West Indies were making such enormous profits that those who wished could return to England and live a life of luxury. They left managers and accountants in charge of running their estates. In order to ensure that they received the maximum profit in their absence, a system of management was developed that shows remarkable similarity to modern academic ideas of scientific management. The earliest known example of this is contained in written instructions sent to his management team in Barbados by Henry Drax (1641–1682), son of the James Drax who founded the estate. He had inherited the Drax Hall estate and Hope Plantation when his brother, also called James Drax (1639–1663), died soon after their father. This was particularly necessary because monocrop agriculture quickly depletes the fertility of the land; nature is not a free gift to big business.

But management was not only by the whip; it also required ideological support, some of which was provided by the Church. Christopher Codrington (1668–1710), another successful Barbados plantation owner, bequeathed part of his estate to the Society for the Propagation of the Christian Gospel, one of the missionary arms of the Church of England. Such a charitable donation provides a lens through which the relationship between Protestant Christianity and enslavement can be examined, particularly the role played by the Church in stabilizing and justifying the whole system of enslavement.

## Soil Depletion

In April 1679, Henry Drax sailed for England. Before he went, he drew up a set of "Instructions which I would have observed by Mr Richard Harwood in the Mannagment of My plantation." He never returned from England, dying there in 1682.[1]

Ken Owen, who uses Henry Drax's "Instructions" in his *Teaching Through Primary Sources*, describes them as follows:

> Drax's instructions are so unremittingly meticulous that the sense of an oppressive, controlling, and inhuman system keeps building for the reader. It is unremittingly clear how slaves were simply seen as cogs in a machine, at every part of the sugar production process, and in every part of plantation life. This is most chillingly seen in the off-hand way that Drax identifies the necessity of replacing as much as 20% of his plantation's workforce on account of death.[2]

Part of the need for such detailed instructions was the deforestation of the Caribbean islands to produce sugar, as well as the soil exhaustion resulting from monocrop, export-based agriculture. As Frederick Engels wrote about the deforestation of Cuba:

> What cared the Spanish planters in Cuba who burned down forests on the slopes of the mountains and obtained from the ashes sufficient fertilizer for one generation of very highly profitable coffee trees—what cared they that the heavy tropical rainfall afterwards washed away the unprotected upper stratum of the soil, leaving behind only bare rock! In relation to nature, as to

society, the present mode of production is predominantly concerned only with the immediate, the most tangible result; and then surprise is expressed that the more remote effects of actions directed to this end turn out to be quite different, are mostly quite the opposite in character.[3]

As the fertility of existing cleared land fell, the landowners ordered the clearing of hillsides and uplands previously thought unsuitable for cultivation, but the heavy rainfall quickly washed away the topsoil. Bridgetown Harbor in Barbados began to silt up, and cane plants were increasingly vulnerable to wind damage.

With the conquest of Jamaica in 1655, new land was opened up for sugar cultivation. As a 1675 report boasted, a sugar works with sixty slaves in Jamaica could make more profit than one with one hundred slaves "in any of the Caribbee Islands, by reason the soil is new." The greater acreage of land available to the Jamaican colonists, in contrast to Barbados, allowed for plantations large enough to have two hundred acres in cane, which was considered the maximum amount that could be handled by one processing plant.

By 1690, where previously it had been possible to harvest three cane crops in succession, planters were now forced to allow exhausted soil to lie fallow.[4] Most plantation owners attempted to preserve the fertility of their land through the constant use of animal dung as manure. They also attempted to prevent soil erosion and depletion through labor-intensive cane hole planting. The first gang would dig a hole between 6 and 9 inches deep and 2 to 3 feet long. They were followed by a second gang who set cuttings of the previous year's cane in the holes and covered them with a mixture of manure and soil. These procedures were extremely taxing on the enslaved laborers ordered to carry them out, not to mention how disgusting it must have been to shovel cow shit all day. Working with large quantities of manure also exposed enslaved workers to an increased risk of disease. Digging cane holes with a hoe was backbreaking work. Weeding cane fields, removing dead leaves, and harvesting the cane subjected the field worker to innumerable leaf cuts, making matters worse.[5]

This increased effort required a more scientific approach to the management of the plantation, and Henry Drax was in the forefront of developing these new methods.

### Scientific Management

These instructions were to form the basis of plantation management throughout the British Empire in the Americas. In 1755 William Belgrove published "A Treatise Upon Husbandry or Planting," in which he writes of the "Pleasure derived from procuring such useful excellent Instructions." Citing Drax, Belgrove stated: "The best Way I know of to prevent Idleness, and to make the Negroes do their Work properly, will be upon the change of Work, constantly to Gang all the Negroes in the Plantations in the Time of Planting." The strongest men and women would be organized into a gang charged with digging cane holes, the "more ordinary" laborers would be tasked with dunging and the children placed in gangs under the oversight of "some careful old Woman." This development of the gang system of labor ensured that the pace of work for each task could be set to that of the strongest, rather than the weakest enslaved worker.[6]

Bill Cooke, who teaches Management Studies at Manchester School of Management (UK), UMIST, argues for a direct connection between the management techniques developed on the slave plantation and modern human resource management practices:

> The industrial discipline which emerged on the plantations was not disconnected temporally, spatially or in substance from that which emerged in other parts of the US economy. The imprint of slavery in contemporary management can be seen in the ongoing dominance from that time of the very idea of the manager with a right to manage. It can also be seen in the specific

management ideas and practices now known as classical management and scientific management...

There was a substantial and growing group of people using what are now seen as management practices, who were known as managers, running plantations. What is also clear, and discomforting, is that white supremacist racism underpinned the creation of the managerial identity....[7]

The result was a calibrated instrument of physical and psychological torture to ensure maximum productivity. As Karl Marx described it:

> Racking to the utmost the toil of the slave—the duration of his life becomes of less moment than its productiveness while it lasts. The most effective economy is that which takes out of the human chattel in the shortest space of time the utmost amount of exertion it is capable of putting forth.[8]

One of the calculations that made the plantation owners disinclined to improve the conditions and treatment of their enslaved laborers was the prospect that this could result in their living longer, into an unproductive old age. The colonial authorities placed a large fine on slaveholders who freed their aging slaves. This was in order to prevent them from manumitting enslaved workers when they had passed their productive life, thereby making them a charge on the local parish.

An Antigua planter who bought some enslaved Africans from a British slave-ship captain told him that his policy was "with little relaxation, hard fare, and hard usage, to wear them out before they became useless, and unable to do service; and then, to buy new ones, to fill up their places." This captain was John Newton, who later saw the error of his ways and wrote many hymns, including "Amazing Grace."[9]

Likewise, the scientific management and cost accounting

introduced by Henry Drax was enhanced and extended over the next two hundred years, as relentlessly efficient overseers determined the maximum sustainable pace of labor and then drove enslaved workers to achieve that maximum.[10]

Karl Marx described plantation slavery as "a calculated and calculating system." Bookkeeping and accounting practices using preprinted reports and forms became universal from about 1780. These imposed accountability and obedience at every level of the chain of command, creating efficient bureaucratic structures with clear duties and responsibilities. Developments in accounting practices paved the way for two other core principles of scientific management: the separation of ownership from management and employee surveillance. These developments enabled plantation owners to return to England and set themselves up on country estates purchased with their profits.[11]

One of the arguments of the abolitionists in their campaign against slavery was that "free labor," with workers paid a wage and free to leave employment when they wished, was more productive than the labor of the enslaved who, it was argued, had no incentive to work unless forced by the whip. Not that the free labor alternative was always expressed in the most tactful way. In 1786 the Reverend Joseph Townsend wrote: "Hunger is not only a peaceable, silent, unremitted pressure, but the most natural motive to industry and labor, it calls forth the most powerful exertions."[12] However, this did not prove to be the case. In 1850 an enslaved laborer picked 200 pounds of cotton a day, but in the 1930s, despite technological advances, a free laborer was picking only 120 pounds.[13] This resulted in many abolitionists, who would not have survived a single day cutting cane under the tropical sun, expressing disappointment at the lack of productivity of the emancipated laborers following the abolition of enslavement.

But the whip is not everything. Ideological justification is required to both undermine the natural resistance of the enslaved and to give confidence to the enslavers. Religion played an important role in this.

## CHRISTIAN SLAVERY

The relationship between the Christian religion and slavery has always been complex. In 1452, even before the arrival of European colonists in the Americas, Pope Nicholas V issued the "Brief Dum Diversas," granting King Alfonso V of Portugal "full and free permission to invade, search out, capture and subjugate the Saracens and pagans and any other unbelievers and enemies of Christ wherever they may be . . . and to reduce their persons into perpetual slavery." This was the original Christian justification for enslavement, long before Europeans had set foot in the Americas, which, of course, begged the question: What is the status of a slave who is baptized?

The original terminology of enslavement had referred to Europeans as Christians, and the enslaved laborers as Negroes or Heathens. European enslavers, both Protestant and Catholic, relied on the infidel status of Africans to justify their enslavement. By their logic, they were afraid that baptism would give their enslaved labor a claim to emancipation. Christian missionaries and their supporters argued that race, rather than religion, was the defining feature of enslavement. Protestant evangelicals in British North America and the Caribbean went to great lengths to reassure slave owners that baptism would not result in their enslaved laborers acquiring any right to emancipation; it would, rather, make them more docile and productive workers.

The Church of England, which was the official church of the British Empire and therefore an arm of the state, only had to consider its position on enslavement when the plantation system started in the British West Indies in the middle of the seventeenth century.[14] The Church struggled with its conscience, but quickly triumphed over any doubts about the legitimacy of the business of slavery. Church officials were greatly assisted in this by Christopher Codrington, a Barbados plantation owner who bequeathed a profitable sugar estate and 315 enslaved laborers to the Society for the Propagation of the Gospel in Foreign Parts, which had been founded by King William III in 1701 as the official overseas "missionary" arm of the Church of England. Thus, the Church's complicity was cheaply purchased.

Even before obtaining control of the Codrington bequest, the Society for the Propagation of the Gospel had already adopted a position that accepted the legitimacy of chattel slavery. During his 1711 annual sermon to the Society, William Fleetwood, Bishop of St. Asaph of the Church in Wales, urged slave owners to Christianize their slaves. Quoting from Saint Paul's "Mission to the Gentiles," Fleetwood stressed a Christian's duty to preach the Gospel, stating that this duty included colonial slaves. He spoke of some misconceptions, held by some slave owners, that baptism could result in manumission and prevent the selling of enslaved Africans who had been baptized. He assured them that baptism did not free the slave, though he urged that Christianity demanded mercy and compassion toward all. "To deal harshly with the slaves was to disobey Christ." Furthermore, "If they could be sold before they were baptized, the Laws of Christ would not deprive the owners of that property after baptism."[15] Above all, he reasserted, the slave owners' right to decide the fate of the oppressed without their consent was paramount. He believed that the ownership of some three hundred slaves enabled the society to preach by example and show fellow slaveholders that a profitable slave plantation was compatible with Christianity.[16]

However, making converts proved incompatible with making profits. With the Bible in one hand and the whip in the other, sixteen years after the death of Christopher Codrington, none of the society's slaves had been baptized.[17] The practice of branding the word *SOCIETY* on the chests of all enslaved laborers coming into the possession of the society can only have added to their alienation at the time that slavery was abolished,

James Heywood Markland, treasurer of the society, was awarded compensation of £8,558 [£10,600,000, $13,462,000] for the 410 slaves that the society still owned on the Codrington estate.

When William Blathwayt, on behalf of the Lords of Trade and

Plantations in London, wrote to the merchants of Barbados to inquire as to "the unhappy state of the Negroes and other slaves in Barbadoes by their not being admitted to the Christian religion," the "gentlemen of Barbados" replied that "the conversion of their slaves to Christianity would not only destroy their property but endanger the island, inasmuch as converted Negroes grow more perverse and intractable than others."[18]

When William Edmundson, a Quaker minister, visited Barbados in 1675, he was criticized for "making the Negroes Christians, and [making] them rebel and cut our Throats." Edmundson replied that "it was a good Work to bring them to the Knowledge of God and Christ Jesus, and to believe in him that died for them, and for all Men, and that would keep them from rebelling or cutting any Man's Throat."[19]

In order to demonstrate their commitment to the whole business of slavery, ministers of the Church of England became the front line of the system's enforcement. In 1661, when the Assembly of Barbados passed "An Act for the good governing of Servants, and ordaining the Rights between Masters and Servants" and "An Act for the better ordering and governing of Negroes," ministers were instructed to read these acts to their parishioners twice a year, so that "no Person may pretend any Ignorance in this Act or Statute, or any Branch, or Clause thereof."[20]

The West Indian parish church also served as a place of public punishment, mainly for enslaved workers, but sometimes also for poor Whites, particularly if they associated with the enslaved. In the 1640s, the Barbados Assembly instructed the churchwardens of every parish to "provide a strong pair of Stocks to be placed . . . near the Church or Chapel." Every Sunday, the constables, churchwardens, and sidesmen were to "walk and search Taverns, Ale-houses, Victualling-houses, or other Houses, where they do suspect . . . debauched Company to frequent." If they found anyone "drinking, swearing, gaming, or otherwise misdemeaning themselves," they brought them to the stocks "to be . . . imprisoned [for] the Space of Four Hours." In 1668 the Assembly passed another law "preventing the selling of Brandy and Rum, in Tipling-houses near the Broad-paths and High-ways." The act targeted "Servants and Negroes" and complained that "on Sabbath-days, many lewd, loose, and idle persons, do usually resort to such Tipling-houses, who, by their drunkenness, swearing, and other miscarriages, do in a very high nature blaspheme the name of God, profane the Sabbath, and bring a great scandal upon true Christian Religion."[21]

According to William Edmundson's 1774 "A Journal of the Life, Travels, Sufferings, and Labour of Love in the Work of the Ministry," the plantation owners were "scarcely noted for their religious zeal" and that they "sank into a hopeless moral torpor, eating, drinking, and fornicating themselves into an early grave."[22] While such behavior is a classic case of ruling-class hypocrisy, it does not mean that owners did not recognize the importance of formal religious observance. In Barbados, they saw themselves as Protestant and used their religious identity to justify their social control. Church-based marriage, baptism, and funerals became integrated into a broader culture of hierarchy that helped to maintain their dominance.

The Christian missionaries, Quaker as well as Anglican, were in the forefront of the racializing of enslavement in order to justify their proselytizing to the enslaved without threatening the source of labor power. The plantation oligarchy eventually sought the best of both worlds. As the language and ideas of racialism replaced religious terms in the British West Indies, the plantocracy was able to use the new forms of racial prejudice in conjunction with the older religious divisions to reinforce their rule. The Irish, who had mainly arrived as indentured servants, might be made to feel that they were better than the Africans, but they were still Catholics and therefore lower on the social ladder than the English Protestants. The change in terminology is illustrated by a 1644 law in Antigua titled "Against Carnall Coppullation between Christian and Heathen," while by 1675 a law on the island of Nevis was titled "White Men Not to Keep Company with Negroes."[23]

Quakers may have been in the forefront of the campaign against slavery in the eighteenth century, but in the seventeenth century, they were as keen as the Anglicans to reconcile religion and enslavement. They argued that Christian influence would help maintain social order, and that enslaved Christians were more docile than others while being more productive.

George Gray, a leading Barbadian Quaker, argued that Blacks were "Heathen by Nature" and urged slave owners to "bring Nigroes unto Christianity or a Christian Life that they may be free men Indeed & in Truth." Masters should encourage their enslaved laborers to keep family meetings and to discourage them from "rudeness, dancing, drinking & having Merry Meetings that are bad examples to all people." He accused the enslaved of "provokeing one another to doe Wickedly" and he urged Quaker slave owners to keep their enslaved laborers busy during the week so they did not have "Liberty to flock & go abroad in Company," which allowed for the opportunity to "do Mischeif & plott & Contrive."[24]

Eventually, the Society for the Propagation of the Gospel inserted into the baptism a ritual for enslaved converts: "You declare in the presence of God and before this Congregation that you do not ask for the holy baptism out of any design to free yourself from the duty and Obedience you owe to your Master while you live but merely for the good of your Soul and to partake of the Graces and Blessings promised to the Members of the Church of Jesus Christ."[25]

However, there was a more practical reason for the plantation oligarchs' opposition to their enslaved workers converting to Christianity. Protestant Christianity traditionally entailed teaching the would-be convert literacy in the English language. The enslavers feared that this would enable the enslaved to advocate legally for their rights and even organize resistance more easily, while the missionaries began to notice that the newly literate enslaved people were starting to place their own interpretations on the Bible.[26]

In 1730 the Rev. Robert Robertson, a Nevis clergyman who was not associated with the Society for the Propagation of the Gospel, published "A Letter To the Right Reverend the Lord Bishop of London from An Inhabitant of his Majesty's Leeward-Caribee Islands," insisting that "there is not a Sugar or Guinea-Trader of any Note in London, Bristol, or Liverpole, but could have told your Lordship that it is impossible Baptism, or any the like Privilege, should destroy the Property the Masters have in their Negro-Slaves, or the Right of selling them again at Pleasure." Rather, he argued, the problem with education and literacy was that they provided the enslaved with skills that they could use to gain access to the legal system to the inconvenience of their masters. More important, literacy gave some enslaved house servants access to planters' newspapers.

In 1815 Nanny Grigg, who worked as an enslaved domestic servant in the Great House of Simmons plantation, read in the newspapers of discussions in the Barbados House of Assembly concerning the Slave Registry Bill in the British House of Commons and, more generally, the activities of the abolitionist movement in Britain. The frenzied denunciations of these by the plantation owners' representatives in Barbados convinced her that freedom was coming, but that the island's authorities were going to deny the enslaved their freedom.[27]

She told her fellow enslaved workers that "the Negroes were all to be freed on New Year's Day" and that "they were all damn fools to work, for that she would not, as freedom they were sure to get." When the promised date passed, she told them: "The only way to obtain freedom was to fight for it. Slave owners would never give up without a fight" and that the only way to obtain their emancipation "was to set fire, as that was the way they did it in St. Domingo."[28] Grigg went on to become one of the leaders of the 1816 Barbados Rebellion.[29]

The missionary work of Christians among the enslaved is often portrayed in a positive light by those modern-day apologists who seek to diminish the stain of slaveowning on plantation owners such as Codrington.[30] However, Christian missionary work and education of the enslaved was in no way altruistic. Rather, it was intended to produce obedient and hardworking enslaved laborers who would accept their position in colonial society with the belief that there was divine authority behind their enslavement. Christianity, as preached by the Church of England and the Society for the Propagation of the Gospel, demonized and outlawed traditional African cultural and spiritual practices, devaluing and demeaning their African ancestry.[31]

Whatever opinions for or against held by individual planters in respect to Christian missionary work among their enslaved laborers, they were united in their hatred of the religious practices that reached back to Africa. They particularly hated and feared drumming. Africans and their descendants, therefore, changed and adapted their belief systems to local circumstances and influences: *Santería* in Cuba, *Obeah* in Jamaica, *Vodun* in Saint-Domingue. Islam also persisted, particularly among the enslaved in Brazil. And the slave owners had good reason to be afraid, as these cultural practices from the old country enabled the enslaved to maintain self-respect and provided a channel for organized resistance.

CHAPTER 4

# Law and Order

The business of slavery had grown many tentacles, and profit came from a number of sources. The most successful businessmen were those who had a finger in many pies: they were suppliers to the British Navy and government contractors, land- and slave owners in the Caribbean; they served as customs officers, commodity traders, and financial speculators. Keeping control of the system required political influence, which during this period meant acquiring estates and country homes in Britain, as landowning was an established route into Parliament. Not only did their new landholdings give them political power and a very comfortable lifestyle, but the associated agricultural land also added considerably to their income. The power, wealth, and political influence that arose from slavery-based money moving into rural Britain enabled the enslavers to take part in the land grab known as the Enclosures, while using the law to defend their newly acquired domains. Controlling the apparatus of law and order was equally important in their drive to maximize profits in London.

By the end of the eighteenth century, when London had become the major port for the import of tropical produce from the Caribbean, London commodity traders were increasingly

# LAW AND ORDER

concerned about the inefficiency and lack of security of the existing docks. So a group of businessmen raised the finance to demolish the old facilities and replace them with the West India Dock, a new dock able to unload more ships at a time, and surrounded by a wall to protect their cargoes. Such a system could only work if it was well-policed; consequently, the West India Dock became the site of the first uniformed official police force in Britain. The "River Police" was not only a security force to prevent theft; it was deeply involved in all levels of industrial relations in the port.

Control of the repressive forces of the state, army, police, and prisons was important, not only to preserve the wealth produced by the business of slavery but also to attempt to conceal the corruption and financial double-dealing involved. This was not always successful as the scandal known as the "South Sea Bubble" reminds us.

## The South Sea Company

Most people who have been to school in England will have heard of the South Sea Bubble of 1720, when the South Sea Company share price crashed and many investors were ruined. Very few people, however, are aware that its principal commercial activity was the slave trade.

The South Sea Company was established by Royal Charter in 1711, as a public-private partnership (PPP) to help manage the national debt, which at that time stood at £9 million [£23 billion]. Government creditors were issued shares in the company, to the nominal value of the debt owing to them. Thus, private holders of British government bonds and annuities converted those state financial assets into shares in the private South Sea Company, in what we would now call a debt-equity swap.[1]

The government made an annual payment to the company of £568,279 [£1,744,000,000, $2,286,602,000], which represented 6 percent interest plus expenses. This was then redistributed to the shareholders as a dividend.[2]

At the end of the War of the Spanish Succession, the Treaty of Utrecht (1713–1714) gave the British government the monopoly of supplying enslaved laborers to the Spanish Empire in the Americas. As part of the process of restructuring the national debt, the British government granted this monopoly, known as the "*Asiento*," to the South Sea Company, which was required to supply 4,800 enslaved Africans every year, using the services of the Royal African Company and the Royal Navy.[3] The Treaty also permitted the passage of one ship per year to Portobello in modern-day Panama for the annual trade fair. Moreover, the company clearly expected that the legal trade would enable and provide cover for a contraband trade, particularly in silver, in defiance of the Spanish government's prohibition in trading with merchants from other nations.[4]

Queen Anne, in her speech to Parliament on June 6, 1712, stated that "I have insisted and obtained that the *asiento* or contract for furnishing the Spanish West Indies with Negroes shall be made with us for thirty years."[5] Indeed, Queen Anne was a substantial shareholder in the new company, attempting to reserve 22.5 percent of the shares for herself, although this was later considerably reduced.[6] When she died in 1714, her shares were inherited by the new king, George I, who appointed his son, the Prince of Wales, as Governor of the Company, although the king took the post back for himself when he realized the money that could be made.

The company's stock certificates were similar to the mortgage-backed securities of the 2008 financial crisis. Similarly, speculators thought that the asset value of the enslaved could only go up, as the Atlantic economy was centrally dependent on enslaved labor. Stock certificates were therefore both a monetization of the national debt and a currency dependent on the business of slavery.[7]

In 1719, the South Sea Company proposed a further debt-equity swap of £1.5 million [£4,233,000,000, $5,375,910,000] in government debt, along with a loan to the government of £554,142 [£1,417,000,000, $1,799,590,000]. In 1720 the company proposed an even more ambitious scheme, which involved the South Sea

Company making a new loan to the government of approximately £7.5 million [£19,180,000,000, $24,358,600,000]. Additionally, the Company acquired £31.5 million [£80,540,000,000, $102,285,800,000] in unconsolidated government debt in exchange for converting the debt into more company shares. The government agreed to pay 5 percent interest on the converted debt. John Trenchard, a financial journalist of the time, warned that directors of the South Sea Company, after having worked up "their Stock by Management to an unnatural Price, will draw out, and leave the Publick to shift for it self."[8] And so it proved. The South Sea Company had to ensure an ongoing increase in the stock value and a continual sale of shares. Daniel Defoe was one of many propagandists for the company, and his writing in contemporary journals, *The Director* and *The Commentator*, were dedicated to boosting the company right up to the crash.

Effectively a Ponzi scheme, the price of the shares rose from £120 [£306,800, $389,636] to nearly £1,000 [£2,557,000, $3,247,390] before crashing back to somewhere near their original value.[9] This stock market crash had winners and losers. Like all such financial crises, those with insider knowledge made a fortune. Sir Isaac Newton was nearly ruined; Sir Thomas Guy sold his shares while they were on the way up and made £45,000 [£115,100,000, $150,910,500].

Economic historians Peter Temin and Hans-Joachim Voth have studied the way in which an important bank of the time, Hoare's Bank, played the market. Having understood the nature of the Ponzi scheme, the bank played it to the limit. Henry Hoare, the senior partner, took £21,000 [£53,690,000, $68,186,300] in profits, while his brother Benjamin made £7,000 [£17,900,000, $22,733,000].[10] King George I lost £56,000 [£143,200,000, $181,864,000], despite being warned of the impending crash by John Aislabie, Chancellor of the Exchequer, who had done much to promote the South Sea Company.[11] Aislabie sold his own shares at inflated values, but was accused of insider trading and "most notorious, dangerous and infamous corruption," when a parliamentary inquiry found that he had been given £20,000 [£51,140,000, $64,947,800] of company stock in exchange for his promotion of the scheme. He was expelled from the House of Commons, fined £45,000 [£115,100,000, $146,177,000], and imprisoned.[12] He was replaced as Chancellor of the Exchequer by Robert Walpole, whose bailout of the company took the form of exchanging its devalued stock for shares in the Bank of England. Thus, central banking has its origins in investments in enslavement.[13] It is worth noting in passing that Robert Walpole had himself made a fortune from his own trading in shares of the South Sea Company, enough to finance the building of Houghton Hall in Norfolk.

These financial games did not matter a jot to the enslaved Africans. The South Sea Company continued trafficking in enslaved Africans until 1739, despite the scandals, and trafficked a total of 64,399 Africans on 538 separate voyages between 1711 and 1740.[14] It is a sad reflection on the state of historical writing in Britain that one can find scores of articles and books on the financial fallout of the South Sea Bubble and its effects on the wealthy investors, but far fewer on the slave-trafficking activities of the company. Isaac Newton may have lost his shirt, but nearly 65,000 Africans lost their liberty and were condemned to a life of backbreaking toil followed by an early death.

### Enclosures

On their return from the West Indies, many slave owners purchased landed estates in Britain. As many as three hundred new country houses were erected during this period, each designed to insert its owner within the established hierarchy, presided over by the English aristocracy. The houses' architecture imitated ancient Greek and Roman edifices in an attempt to conceal the origins of the owners' wealth from the brutal exploitation of African labor on the colonial plantations.[15]

These stately homes were always more than just places to live, they were also public relations exercises. They represented power, permanence, and a self-justified entitlement expressing, in stone, bricks, and mortar, the determination of the ruling class to retain and expand its wealth, no matter how it was acquired. This sanitizing of the process of the accumulation of capital has become an important part of the capitalist ideological offensive, part of the definition of being British. The significance of this historical legacy can be seen by the considerable part of the license fee money that the BBC spends on lavish costume dramas such as *Downton Abbey*, as well as the ruling-class fury whenever there is the slightest reference to the colonial origins of the money that created these ostentatious displays of landed wealth.[16] The outcry from the right-wing newspaper *Daily Mail* over the National Trust's recently published "Interim Report on the Connections between Colonialism and Properties now in the Care of the National Trust, Including Links with Historic Slavery," shows the importance of such whitewashing.[17] This is akin to the outrage expressed by right-wing Texan politicians when anyone suggests that the secession of White settlers in Texas from the Republic of Mexico was a slaveholders' revolt provoked by the Mexican government's abolition of slavery in 1829.[18]

By the middle of the eighteenth century an increasing number of businessmen had made vast sums of money from all aspects of the business of slavery, as well as from the profits generated from the exploitation of India through the East India Company and by supplying the Royal Navy. They had enough money to buy land and were starting to do so, thinking that they could thereby buy their way into the ruling elite.[19]

However, in the 1750s, there was still political animosity between those who made their money in the business of slavery and the old landed aristocracy over the question of war. The West Indian enslavers wanted to ensure the defense of the colonies, while the landed aristocracy resented paying the increased taxes that would be necessary to fund the succession of wars between rival European imperialisms, largely in disputes over colonial territories. Both factions did, however, agree on the need to privatize land that had previously been held in common by ordinary country people.

The Enclosures in Britain were the expropriation and privatization of the subsistence farms of peasant producers, as well as the woodlands, meadowlands, and marshlands that were customarily shared communally. This land expropriation process ran parallel to the development of the slave-based economy in the Americas, and many of the planters and businessmen engaged in enslaving Africans seized the land of the Indigenous nations of the Americas while they were also enclosing rural Britain. Thus, the development of capitalism was achieved by both an agricultural revolution and an industrial revolution, both of which were deeply entwined with the business of slavery.

Karl Marx writes of the origins of capitalism:

> The spoliation of the church's property, the fraudulent alienation of the State domains, the robbery of the common lands, the usurpation of feudal and clan property, and its transformation into modern private property under circumstances of reckless terrorism, were just so many idyllic methods of primitive accumulation. They conquered the field for capitalistic agriculture, made the soil part and parcel of capital, and created for the town industries the necessary supply of a "free" and outlawed proletariat.[20]

Imogen Tyler, author and sociology professor, argues for a view of enclosures that stretches across the British Empire. Seeing the enclosures in Britain as a land grab, or systematic privatization, she extends the concept to see the land grab occurring in the Americas, the colonization process, as part and parcel of the same phenomenon. The same class in England that initiated the enclosures also organized the colonization of North America and the Caribbean, as well as the start of the Atlantic slave trade.[21]

Across Britain, industrialization needed to turn people into wage workers. Within the commons, or shared arable land, local people had long enjoyed traditional and collective rights of access in order to pasture animals, harvest meadow grass for winter animal feed, fish, collect firewood, or otherwise benefit. By enabling the privatization and expropriation of agricultural land that had previously been worked on a small scale by family units, the enclosures enriched the landowners who gained increased holdings. It also rendered independent farming inaccessible to most ordinary country people, who previously had access to the commons, thereby depriving agricultural laborers of their means of subsistence and turning them into paupers and proletarians who could survive only by selling their labor power in the towns.[22]

This was a lengthy historical process, beginning in the fourteenth century. The expropriation of the agricultural producer, wrote Marx, "went hand in hand with the genesis of the capitalist farmer and the industrial capitalist."[23] In England, the nobility, which was already moving toward a money-based economy, transformed much arable land to sheep pasture, as more money could be made from selling wool to the early textile industry than in collecting rent from the peasantry.

Also enclosed were areas of land known as "wastes." In this period, the term waste had two meanings: the common usage of today of something that is useless and an older meaning of uncultivated land. This uncultivated land was far from useless as far as the rural workers were concerned, as they could collect wild products from these wastes. Landowning gentry, however, applied the other meaning, seeing these lands as useless, as they could not make a profit from their exploitation.

From the beginning of the eighteenth century to the end of the nineteenth, there was a trend toward increasingly large holdings of land in the hands of a decreasing number of families and individuals.[24] This was a period of extensive enclosures of common land and the expropriation of small-scale peasant landholders. The Enclosure Acts were a series of parliamentary acts between 1750 and 1860, privatizing the previously common land, where the ordinary country people had made their living.[25]

As Karl Marx wrote of one of the most notorious enclosing landlords of the early nineteenth century:

> As an example of the method used in the nineteenth century, the "clearings" made by the Duchess of Sutherland will suffice here. This person, who had been well instructed in economics, resolved, when she succeeded to the headship of the clan, to undertake a radical economic cure, and to turn the whole county of Sutherland, the population of which had already been reduced to 15,000 by similar processes, into a sheep-walk. Between 1814 and 1820 these 15,000 inhabitants, about 3,000 families, were systematically hunted and rooted out. All their villages were destroyed and burnt, all their fields turned into pasturage. British soldiers enforced this mass of evictions, and came to blows with the inhabitants. One old woman was burnt to death in the flames of the house she refused to leave. It was in this manner that this fine lady appropriated 794,000 acres of land which had belonged to the clan from time immemorial.[26]

The money to fund this clearing was deeply entwined with the business of slavery. The Duchess of Sutherland had inherited £5,000 [£5,789,000, $7,590,000] from her paternal grandfather, William Maxwell, whose estate consisted "mostly in trade and plantations in Jamaica," while her maternal grandfather was involved in the slavery-based economy through investments in tobacco in Virginia.[27]

Historian Corinne Fowler writes: "The period of enclosure and agricultural improvement, was also the period of empire and slavery. Commodifying land and commodifying people went hand in hand."[28] A prime example is John Sawbridge Erle Drax (1800–1887), part of the Drax dynasty of enslavers and landowners in Barbados, who enclosed Sturminster Marshall Common Field and some of its neighboring land, thereby extending his Charborough Park and diverting the existing town of Wimborne to Dorchester Road, today the major road from London to the West Country.[29]

As well as increasing his income from agricultural production, this expansion was doubly profitable, as it enabled the construction of a toll road, of which Drax was the chief promoter and investor. Meanwhile, the Drax Hall plantation in Barbados still made him an average yearly net profit of £3,591 [£3,984,000, $5,223,500], and when compensation was paid following the abolition of slavery, he received just over £4,293 [£4,866,000, $6,380,000] in compensation for his 189 enslaved laborers.

Enclosure of common land had started slowly in the twelfth century, and initially it was mainly by agreement. The process accelerated remarkably in the eighteenth and early nineteenth centuries and was then mainly forced through by parliamentary action. There were 4,041 such parliamentary enclosures between 1730 and 1839, dispossessing former occupiers from a further 30 percent of England's agricultural land.[30] Rural laborers who lived on the margin depended on open fields and the wastes to supplement their meager incomes. Enclosure left three alternatives: to work like serfs as tenant farmers for large landowners; to emigrate; or to move into already crowded towns and cities, where they pushed down one another's wages by competing for a limited number of jobs.[31]

As E. P. Thompson put it:

> And first we should remember that the spirit of agricultural improvements in the eighteenth century was impelled less by altruistic desires to banish ugly wastes or—as the tedious phrase goes—to "feed a growing population" than by the desire for fatter rent-rolls and larger profits.
>
> Enclosure (when all the sophistications are allowed for) was a plain enough case of class robbery, played according to fair rules of property and law laid down by a parliament of property-owners and lawyers.[32]

In the late eighteenth century and early nineteenth, the main motive for enclosure was to develop large country estates by privatizing open fields, common pastures, and areas of uncultivated land such as woodlands, moors, marshes, bogs, heaths, downs, fens, and converting them into arable or mixed farmland. Between 1750 and 1830, almost all the remaining 25 percent of Britain that was still unenclosed was brought into private ownership through the passage of further enclosure acts.[33] The enclosure of common pastures and wastes meant that land could be repurposed for intensive agricultural use, making possible the consolidation of landholdings and a market for land speculation. This provided the conditions for developing agricultural businesses and investing in new agricultural methods, technologies, and infrastructure without regard to the rights of commoners.

The big landholders, aided by their parliamentary and legal allies, reframed debate about the legitimacy of removing common rights. Once having argued for their individual self-interests, they now stressed that enclosure was in the national interest. John Arbuthnot, eighteenth-century man of letters, wrote, for example:

> However beautiful it may be in theory to raise the lower orders to a situation of comparative independence, the line between the proprietor and the laborer must be firmly drawn. Without it, neither agriculture nor commerce can flourish.[34]
>
> If by converting the little farmers into a body of men who must work for others, more labour is produced, it is an advantage which the nation should wish for: the compulsion will be that of honest industry to provide for a family.[35]

The term "improvement" became a euphemism for the wholesale privatization involved in the enclosures. Improvement became central to the ideological justification of eighteenth-century agrarian capitalism. It meant enlarging farms and enhancing the productivity of land through investment in technological innovations and agricultural science, along with a more profit-oriented approach to land management. This "improvement" also had the effect of establishing the sanctity of private property and disparaging common lands as terrains of idleness, destitution, and crime, which, it was argued, furthered the national economic interest.[36]

However, as Marxist economist Utsa Patnaik counters:

> The first industrial nation, Britain suffered a food deficit by the 1790s even before the first phase of the Industrial Revolution had got underway, and only increasing food imports from its nearest colony, Ireland, and food and raw material imports from its tropical colonial possessions in the West Indies and India, allowed its industrial transition to proceed at all.[37]

The problem was caused, in part, by the fact that many landowners could make greater profit by turning their land over to livestock farming, beef, and wool, rather than the grain production needed to feed the working class. Capitalist improvement meant increasing profits, not increasing useful production:

> The "agricultural revolution" was a revolution by and for the landlords. For the great majority it was a great reversal, a counter-revolution in which the people who best knew the land, and who had worked hard to make it more productive, were expropriated by a tiny class of rentiers whose primary interests were increased rents, political power and luxurious lifestyles.[38]

Another link between the enclosures and industrialization was the need for coal to power the new industries, which led to another form of Enclosure: the expropriation of mineral rights under common land. John Nef, in his history of the early British coal industry, tells us:

> Wherever coal-mining became important, it stimulated the movement towards curtailing the rights of customary tenants and even of small freeholders, and towards the enclosure of portions of the wastes . . . Not only must the tenants be prevented from digging themselves, they must be stripped of their power

to refuse access to minerals under their holdings, or to demand excessive compensation.

Nef adds that tenant farmers "lived in constant fear of the discovery of coal under their land," and enclosures to establish new mines were often resisted by sabotage and violence.[39]

The enclosures were, therefore, according to Marx, a doubly important element in the process of industrialization:

> For large-scale landed property, as in England, drives the overwhelming majority of the population into the arms of industry and reduces its own workers to total misery.[40]

Capitalist development did not only happen in manufacturing industry; the political economy of agriculture was also transformed, and the capital accumulation derived from the business of slavery was used to finance the changes taking place in the British countryside.

The British rural economy changed during the seventeenth, eighteenth, and nineteenth centuries from subsistence farming with a small surplus, to commodity production on a fully capitalist basis. Many of the absentee West Indian plantocracy had used their profits to purchase landed estates in Britain as a diversification of business interests, a capital investment, and the acquisition of political influence, as well as conspicuous consumption. Just as this transformation of rural England can be seen as part of the development of capitalism, it is also very much part of the history of the business of slavery, as we follow the money.

## The Black Act

Some commoners moved from subsistence agriculture directly into industrial employment, although "acceptance of wage labor was the last resort open to those who had lost their land, but many regarded it as little better than slavery."[41]

Ian Angus states: "Not only were wages low and working conditions abysmal, but the very idea of being subject to a boss and working under wage-discipline was universally detested."[42] Socialist historian Brian Manning argues:

> Piracy, highway robbery, smuggling and poaching were all strategies developed by the impoverished to survive without submitting to the discipline of full-time wage labor increasingly being imposed by the advance of capitalism. . . . Resistance by means of poaching was an aspect of class struggle between peasants and landowners.[43]

These changes in social organization required extensive changes in the law, as country people, who previously had supplemented their income by hunting and gathering on common land, had to be forcibly dissuaded from continuing the practice on the newly enclosed private property. The Black Act was passed by Parliament in May 1723 with no serious debate or objection. At a stroke, it introduced fifty new crimes for which the death penalty could be applied, almost all relating to forms of game poaching. In particular, the law was aimed at those who blackened their faces in disguise to avoid identification by the authorities and the resulting repression—thus, the title of the act.

Were these poachers such a threat to the lives and property of the ruling class of the time that such extraordinary legislation was necessary? E. P. Thompson found no evidence of any such emergency in contemporary printed media; indeed the perceived threat seems to have been restricted to the forests of Windsor, Enfield, Kingston, and Waltham in Hampshire. The main hunting grounds affected seem to have been the private domains of the king and the prime minister, Robert Walpole, as well as a number of their close associates. So we have to look elsewhere for the real reason for the law.

For it was not just the notoriously corrupt Walpole and his circle that supported this heavy-handed act; its easy passage through

Parliament seems to indicate that it struck a chord with the perceived interests of the ruling class in general. As the increasing dominance of the capitalist economy and the enclosures of common land deprived peasant farmers of their means of subsistence, the old methods of class control were becoming ineffective and needed to be replaced by terror: poverty wages and the death penalty. With the changing nature of the economy and the impoverishment of ordinary country people due to advancing capitalist agriculture poaching was not a luxury for many rural households but an essential to put food on the table.

There was also a direct connection between authoritarianism and corruption. The Walpole administration, not only responsible for an absolutely draconian increase in the use of judicial terror, was also noteworthy for institutionalizing the means of corruption. The Duke of Wharton, asked why a highway robber "committed, perhaps for a trifle, or the mere relief of his necessities" should be executed,

> whilst another, who has inriched himself by continual depredations, for a course of some years, at the expense of his country, shall not only escape with impunity, but, by a servile herd of flatterers and sycophants, have all his actions crowned with applause.[44]

With the generalization of paid employment, the product of a worker's labor became the absolute property of the employer, defended by the gallows. Consequently, the Black Act was used to prosecute all manner of other offenses against property and bourgeois order.[45] And the origins of policing in Britain are directly linked to the West Indian trade.

### West India Dock and the River Police

In 1793 plans emerged for a new dock in London dedicated to the West Indian trade. There were two main reasons behind this enterprise. First, many commodity traders were increasingly concerned at what they considered pilfering and theft by the dock workers, although the dockers themselves saw this as merely their entitlement, their perquisites. Second, the size of the slavery-originated trade into London had grown to overwhelm the existing facilities.

By the end of the eighteenth century, two-thirds of Britain's total sugar imports came through London. The City of London financial services industry provided the banking system for the West Indies, and West Indian trade accounted for a third of the total London trade by value. Moreover, the business of buying and selling enslaved Africans in the West Indies, extending credit to plantation owners, and brokering return shipments of slave-grown commodities was organized and funded from the City of London.[46] The West India Dock Company, based on the Isle of Dogs, an East London peninsula, would become a dedicated port facility with a statutory monopoly on goods—mainly sugar and rum—produced by Caribbean slavery. A large part of the business's initial investments came from persons already involved in the West Indian trade, but the West India Dock Company also gave others, latecomers, the opportunity to profit from the business of slavery.[47]

The originator of the concept of an enclosed dock for the import of the products of Caribbean enslaved labor was William Vaughan, heir to estates in the West Indies and a director of the Royal Exchange Assurance. He argued for greater control over the movement and unloading of ships to reduce the costs of delay, as well as for a reduction of what he referred to as the depredations by the dockworkers. In association with two City of London Aldermen, Sir John Eamer and George Hibbert, Vaughan launched a subscription on December 22, 1795, raising £800,000 [£1,227,000,000, $1,609,867,000] in support of the West India Dock project.

The building of the West India Dock necessitated the compulsory purchase of a considerable number of existing dwellings and warehousing. From this process, George Hibbert, as well as being chairman of the company, managed to secure compensation of £33,408 [£38,680,000] for what was effectively the upgrading of his own previous warehouses in Wapping, in the East End of London, thereby profiting from both ends of the process. The West India Dock Company was extremely profitable, paying a dividend of 10 percent per annum from 1806 to 1823, and became one of the ways in which the City of London financial services industry profited from the slavery-based economy.[48]

The West Indian merchants believed that the delays to landing and unloading that occurred before the West India Dock was built were responsible for giving the opportunity for the river workers to, as they put it, plunder their cargoes. The river workers, known as "lumpers," were poorly paid and frequently cheated of even their underpayment by the foremen and ships' captains. So their perquisites were essential to their economic survival and, over time, came to be considered as their customary rights, with many of their employers recognizing these perks as a form of payment in kind. The problem with such a system is that it removes the control of wage rates from the employer and makes wage cuts almost impossible to implement. Part of the reason for such expenditure on the new dock—surrounded by a thirty-foot-high wall, a moat, and guarded by a new river police force—was to break this system.

In 1798, to control access to the docks, the Committee of West Indian Merchants financed and encouraged a Scottish merchant, Patrick Colquhoun, to set up the new Marine Police Office, which was backed up by a further military contingent permanently stationed on the dock.[49]

Patrick Colquhoun spent his teens and early twenties in colonial Virginia, then served as an agent for British cotton manufacturers, and was the London agent of the slaveholders of Saint Vincent, Nevis, Dominica, and the Virgin Islands. He also owned shares in sugar plantations in Jamaica. He was extremely influential in the development of policing in Britain, writing extensively on the relationship between the law, property, and class.[50] His main concern was in protecting bourgeois property relationships and disciplining the working class, which he clearly saw as the enemy, but an enemy necessary for the production of wealth, an attitude not dissimilar from that exhibited by the slave owners who employed him in the Caribbean as their agent. For Colquhoun, the best way to organize labor was an amalgamation of policing and human resource management.

The Marine Police Office, situated in Wapping New Stairs, near the new West India Dock, served as both a police station and a hiring hall for the workers who would unload the ships. The dockers were paid from the Marine Police Office at wages determined by the magistrates. The unloading at the dock was organized from the Wapping Police Office, and the shipowners were charged directly. Employed in this new police force, which came to be known as the River Police, were fifty constables, armed with cutlasses and truncheons. Their main task was searching those employed in unloading the ships to ensure that they did not take their customary perquisites. This system resulted in a serious lowering of the standard of living of the river workers, whose wages were now their sole income and did not compensate for the previous system whereby they had effectively been paid in kind.

This new enforcement system was not accepted quietly and, in October 1798 a large crowd attacked the Wapping Police Office following the arrest and conviction of a coal heaver who had been found with coal in his possession. Marxist historian Peter Linebaugh argues: "The international circuit of sugar brought the violence of its social relations back to London."[51]

Although the River Police became the forerunner of the Metropolitan Police, set up in 1829 by Home Secretary Sir Robert Peel, the origins of policing are not just connected to the business of slavery through the London end of the West Indian trade. The colonial experience was formative in other ways.

Early colonial policing was shaped by slavery. Long before the London Metropolitan Police were formed, colonial cities in the slave colonies had paid full-time police forces, derived from slave patrols. In Cuba, from the beginning of colonization, armed Spanish bands called *hermandades* had hunted those escaping from enslavement, a practice that was adopted by the English in Barbados a century later. South Carolina, founded by slave owners from Barbados, set up its first slave patrol in 1702; Virginia followed in 1726; North Carolina in 1753. Serving in the slave patrol was mandatory for all able-bodied White men in slave societies generally. Patrick Colquhoun was familiar with slave patrols from his time in the West Indies, which helped to form his theories.[52]

While most slave patrols operated in rural areas, urban patrols like the Charleston, South Carolina, City Guard and Watch became a formal paid force as early as 1783. These heavily armed police regularly inspected the passes of the enslaved and the papers of free Black people. The only limit on police power was the fact that enslaved people were someone's property, so killing one could result in civil liability to the owner.

Although there is widespread acceptance of the slavery-based origins of policing in the United States, little is said of similar beginnings in British policing. The Barbados Slave Act of 1661 made it the legal duty of all White persons to watch, apprehend, and punish enslaved Africans, forming, in effect, a collective police force. A mounted and uniformed militia patrolled Barbados estates, performed twice-monthly searches of homes of the enslaved, pursued runaways, and supervised gatherings of enslaved people at markets, funerals, and celebrations. Between 1696 and 1702, the Barbados Assembly introduced the tenant militia, offering indentured servants rent-free land to serve as live-in plantation police.[53] These slave-catchers were granted immunity by An Act for the Governing of Negroes, 1688:

> If any poor small free-holder or other person kill a Negro or other Slave by Night, out of the Road or Common Path, and stealing, or attempting to steal his Provision, Swine, or other Goods, he shall not be accountable for it; any Law, Statute, or Ordinance to the contrary notwithstanding.[54]

In 1812 Sir Robert Peel was appointed Chief Secretary for Ireland. The Peace Preservation Act of 1814 authorized the Lord Lieutenant of Ireland to appoint additional magistrates, who were authorized to appoint paid special constables. Peel thus laid the basis for the Royal Irish Constabulary, which played a central role in maintaining British rule over Ireland. Combining this colonial experience with the theoretical ideas of Patrick Colquhoun, Peel set out the main duties of the Metropolitan Police, which were to protect property, maintain order, quell riots, put down strikes and other industrial actions, and produce a disciplined industrial workforce.

The London model was imported to Boston in 1838, and then spread through northern U.S. cities over the next few decades. If a local businessman had close ties to a local politician, he had only to go to the station and a squad of police would be sent to threaten, beat, or arrest his employees. The primary role of early detectives was to spy on political radicals and other troublemakers. Pennsylvania was home to some of the most militant trade unionism in the United States during the late nineteenth and early twentieth centuries. The initial response of the mine and factory owners there was to set up a private police force called the Coal and Iron Police. This force committed many atrocities, such as the Latimer Massacre of 1897, in which police killed nineteen unarmed miners and wounded thirty-two others. Although the Coal and Iron Police continued to exist until 1931. the state increasingly took responsibility for social control, starting with the formation of the Pennsylvania State Police in 1905, the first state police force in the country. Their behavior, however, was much the same as police everywhere: strikebreaking and killing workers, as in the Westmoreland County Coal Strike of 1910–1911, where they earned the nickname of Pennsylvania Cossacks.

The Pennsylvania State Police were modeled on the Philippine Constabulary. Jesse Garwood, a major figure in the U.S. occupation forces in the Philippines, used repressive measures originating in the colonies in confrontations with Pennsylvania miners and factory workers. Marine General Smedley Butler, who once described himself as "a high class muscle-man for Big Business," served as police chief of Philadelphia in 1924. He was removed from office after a public outcry over his heavy-handed methods.

The United States also had its own domestic version of colonial policing, the Texas Rangers. In the same tradition as the Carolina Rangers, the Texas Rangers were trained to protect the interests of the White colonists when Texas seceded from Mexico in 1836, following the Mexican government's abolition of slavery. The Texas Rangers were a major force for White Anglo-Saxon Protestant colonial settler expansion, hunting down and killing the Indigenous population, as well as violently driving out the Mexican inhabitants. In effect, they served as the front line in the ethnic cleansing of Texas and, having secured the land, they became labor enforcers for the landowners.[55] One of their primary roles was to act as a slave-catching patrol, which led, in the twentieth century, to their violent opposition to the civil rights movement. In the 1960s and 1970s, the Rangers played a central role in suppressing the United Farm Workers of America, arresting and beating pickets and union officials.[56]

The control of working-class activity was equally important for policing in Britain, particularly after the Hyde Park riots of 1866, which involved three days of fighting between the police and workers demanding suffrage by supporting the Reform League.[57] Political reformers made comparisons between the way workers were treated in Jamaica and their own struggle for parliamentary reform. For example, the newspaper *Reynold's News* attacked both the repression in Jamaica following the 1865 Morant Bay rebellion and the treatment of the Fenians in Ireland:

> Let Englishmen think of these things; for, although Irishmen and Negroes are the present victims, who knows who may be the next people exposed to the tender mercies of the Hobbs's, the Eyres, and the Wodehouses.[58]

> The chief end and object of all royal and aristocratic governments is to enslave the masses of mankind . . . it behooves people of England to demonstrate . . . that they did not identify themselves with acts which had disgraced the British name.[59]

Today, neoliberal politicians see all social problems as police problems. Governments see no need to pursue social policies that might address social problems without the use of the police, abandoning poor neighborhoods to market forces, backed up by a repressive criminal justice system, leading to gentrification and social cleansing. Modern policing does nothing to make poorer communities safer places to live. Indeed, for young Black men in particular, it does quite the reverse.[60]

CHAPTER 5

Finance and Industry

In 1944, Eric Williams, a future prime minister of Trinidad and Tobago, published *Capitalism and Slavery*, a book that put forward, among many other groundbreaking arguments, the proposition that "the profits obtained [from slavery] provided one of the main streams of that accumulation of capital in England which financed the Industrial Revolution." This made uncomfortable reading for the British bourgeoisie, but thereafter it has inspired civil rights and anticapitalist activists. The financing of industrial development cannot be separated from the more general banks, investment houses, lenders, finance companies, real estate brokers, and insurance companies, commonly known as the financial services industry. After all, a considerable part of the capital required to start up industrial enterprises and provide credit for their continuation also came from banking institutions that made their money through slavery-based commercial activities, even if loan recipients were unaware of these origins. The modern insurance industry, in particular, has its roots in insuring the risks involved in trafficking enslaved Africans.

The connection between industrialization and slavery is well illustrated by the origins of the finance that enabled the expansion of the Welsh slate quarries at the end of the eighteenth century. Let us look at the most blatant case of the use of profits from enslavement to fund the industrial takeoff: the Pennant family of North Wales and Liverpool.

Richard Pennant, a Liverpool businessman active in the West India trade, acquired, by marriage, a half-share of the Penrhyn estate in North Wales; he then bought the remaining half.[1] The money Pennant generated from sugar and slavery in Jamaica was invested in building roads, railways, and port infrastructure, as well as expanding the slate industry in Wales, in particular his Penrhyn slate quarry. By the 1790s, the quarry was employing four hundred men, working in harsh and dangerous conditions. Slate had to be pried off the rock face, with the workers hanging from ropes over the edge. The dust was extremely damaging to their health; there were frequent accidents, injuries, and deaths. But health and safety were not one of Richard Pennant's priorities.[2]

When Richard Pennant died, the estate passed to his cousin, George Hay Dawkins-Pennant (1764–1840), who, when slavery was finally abolished, received £14,683 [£18,180,000, $23,000,000] compensation for the 764 enslaved laborers on the Pennant family's Jamaican estates. The family wealth not only enabled the expansion of the slate industry, but also enabled the construction and lavish furnishing of Penrhyn Castle, a mock-Norman castle, complete with arrow slits and a moat, presumably intended to give the impression of the family's long, respectable lineage.[3]

By 1890 the Penrhyn estate—comprising the castle, 41,348 acres of agricultural land in Caernarvonshire, the slate quarry employing three thousand men, and the Jamaican plantations—was owned by George Sholto Gordon Douglas Pennant, Second Baron Penrhyn (1836–1907). His refusal to recognize the slate workers' trade union, the North Wales Quarrymen's Union, led to the longest strike in British history, nearly three years, from 1900 to 1903.[4]

Penrhyn Castle is now owned by the National Trust, whose website speaks of the way in which "Penrhyn Castle's foundations were built on a dark history. One of exploitation, Jamaican sugar fortunes and the transatlantic slave trade."[5] There is also an account of the great strike and the admission that "many in the local community will still not visit Penrhyn Castle because of what it represents."[6] The Transport and General Workers' Union erected a memorial to commemorate the great strike. Presently, there is no memorial to the thousands of enslaved Africans who labored and died on the Pennant Jamaican plantations, producing the original wealth that allowed the Pennant family to continue their exploitation of labor in Wales.

## Sugar and Health

There is another connection between the proletarianization of rural people in Wales and the business of slavery. The workforce of the Pennant slate quarries, along with much of the rest of the working class in Britain during the eighteenth and nineteenth centuries, lived on a poverty diet of white bread and jam, washed down with tea sweetened by sugar, produced initially by enslaved workers in the West Indies and later by indentured workers in British colonies, and by enslaved labor in Brazil or Cuba.[7] Anthropologist Sidney Mintz has demonstrated how sugar, as a significant source of calories, became a crucial part of the diet of industrial workers in Britain.[8] British sugar consumption rose by 44 percent between 1770 and 1849, and accelerated sharply thereafter. Annual per capita consumption increased from twenty pounds a year in 1800 to eighty pounds by 1914.

Sugar has become ubiquitous in the modern diet, with 40 percent of sugar being consumed in processed and preprepared food. The most obvious example is breakfast cereals, the great success of the Big Food corporations. Some cereals contain more than half their weight in sugar. Sugar is, in general, the key to the commercial success of a food or drink product. It is also an essential ingredient of processed meat—what makes Kentucky Fried Chicken appear edible.

There is now an epidemic of obesity. The World Health Organization estimates that two billion people in this world are overweight, with 600 million classified as obese. This has devastating implications for their health: diabetes, hypertension, myocardial infarction, angina, osteoarthritis, stroke, gout, gall bladder disease, colonic and ovarian cancer, breathing difficulties and back problems, for which the vast amount sugar in the modern diet is largely responsible. Sugar is also responsible for the widespread dental problems in young people and many diseases of the pancreas. The addiction to sugar works in the same way as other addictions: people like the sweet taste and crave more, and frequently then ignore the substandard taste of the food it drowns.[9]

This public health situation is one of the continuing legacies of the business of slavery, going back to the earliest origins of urban industrialization. Sugar refining was one of the first urban industrial processes to develop in European cities, starting in Antwerp in the sixteenth century.

## Origins of Industrial Capitalism

Adam Smith's account of the original accumulation of capital necessary for the startup of the capitalist economy spoke of some people working harder than others and gradually building up wealth, eventually leaving the less diligent workers to accept wages for their labor. Karl Marx described this as a nursery tale, akin to the biblical myth of "original sin":

> This primitive accumulation plays in political economy about the same part as original sin in theology. Adam bit the apple, and thereupon sin fell on the human race. Its origin is supposed to be explained when it is told as an anecdote of the past. In times long gone-by there were two sorts of people; one, the diligent, intelligent, and, above all, frugal elite; the other, lazy rascals, spending their substance, and more, in riotous living.... Thus it came to pass that the former sort accumulated wealth, and the latter sort had at last nothing to sell except their own skins. And from this

original sin dates the poverty of the great majority that, despite all its labor, has up to now nothing to sell but itself, and the wealth of the few that increases constantly although they have long ceased to work. Such childishness is every day preached to us in the defense of property.[10]

When describing his preferred term, "original expropriation," Marx wrote::

The discovery of gold and silver in America, the extirpation, enslavement and entombment in mines of the aboriginal population, the beginning of the conquest and looting of the East Indies, the turning of Africa into a warren for the commercial hunting of black-skins, signalized the rosy dawn of the era of capitalist production. These idyllic proceedings are the chief momenta of primitive accumulation. On their heels treads the commercial war of the European nations, with the globe for a theater.[11]

Colonial commerce, including the business of slavery, was one of the driving forces of the capitalist economy from its earliest manifestation, encouraging the expansion of a manufacturing economy. Exports from Britain accounted for around half of all industrial production in the eighteenth century.[12] Economic historian Joseph Inikori tells us that in 1770 the slave trade and the plantation economy furnished as much as 55 percent of gross fixed capital formation investment in Great Britain.[13]

The increased rate of industrial growth based on exports depended on purchasing power generated by the British West Indies. Demand stemming from Africa, the Caribbean, and North America based on the sugar industry was responsible for more than half of the growth of English exports in the third quarter of the eighteenth century. The business of slavery greatly contributed to increasing investment in the British Empire, particularly the construction of the infrastructure that such trade required. Additionally, the re-export of sugar to Europe brought enormous profits.[14] Half of the nonagricultural workforce in England and Wales was employed in production for export, accounting for much of the growth in manufacturing output.[15]

The initial outlay required to start an individual industrial enterprise was relatively small but, on a day-to-day basis, copious amounts of working capital or credit were needed, much of which came from the Atlantic trade.[16] Considerable capital investment and government support was required for the construction of the necessary infrastructure: canals, roads, harbors, docks, warehouses, and shipping. Moreover, according to Marx:

> During the historical genesis of capitalist production . . . the rising bourgeoisie needs the power of the State, and uses it to "regulate" wages, i.e. to force them into the limits suitable for making a profit, to lengthen the working day, and to keep the worker himself at his normal level of dependence. This is an essential aspect of so-called primitive accumulation.[17]

The textile industry depended on a particularly close connection between merchant capital, plantation owners, and manufacturers. Cheap raw cotton from the southern U.S. states was central to the growth of industrialization in Britain which, in turn, encouraged the growth of U.S. slavery.[18]

The use of the term "so-called primitive accumulation" is open to confusion, and can imply that the initial expropriation, which generated the finance to enable the early manufacturing start-ups, was only present in the early stages of the development of industrial capitalism and was then replaced with exploitation of employed workers. In fact, the combination of expropriation and exploitation has been characteristic of capitalism throughout its history.[19]

## Guns, Steam, and Steel

The institution of slavery has its origins in the pre-capitalist era, but the form that it later took in the Americas, plantation slavery on an industrial scale, was geared to the mass production of commodities and flourished as a result of market forces. It not only enabled the initial development of capitalism, but also became an important component of the mature capitalism of the late eighteenth and nineteenth centuries. Until it was finally abolished in Brazil in 1888, slavery was a central feature of the capitalist economy.

As early as 1550, the citizens of Antwerp were complaining about pollution from the city's nineteen sugar refineries. The stench of sugar refining also became a common complaint in Amsterdam, where the number of refineries increased from forty in 1650 to one hundred by 1770. Later, the industry spread to England, where Bristol had twenty factories refining sugar, processing 21,000 tons of raw sugar a year, while London had over one hundred refineries.

In Bristol, sugar refining began in 1609, when the town began importing raw sugar from the enslaved labor camps run by the Portuguese in Madeira and the Azores.[20] Following the conquest of Jamaica, when mass production of raw sugar really accelerated, Bristol became the center of the refining industry. Sugar dust is highly flammable; consequently, in 1769, the sugar refiners established the Bristol Fire Insurance Office, another link between financial services and the business of slavery.[21] These connections are best illustrated by William Miles (1728–1803), who based his fortune on sugar refining, then went on, in 1794, to buy a leading partnership in the old banking house of Vaughan and Barker, which continued trading as the Miles Bank and which, after a series of mergers and acquisitions, became part of the NatWest Group. Miles was also a slave factor, which was the term used for someone who bought enslaved Africans from the traffickers in the Caribbean ports and sold them at a profit to the plantation owners. He later became owner of a plantation in Jamaica run by enslaved labor, finally returning in the 1790s to become a financier of the slave trade in Bristol, using his wealth to buy a landed estate in Somerset.[22] William Miles's son, Philip John Miles (1774–1845), continued in the business of slavery and banking, receiving £17,850 [£23,610,000, $30,000,000] compensation for 663 enslaved laborers at emancipation in 1838.[23]

The productivity of the sugar refining process was vastly increased at the end of the eighteenth century by mechanization, including the use of vacuum pans for rapid evaporation at low temperatures, air pumps, and steam engines. James Watt, whose patents for improvement of the steam engine made it practical for widespread industrial use, was the son of a West Indian merchant and slave trader who supported Watt in his career. Watt himself worked for his father as a mercantile agent in Glasgow during the 1750s. Caribbean plantation owners who needed to process sugarcane were significant customers for James Watt's steam engines. This mechanization of sugar processing, far from making the lives of the enslaved laborers easier, made their labors more relentless, as the increased pace of the steam-powered machinery forced an increase in productivity by the workers; in this context, productivity increase meant even harder work, driven by the whip.[24]

Why did the steam engine come to dominate capitalist development in the early nineteenth century, when water power was readily available and cheaper? There was one major factor: control of labor.[25]

At the end of the eighteenth century, most cotton mills were water-powered, but water flow sufficient to power a mill was located far from the major population centers and this gave an edge to labor in its struggle for higher wages and better conditions. Mill and factory owners attempted to compensate for the labor shortage by creating colonies of workers, model villages around the water-driven mills. But creating these villages required additional capital expenditure and, once the workers had organized themselves into trade unions, their very isolation and community solidarity made them harder to defeat. Thus, according to poet and novelist Sir Walter Scott:

> The manufactures are transferred to great towns, where a man may assemble five hundred workmen one week and dismiss

them the next, without having any further connection with them than to receive a week's work for a week's wages, nor any further solicitude about their future fate than if they were so many old shuttles.[26]

Following a stock market crash in 1825 caused by overenthusiastic speculation in South America, leading to a general economic crisis, the need to extract the maximum profit from the workforce became critical in the heightened competition, and this was, in turn, dependent on coal-powered steam engines. The workers themselves, of course, resisted, and the early trade unions and workers' associations organized a general strike in 1842, in large part as resistance to increased automation, de-skilling, and unemployment. The strike was accompanied by widespread sabotage, which included pulling the plugs on the steam engines.[27] Nevertheless, steam-driven mechanization became central to the ideology of the industrial capitalist class.

The upshot of all this was to become the complete dependence of capitalist industry on fossil fuels, with oil added into the package in the twentieth century. Just as employers in the nineteenth century moved their operations into the cities to obtain cheap labor, they were moving to the Third World in the mid-twentieth in an attempt to avoid the trade union organization in the metropolitan counties that pushed up wages. The outsourcing of production by the textile industry from Europe and the United States to Bangladesh and Haiti is just one example. The dominance of fossil-fuel-based power is a consequence of the class struggle, and an essential driver in capital's need to extract greater surplus value from labor.[28]

The economic transition brought about by coal-based steam power was initially based on the accumulation of capital through a combination of Caribbean slavery and colonial exploitation, accompanying the proletarianization and immiseration of labor in the metropolitan counties. Even after the abolition of slavery in the British Empire, the steam-driven cotton industry in Britain was still dependent on cotton from the United States that was picked by enslaved labor. Continued slavery in the United States was, conversely, greatly assisted by investment and loans from the British financial services industry. With the approach of the U.S. Civil War in the mid-1800s, the British imperial state would likely have intervened in support of the Confederacy, were it not for popular opposition. There was also substantial investment of British capital in its own informal empire in Latin America, particularly in Cuba and Brazil, which were the last countries in the Americas to abolish slavery.

The textile industry, the bedrock of capitalist industrialization, has been connected to slavery at every level. Samuel Greg (1758–1834), who set up the first water-driven yarn-spinning factory in England at Quarry Bank near Manchester in 1784, also owned Hillsborough Estate, a large sugar plantation on the island of Dominica. He had other family connections to the transatlantic slave trade, including his brother-in-law Thomas Hodgson, who owned slaving ships, and another brother-in-law, Thomas Pares, a banker whose family had also made their fortune through slavery. Samuel's brother Thomas married Margaret Hibbert (1749–1818), the sister of West Indian merchant William Hibbert of Hare Hill, and provided insurance for his brother-in-law's transatlantic trade as a member of Lloyd's of London.[29]

The demand for guns to trade for kidnapped Africans, as well as shackles to imprison them, meant that metalworking and the arms industry in Britain profited from massive expansion. Between 1750 and 1807, between 283,000 and 394,000 muskets were exported annually, totaling nearly twenty million weapons during this period.[30]

But enslaved Africans had a more direct impact on the Industrial Revolution. The Cort process, named after English businessman Henry Cort who patented it, enabled scrap and poor-quality iron to be converted into wrought iron on an industrial scale. In fact, Cort merely purchased the factory machinery of a Jamaican enslaver, John Reeder, had it transported to England, and then patented it as if it were his own idea. Furthermore the inventor of this metal-conversion process was not Reeder himself but his enslaved African laborers, who had brought the knowledge of ironworking with them from West Africa, home to some of the most important ironworking civilizations in history.[31] Not content with robbing the ideas of enslaved Africans, Cort embezzled £39,676 [£38,150,000, $48,300,000] from the Royal Navy. In response, the British government confiscated his patents and made them public, enabling the widespread use of the process in British industry.[32]

Brass was also much in demand as a trade good on the West Coast of Africa. John Coster (1647–1718) of Bristol developed the use of coal to replace charcoal in the smelting of copper as part of the brass-making process, later supplying the copper sheathing attached to the undersides of ships—mainly Royal Navy vessels, sugar importers, and slave traffickers—to prevent tropical mollusks from attacking the wooden hulls. Later, copper stills were used for the distillation of rum. Not content with merely supplying the business of slavery with the tools of its trade, John Coster's son Thomas (1684–1739) owned shares in several slaving vessels.[33]

Professor of economic and social history Nuala Zahedieh provides us with a useful case study on the relationship between copper, industrialization, and the plantation.[34] William Forbes, she writes, was a coppersmith who moved from Aberdeen to London in 1771 to set up a copper-founding business. By 1775 he had installed copper machinery for eleven London sugar refiners. In 1776 he supplied slaveholders in Antigua, Barbados, Dominica, Grenada, Jamaica, and Tobago; his works produced all the essential metallic parts of the sugar-refining process. The Forbes workshop was also heavily committed to supplying the Royal Navy with copper sheathing for their vessels. So, while Forbes made no direct investment in the business of slavery, he made his fortune by supplying the sugar plantocracy and the navy with their necessary equipment. At this time, most copper ore came from Cornwall, and the Cornish copper-mining industry became one of the principal markets for James Watt's improved steam engine; forty had been purchased in the county by 1780. These engines required coal, which was imported from South Wales, thereby giving an impulse to a new coalfield development. Forbes returned to Scotland, where he used his capital to acquire a landed estate of six thousand acres in Stirlingshire. He evicted tenants, enclosed common lands, and created new farms, which he let out at exorbitant rents. He had woodland cleared, sold the timber, and exploited a local coalfield. This process of using capital investment to exploit landed estates is frequently known as "improvement," a term which became a euphemism for the wholesale privatization involved in the enclosures, although this was the opposite of improvement in the lives of the villagers on his estate.

The link between copper and slavery continued in Cuba for years after the abolition of enslavement in the British Empire. There was a rich source of copper in eastern Cuba, with mines in the area around the town of El Cobre. Even the town's name came from the Spanish word for copper. These had fallen into disuse, but were reopened in the late 1830s by two British companies, the Company of Proprietors of the Royal Copper Mines of Cobre, and the Santiago Company, both financed by capital originating in the City of London. Copper was shipped from Santiago de Cuba to Swansea in Wales, in a fleet of specially constructed ships. While the skilled miners and overseers of El Cobre were Cornish or Welsh, the rest of the manual laborers were enslaved Cubans of African descent, either owned by the Santiago company directly or leased from local Cuban plantation owners. By 1841 the Cobre Company was extracting 25,000 tons of copper ore per year, with a monthly profit of £12,000 [£16,060,000, \$20,339,000], a 30 percent return on investment.[35] The slave-based mining continued until the Cuban war against Spanish colonialism, known as the Ten Years' War (1868–1878), during which the rebel army captured El Cobre and freed the enslaved miners, most of whom went on to join the rebel forces and fight against slavery and the colonial domination of the Spanish Empire.

Thus the exploitation of the enslaved labor force in the

various slave-based economies of the Americas stimulated Western European and North American industrial development. It is now well established that the origin of the current crisis of global warming can be traced back to the widespread adoption of the coal-powered steam engine by the British textile industry in the early nineteenth century. Since then, the drive for profit has been linked to the vastly increased use of fossil fuels, resulting in massively increased production of greenhouse gases and other pollutants.

This increasing reliance on fossil fuels is based on a mutually reinforcing relationship between slavery and industrialization, with the one feeding the other. Many slave traders, planters, and merchants did diversify into manufacture, agricultural improvement, and infrastructure, or else kept their money in banks and finance houses that extended credit to the developing capitalist economy. However, as the slave economy expanded the need for credit, banking, and insurance, the main beneficiary was, as always, the financial services industry.

### Financing the Business of Slavery

The close relationship between West Indian slave-grown cotton and the Lancashire textile industry had resulted in the early development of Liverpool cotton brokers who later influenced cotton brokering in the United States. Slaveholding was absolutely intertwined with cotton manufacture as well as cotton trading, often participating in parallel streams of business activity based ultimately on slavery.[36]

Slave trading required credit in order to finance expeditions to the African coast and, given the risks involved, the interest demanded by those who lent the money was significant. The purchase of enslaved laborers, when they reached the Americas, required further credit, as few slave owners had sufficient capital to buy the number of laborers they required. In turn, in a very modern format, these loans were often secured by mortgages on the estates, effectively a mortgage on the enslaved people themselves, as they represented an estate's most valuable asset. Given the links between the production of raw cotton by enslaved labor in the United States and the growing textile manufacturing industry in Britain, it is useful to examine the role of the London-based financial services industry in this relationship.

Let us take the example of the Consolidated Association of the Planters of Louisiana (CAPL), which used enslaved Africans as collateral to raise capital overseas in order to build a lending institution under slave owner control. CAPL was chartered by the Louisiana State Legislature in 1827 and used the famous Baring Brothers of London as its European brokers. U.S. state administrations issued bonds that turned slave mortgages into securities to be marketed to European investors. These securities produced credit to buy more enslaved workers.

By 1836 New Orleans had the densest concentration of banking capital in the country. Other states followed suit, supporting banks that offered slave-based bonds to Europe; Alabama, for example, sold most of its bonds to Rothschild Frères of Paris. In the U.S. southwestern states these sales generated a speculative bubble, which burst in 1839, resulting in the collapse of most of the region's state-sponsored banks. The state governments had guaranteed these banks and, after the crash, increased taxes to redeem the bonds, thus privatizing the gains but socializing the risks. In the event, eight states and the territory of Florida defaulted on their sovereign debts.

In the recovery from these collapses, southern U.S. slave owners became dependent on northern credit, but they held a vast capital investment in three million enslaved workers. A new system then developed, based on northern capital coming south to buy cotton. Lehman Brothers of London, the same banking corporation that went bankrupt in 2008, started life lending money to slave owners on the security of future crops, and mortgages on the enslaved workers themselves. These factors borrowed from New York banks such as Brown Brothers. It is interesting to see how many entities in the financial services industry that started this way became household names.

Slave trafficking was a risky business; in addition to the normal hazards of sea voyages during the eighteenth century, there was the ever-present possibility of revolt by the kidnapped Africans. The insurance industry developed initially in order to spread these risks among a number of investors.[37] Insurance against rebellion at sea, however, did not cover the deaths incurred in putting down the insurrection if less than 10 percent of the enslaved cargo were killed. Insuring aspects of the business of slavery is an early example of the principle of putting a monetary value on human life.

In 1790 the slave trade and the transportation of slave-grown produce from the West Indies was the single most important marine insurance sector, accounting for at least a third of the premiums of the London Assurance Company. Insurance played an important role in the takeoff of London-based finance capitalism and, in the eighteenth century, such insurance enterprises boomed, taking on a capital accumulation logic of their own. These insurance companies are still with us today. For example, the 1720 act of Parliament that allowed the formation of two joint-stock insurance companies, both heavily involved in insuring the slave trade, facilitated the formation of Royal Exchange Insurance, later Guardian Royal Exchange, and currently part of AXA, along with London Insurance, later incorporated in Royal and Sun Alliance. The most important business of Lloyds of London, still with us today, was the West India trade.[38]

British banking was deeply involved in the expansion of slavery in the U.S. South. Barings Bank enabled the Louisiana Purchase in 1802, doubling the landmass of the United States and vastly increasing the land available to the slavery-based cotton economy. Both Barings and Rothschild had major investments in plantation banks, centered in New Orleans, and provided the credit for consignments of cotton throughout the pre–Civil War period. British capital also provided credit for the purchase of land in the newly acquired territories and the expanded internal trade in enslaved laborers, thereby enabling the expansion of the business of slavery.[39]

Slavery is a capital-intensive business, and the expansion of U.S. cotton agriculture depended on large sources of credit, most commonly the London money market, where loans were frequently secured on mortgages on enslaved Africans. More ingeniously, these mortgages were then turned into bonds that could be sold to European and U.S. investors in a manner that both spread the risk and commodified the enslaved worker, making slave owning more acceptable to early Victorian gentlefolk. It is hardly surprising, therefore, to see Baring Brothers Bank at the center of this financial web, being one of the prime issuers of such bonds.

Another modern financial tool produced by slave-based agriculture was the idea of the futures market, as financiers who traded in cotton (and the Barings were among the most important of these) traded in shipments, not yet arrived, while they were still on the high seas. Social anthropologists Erika Brodnock and Johannes Lenhard see the origins of modern venture capital in colonialism and the business of slavery.[40]

But if the profits from enslavement and the financial instruments developed to process those profits were important factors in the development of industrial capitalism, by the beginning of the nineteenth century, the business of slavery had started to outlive its usefulness to the manufacturing bourgeoisie, who now needed a different form of state, with different economic priorities. The struggle over the abolition of enslavement was one of the battlegrounds for political control of the state.

CHAPTER 6

## Amelioration, Resistance, and Emancipation

*Great mass movements show a curious affinity with the rise and development of new interests.*

—Eric Williams

This chapter considers the process of emancipation in greater complexity than the simplistic "Wilberforce freed the slaves," which many of us were taught in English schools.[1] That view of the abolition movement gives all the credit for the ending of enslavement in the British Empire to the work of a few upper-class, Evangelical Anglican campaigners led by William Wilberforce and Thomas Clarkson, collectively known as the "Clapham Sect" after the church where they worshiped in Clapham in South London. William Wilberforce (1759–1833) led the parliamentary campaign against the British slave trade for twenty years until the passage of the Slave Trade Act of 1807. The campaign for complete abolition was launched in 1823 with the founding of the Society for the Mitigation and Gradual Abolition of Slavery (later known as the Anti-Slavery Society), which eventually took a position in favor of immediate emancipation. One of this group's leading figures was Thomas Clarkson, who traveled an estimated 10,000 miles up and down the country campaigning against the evils of enslavement. The official view is summed up by the inscription on Wiberforce's tomb in Westminster Abbey which reads:

> In an age and country fertile in great and good men, he was among the foremost of those who fixed the character of their times.... His name will ever be specially identified with those exertions which, by the blessing of God, removed from England the guilt of the African slave trade, and prepared the way for the abolition of slavery in every colony of the empire.

The belief that abolition was the work of a few great men solely motivated by Christian charity was almost universally held in Britain until Eric Williams, in *Capitalism and Slavery*, argued that the profitability of slavery, the slave trade, and the Caribbean colonies had declined in the aftermath of the American Revolution, and that this decline was an important factor in the British Parliament's decision to abolish the slave trade and later to emancipate the enslaved in the British West Indies. Williams's analysis challenged the previous widely held view that abolition was an act of unselfish humanitarianism. Predictably, this rejection of the comfortable notion of British establishment benevolence has been widely criticized, with a number of authors producing data to prove that the profitability of slavery was not in decline.[2] But we can also understand "decline" in relative terms, as the plantation economy, while still profitable, was overtaken by the manufacturing industry it had helped to establish.[3]

The United Kingdom's 1838 emancipation of the enslaved can be seen as part of a dispute within the British ruling class over which interest group controlled the levers of power. The rising industrial bourgeoisie contested political control with the established landowning gentry and businessmen who made their money through the business of slavery. Both of these groups required protection of their agricultural produce from foreign competition through import tariffs. Industrialists had a much greater interest in free trade, as protective import duties forced up the price of food for their employees and thereby meant that wages, even poverty wages, had to be higher, which cut into their profits. Moreover, workers and radicals in Britain were fighting for their civil rights, and many activists linked the struggle for universal suffrage and trade union rights to the campaign for emancipation of the enslaved. At the same time, increased resistance by the enslaved laborers themselves was making the whole system untenable. Their endeavors to secure their own freedom gave rise to three major rebellions in the early part of the nineteenth century.

In 1783 absentee plantation owners, businessmen trading with the West Indies, and colonial agents organized themselves into a formal lobbying group called the London West India Committee. Between 1783 and 1833, this committee acted as a political pressure group for the slavery business in Britain and the absentee landlords, as well as for the slave owners living in the West Indies. Initially they lobbied the government against restrictions on the slave trade, then lobbied against measures to ameliorate the working conditions of their enslaved workers and against free trade in sugar. They went on to fight a defensive action against the abolition movement and, after emancipation, campaigned for and won increased compensation for their loss of the property in enslaved laborers.[4]

If Prussian military strategist Karl von Clausewitz saw war as politics by other means, many slave-owning families saw politics as business by other means. Their representation in Parliament was vital to defending slavery-based property relationships for as long as possible, then obtaining the maximum compensation from the public purse when that defense was no longer possible.

The slave owners did not surrender without a fight, and their supporters started discussing the improvement of the conditions of their enslaved laborers. When this delaying tactic finally failed and abolition became inevitable, they still managed to get compensation for their loss of property, which they were able to invest in the new post-slavery economy. This compensation of slave owners was one of the biggest bailouts in British history and the financial basis for a reorganization of the economy.

## A Different Kind of State

At first sight, the case for the continued profitability of slavery in the British West Indies seems to have been well made. Not only are the economic statistics convincing, but a logical argument could be made that the massive abolitionist campaigns would not have been necessary if there was a real decline within the Caribbean colonies after the loss of the North American colonies. It would have been sufficient to allow the practice of slavery to die the death of a declining industry. When we look at slavery in the United States, that logic is reinforced, as one cannot imagine the need for the Civil War, with its great losses of life and huge expense, if enslaved labor, over which it was fought, was on its way out.

Another indication of the continued profitability of the slave economy was the decision to build, between 1800 and 1802, the West India Dock in London, specifically to deal with the trade in tropical products from the Caribbean. At this time, the West Indian trade represented one-third of London's overseas trade by value and the slave economy was an important contributing factor in the growth of the City of London as a financial center.[5]

Capitalism requires continuous expansion; witness the modern obsession with economic growth. British slavery was based in the Caribbean islands, and this meant that there was a physical and geographical limit to the growth of the sugar economy. We have also seen earlier the problems of soil erosion and reduced agricultural productivity. This lack of possible expansion was offset by protectionist legislation that artificially increased the price of sugar and thereby maintained the plantation owners' profits.

The early stages of the development of any capitalist economy require protection from the competition of rival producers in other parts of the world, but once the new economy has become established this protection inhibits further growth.

Agriculture in mainland Britain was similarly protected on one hand by the tariffs that restricted the import of cheaper food from abroad, known as the Corn Laws. On the other hand, while manufacturing industry, particularly textiles, had benefited from similar protective legislation in the early days, by the end of the eighteenth century, the manufacturing bourgeoisie no longer needed such help and came to see their business as restricted by the protection still afforded agriculture in general, and sugar in particular. The essence of the matter was that manufacturing required a different form of state, one that would implement policies that were incompatible with the slave-based "West Indian Interest," a general term used at the time to describe those people and businesses in Britain and the colonies whose profits came from the business of slavery.[6]

Thus, one aspect of abolition can be seen as part of a struggle between two factions of the British ruling class with conflicting interests. Nevertheless, in order to win that campaign, those capitalist interests opposed to slavery had to reach a compromise with the still-powerful West Indian landowners. The situation was complicated by slave-produced cotton.

Cotton fabrics were linked from the outset with slavery, as cotton cloth from India was a popular trade item at the African end of the slave trade. This produced considerable profit for the East India Company, but English businessmen coveted this market and the replacement of Indian imports by home-produced exports from Britain became a priority. Since cotton fabrics originating in India proved very popular in England, the English Parliament, in 1685, imposed a duty of 10 percent on cloth imported from India; this was doubled in 1690, and, in 1701, the import of Indian printed cotton was banned altogether.[7]

The riches generated by slavery came from the combination of the exploitation of enslaved labor in the Caribbean and a protected British market with regressive taxes on items of everyday consumption, which, like all such consumption-based taxation, fell disproportionately on the poor.[8] As textile production became more mechanized, technology overcame the relatively high cost of labor in Britain, compared to that of India, while, at the same time, the British Empire deliberately undermined textile production in India. The British cotton industry thereby lost the need for economic protectionism, and its owners became convinced of the advantages of free trade.

To achieve this "free trade," the cotton bourgeoisie needed political power and representatives in order to control the state in the face of competing elites, principally the British landed gentry and the West Indian interest, whose profits were maintained by import tariffs on corn and sugar. Conversely, manufacturers sought to maximize their profits by reducing the wages they paid to their laborers. But these wages had to be sufficient to feed and clothe workers and their families, thus high grain and sugar prices necessitated increased factory wages.

Therefore, one factor driving the campaign for the abolition of slavery was the internal rivalry within the ruling class. Victory in the struggle for ascendancy by the manufacturing bourgeoisie over the previously dominant agricultural landowners' interests and their slaveholding allies was achieved legislatively, through the Abolition of the Slave Trade in 1807, the Reform Act in 1832, the Abolition of Slavery in 1833, the New Poor Law of 1834, and the Importation Act of 1846. This last, popularly known as the Repeal of the Corn Laws, was passed at the same time as the Sugar Duties Act of 1846, which removed protection for the sugar produced in the British Caribbean colonies. This law restored the link between sugar and slavery in Cuba and Brazil, as it gave a boost to cheaper sugar produced by enslaved labor there. Indeed, free trade allowed generally uninterrupted access to raw materials produced by forced labor of all kinds.[9]

But the abolitionist movement was much more complex than the story of bourgeois philanthropists like Wilberforce handing down freedom from on high. If the elite abolitionist movement aimed at the transformation of British capitalism from an agricultural to a manufacturing and financial services economy, there was another current within the movement that saw it as part of a struggle for reforms that would empower ordinary working people.

### Radical Abolitionists

In 1819, at a meeting in his Hopkins Street Chapel in Soho, radical "freethinker" Robert Wedderburn asked the congregation, "Has a slave an inherent right to slay his master, who refuses him liberty?" Following a discussion, "nearly the whole of the persons in the room held up their hands in favor of the Question." Wedderburn then exclaimed, "Well Gentlemen, I can now write home and tell the Slaves to murder their masters as soon as they please."[10] Wedderburn was the son of a Jamaican slave owner and an enslaved African woman named Joanna. To escape poverty in the West Indies, he joined the Royal Navy, eventually settling in London in 1779. He quickly became involved with a revolutionary current led by Thomas Spence. When Spence, on two occasions, was imprisoned for treason and seditious libel, Wedderburn became the effective leader of this radical movement, although he was imprisoned himself on several occasions. His most influential publication as titled *The Horrors of Slavery*, published in 1824.[11]

He was not alone in taking a radical stand in the struggle against enslavement. One of the first abolitionist petitions was launched by the Manchester Society for Constitutional Information in 1787, and petitioning would go on to become an important tactic, not only against enslavement and the slave trade, but also for many other radical and working-class causes such as parliamentary reform. Thomas Paine, author of *The Rights of Man*, was a leading member of the Society for Constitutional Information, which played an important part in setting up the London Corresponding Society, one of the first radical working-class political organizations in Britain. Thomas Hardy, founder of the Society, shared a house with Olaudah Equiano, the formerly enslaved African abolitionist. Equiano was part of the abolitionist group the Sons of

Africa, whose members were Africans living in Britain. His widely circulated autobiography, *The Interesting Narrative of the Life of Olaudah Equiano*, published in 1789, was an important campaigning tool in the fight for abolition.[12]

Olaudah Equiano was important in the development of the London Corresponding Society, as he provided a link between the radicals in London and militant workers in Manchester and Sheffield, whom he knew through his abolitionist campaigning. The Sheffield cutlery workers made a particularly firm connection between abolition of slavery in the colonies and reform at home; a mass meeting in Sheffield in 1794, the largest ever in the town, called for total abolition of slavery at a time when William Wilberforce and the "Clapham Sect" were merely calling for the end of the slave *trade*.[13]

The London Corresponding Society explicitly linked the slave owners to the corrupt political establishment they were fighting in Britain, and argued that the end of slavery would reduce the reactionary political base of the "Old Corruption," as the political regime controlled by the landed aristocracy and their allies was widely known at the time. Many rich men who had made their money from exploiting enslaved labor in the West Indies controlled the parliamentary constituencies known as "Rotten Boroughs," where the member of Parliament was effectively appointed by a rich man who controlled the few electors with the right to vote. Any attempt to reform the undemocratic electoral system in Britain would bring the reformers into head-on collision with the entrenched landed elite and their allies among the slaveholders.[14]

Thus, the demand for parliamentary reform in Britain and the campaign for the abolition of slavery became linked to the radical popular democratic movement of the late eighteenth century, with its demands for political and human rights. However, the British government also saw the connection, and Thomas Hardy was put on trial for high treason, along with John Horne Tooke and John Thelwall. In this case, politically opposing the government was defined as treason. Despite threats from the judge, the jury failed to convict them, and they were released, to public rejoicing. In order to tighten the law and make future acquittals of radicals less likely, the government brought in the Treasonable and Seditious Practices Act and the Seditious Meetings Act 1795, following with a Parliamentary Act of 1799, "For the more effectual suppression of societies established for seditious and treasonable purposes; and for better preventing treasonable and seditious practices," which banned all reformist associations, specifying the London Corresponding Society by name. William Wilberforce voted for all these "Gagging Bills," as well as the "Act to prevent Unlawful Combinations of Workmen" in 1800, which suppressed trade union activity.

Radical antislavery activists suffered severe government repression, along with the rest of the reform movement and so, when merely the *trade* in enslaved Africans was abolished in 1807, there was little space in which those who thought the measure too moderate could campaign for full emancipation. In the slightly more relaxed political atmosphere after the end of the Napoleonic Wars in 1815, antislavery petitions revived radical political activity. Radical activity was again repressed after the 1819 Peterloo Massacre, when cavalry charged into a crowd of around 60,000 working-class people in Manchester who were demanding the reform of parliamentary elections, killing eighteen and injuring between four hundred and seven hundred. The Seditious Meetings Prevention Act and the Blasphemous and Seditious Libels Act of 1819 curtailed the right of assembly and free speech and were passed with the support of William Wilberforce.

Once the Seditious Meetings Act was repealed in 1824, however, antislavery campaigning became inextricably linked with agitation for parliamentary reform and trade union rights. So much so that, in 1832, the political opportunist William Cobbett, when seeking parliamentary election in Oldham, with its strong working-class militant traditions, had to espouse antislavery sentiments, despite his own racist views.[15] From 1831 to 1832, over one and a half million names were added to antislavery petitions.

At a rally in Birmingham in 1838, where 200,000 people gathered to launch the national petition for universal suffrage, the main speaker began his speech by saying, to loud cheers, that he had attended the Birmingham Town Hall to "celebrate the emancipation of the blacks in Jamaica" and was now campaigning "to work out the emancipation of the whites at home."[16]

Women antislavery activists were frequently more radical than the men and, following the publication of Elizabeth Heyrick's 1824 pamphlet "Immediate Not Gradual Abolition," women's antislavery groups, such as the Birmingham Ladies Society for the Relief of Negro Slaves, led the way in establishing the movement's aim as immediate rather than gradual emancipation, despite the foot-dragging of the (male) national abolitionist leadership. One of the founders of the Ladies' Association in Colne, another antislavery group, expressed the hope that no Ladies' Association would ever be found with the word "gradual" attached to it.

## Breaking Their Own Chains

It would be a mistake to see emancipation as arising merely from British politics, whether radical, moderate, or conservative. The enslaved played an essential part in their own liberation. The revolution in Haiti not only abolished enslavement, in what was the most important sugar colony of the time; it also made slave owners on other islands realize the precarious nature of their position, which required increasing militarization of the region.

Revolts, escapes, and similar acts of resistance undermined the attractiveness of slavery as an investment proposition, while also heartening radical abolitionist opinion back in Britain. Throughout the history of slavery in the Americas, the enslaved made constant attempts to escape. Some, known as Maroons, went to live in remote and well-defended communities away from White society; many hid among the free population of the formerly enslaved in the towns; others lived as gangs of outlaws. A common form of escape in the Caribbean was to flee to the next island by canoe, stow away on a merchant vessel, or join a pirate company. Nowhere did Maroonage end slavery, but it considerably weakened the institution. Escapes proved costly, both through the loss of the enslaved who successfully fled, and through the need for slave catchers and soldiers to prevent more from running away.

Meanwhile, the plantation owners lived in a state of insecurity and fear of their enslaved laborers—with good reason, as there were many small-scale revolts. Attempts at mass escape sometimes resulted in the death of a planter and his family. Maroons provided a disruptive role model for the enslaved. The penalties they faced for escape—torture, mutilation—rendered recaptured Maroons less valuable and less productive.[17] The owners' frequent decisions to execute rebels put them in a contradictory position, as they thereby lost property. For investors, revolts, escapes, and similar acts of resistance undermined the attractiveness of slavery as a lucrative proposition, while heartening the opinion of radical abolitionists back in Britain.

Massive revolts were exceptional and depended on exceptional situations, reflecting the understanding by the enslaved of the odds against them and their ability to plan for the moment when they stood the best chance. Despite the cruel punishments for rebellion and resistance, there were important, if not successful, revolts and conspiracies in Barbados in 1649, 1675, 1686, 1692, 1708, and 1816.[18]

There were three major rebellions in the early part of the nineteenth century. The 1816 rebellion, known as Bussa's War, was a well-organized uprising, carefully planned, that started in Saint Philip parish, then quickly spread throughout most of the southern and central parishes of Christ Church, Saint John, Saint Thomas, Saint George, and parts of Saint Michael. Damage estimated at £175,000 [£203,900,000, $260,000,000] was caused during the uprising, for which the Drax Hall Estate claimed £4,084 [£4,758,000, $6,000,000] compensation. Twenty-five percent of the year's sugarcane crop was burned, as arson was used extensively by the rebels to undermine the economic base of the colony.[19] The revolt was defeated militarily by the militia, aided by imperial troops. A contemporary account speaks of "a little short of 1,000 slaves were killed in battle and executed at Law."[20]

Barbadian historian Hilary Beckles wrote:

> The rebellion failed to fulfill its immediate objective, but the anti-slavery movement in the metropolis succeeded in pushing emancipation bills through Parliament in 1833 and 1838, legally ending slavery and terminating almost half a century of intense and heated debate. The rebellion was the contribution of Barbadian slaves to that debate. It was their attempt to influence the future path of their society. They proved to the English Parliament that, contrary to the planters' assertions, they were not content with their status as slaves, and that their intention was to free themselves by force of arms, as imperial reformist means seemed unduly slow, if not unreliable.[21]

There were two further major uprisings in the British West Indies during the early nineteenth century, the Demerara Rebellion of 1823, involving more than ten thousand enslaved people, which took place in the colony of Demerara-Essequibo (Guyana); and the Baptist War, as the Jamaican uprising of 1831 became known. These three revolts can be credited with concentrating the minds of the British government to face the fact that increasing rebelliousness was causing the whole system to fail.[22] The slave-owning oligarchy would equally have been aware of Nat Turner's rebellion of enslaved people in Virginia, which also occurred in 1831.

But, in an attempt to head off the emancipation movement, the slave owners and their parliamentary representatives offered to improve the conditions under which their enslaved laborers toiled, a process known as amelioration. It may be useful to examine these developments in London, before returning to the revolts of 1823 and 1831, as parliamentary debates had an important influence on these rebellions.

## Amelioration

The abolition campaign in Britain, after a relative lull in activity following the abolition of the slave trade in 1807, was relaunched in 1823, when the Society for the Mitigation and Gradual Abolition of Slavery Throughout the British Dominions was founded, and Thomas Fowell Buxton moved a resolution in the House of Commons condemning enslavement as "repugnant to the principles of the British constitution and of the Christian religion," and calling for its gradual abolition. Despite the efforts of George Canning, foreign secretary and later prime minister, Buxton also urged the government to send dispatches to the colonies to improve the treatment of the enslaved.[23]

Sir John Gladstone was a Member of Parliament from 1818 until 1827, chairman of the Liverpool West India Association, as well as a close friend and colleague of George Canning. Together, Gladstone and Canning, realizing that there was a need to undermine the activities of the abolitionist faction in the House of Commons, proposed a series of reforms collectively known as Amelioration.[24] In 1823, therefore, resolutions were sent to the colonial assemblies, urging them to pass legislation ameliorating the conditions under which enslaved laborers worked. Lord Bathurst, the colonial secretary, drafted a series of measures for, to use his words, the "improvement" of the enslaved.[25]

The proposals included:

- Better provision for the religious instruction of the slaves.
- Abolishing Sunday markets so that the enslaved could attend church.
- Regulation of the punishment of enslaved men.
- The whip should not be used casually in the field.
- The flogging of enslaved women was forbidden.
- Families should not be separated.
- Legal recognition of the right of the enslaved to hold property

and the admission of their evidence against White colonists in court.
- Encouraging the manumission of those who could afford to buy their own freedom.

Before the Toleration Act of 1812, the Nonconformists, Protestant Christians in England who were not members of the established Church of England, were subject to a number of social and political restrictions. The Toleration Act removed these restrictions and opened the way for the Baptists and Methodists to form missions in the West Indies. These Nonconformists were in the forefront of that part of the amelioration program concerned with giving religious instruction to the enslaved. Although the planters mistrusted the missionaries, some were prepared, on the advice the Committee of West India Planters and Merchants, to compromise on the issue of religious instruction and, on their own terms, to tolerate the missionaries. Other planters advocated outright opposition to the reform program and were therefore hostile to the missionaries, who were seen to be implicated in the proposals.[26]

## Demerara Rebellion

Amelioration, as an attempt to head off demands for the eventual abolition of slavery, was widely misunderstood by the plantocracy in the Caribbean who saw it as unjustified interference in their right to private property—that is, their profits. In Demerara, the colonial authorities discussed the resolutions but made no public declaration as to their intention to implement them. Nevertheless, word of the existence of these instructions from London quickly reached the ears of the enslaved workers. Believing that the British Parliament had legislated their freedom, they planned militant activity to secure what they saw as their rights that were being withheld by the plantation oligarchy.

In August 1823, in the colony of Demerara, on Le Success plantation owned by Sir John Gladstone, there was a strike organized by two of Gladstone's enslaved workers, Jack and his father Quamina, which quickly spread to neighboring estates as large groups went from one plantation to another, calling the enslaved workers to join them. The Demerara rebels made no move to kill or injure the plantation management, merely locking the overseers, managers, and bookkeepers in the stocks and commandeering any weapons they found. There was some looting, ransacking of buildings, and cane fields were set on fire. Where owners, managers, or overseers resisted and firefights developed, a few were wounded or killed, but the leaders of the uprising did their best to prevent unnecessary loss of life among the enslavers, and, as a result, there were surprisingly few casualties among plantation management, although many of the most hated were abused, humiliated, and slapped while in the stocks, particularly by the enslaved women.[27]

The rebels of Demerara, numbering between nine thousand and twelve thousand, attempted to negotiate with the governor of the colony and the commander of the troops about their rights to wages, days without labor, and freedom, an example of the ways in which actions by enslaved workers represented a form of collective bargaining by riot.[28] Considering the circumstances, little damage was done to property.

Despite the relatively peaceful nature of the action, the colonial authorities brutally suppressed the revolt, killing hundreds of rebels, both in combat and by execution following impromptu field courts-martial. There were also a series of show trials, followed by public executions, performed as a grisly pageant designed to terrify the enslaved workers and reassure the enslavers, who had been badly frightened.

The nature of this uprising has been much debated in its historiography, with some seeing it as an attempt at the revolutionary overthrow of the whole institution of enslavement, while others view it as an armed, but reformist, demonstration intending to secure rights that were legally theirs.[29] I would argue that both these positions oversimplify the dynamic of the class struggle: revolutionaries frequently lead strikes and demonstrations with reformist aims when they see no possibility of immediate revolution, while reformist workers, in the heat of the struggle, frequently shift to revolutionary positions.

Editor and historian Mary Turner suggests that in order to improve the understanding of enslaved labor rebellions they should be placed in the "'context of chattel labor relations: not just the heroic moments of action but the protracted daily struggles at the point of production."[30] She further contends that enslaved workers would often engage in forms of protest, not dissimilar from the forms of industrial action taken by employed workers, in order to obtain increased provisions, lighter workloads, the removal of hated overseers, greater access to provision grounds, and other reforms to their working conditions. For instance, they would all gather at the boundary of the estate and refuse to work, but not leave the premises so that they could not be accused of trying to escape.[31] Although such day-to-day individual and collective resistance helped build the solidarity necessary for the uprising, which cannot be traced to any single cause, at bottom it was the very institution of slavery and the years of frustration that finally spilled over into revolt.

The terrified slave owners painted a picture of the rebels as violent, bloodthirsty brutes.[32] Meanwhile, the *Edinburgh Review*, an antislavery journal, wrote:

> In Demerara, a slight commotion was occasioned among the Negroes ... and far more resembling a combination of European workmen to strike for wages, for time, or other indulgence than a rebellion of African slaves.[33]

Reversing the allegations by the enslavers that the abolitionists in London had inspired the revolt, Trinidadian historian and scholar Gelien Matthews places the initiative with the enslaved themselves: "The slaves seemed to make a point of identifying their overt resistance with the debates taking place in Britain on their behalf by timing their risings to follow each wave of abolitionist activity."[34] The racist contempt of the plantation owners meant that they could not believe that the rebels were responsible for such a sophisticated strategy. On August 28, 1823, the editor of the *Demerara Gazette* concluded: "The plans and arrangements of the rebels were most extensive and well made—too well made indeed to admit of a doubt but a superior order of people had laid the original foundation."[35]

Demerara society found a convenient scapegoat in the Reverend John Smith, an English missionary and abolitionist who was the preacher at the church where Jack and Quamina worshipped. He was sentenced to death but died from conditions of his imprisonment before he could be executed. Typically, John Smith's judicial murder caused more outrage among elite London abolitionists than all the hundreds of the African dead. Sir John Gladstone, however, advanced the opinion, "I was not sorry to hear of Smith's death as his release would have been followed by much cavil and discussion here."

Nevertheless, some workers in Britain adopted a position of solidarity with the enslaved in this uprising. As a tract of the Anti-Slavery Society put it:

> The agricultural labourers, who in open day have been proceeding in bodies to the destruction of threshing machines, and to other acts of destruction of lawless violence; or that of the Luddites or, that of the Blanketeers. And let us ask whether it would have been endured that even these individuals should have been dealt with as the poor, ignorant, oppressed, cart-whipped slaves of Demerara have been dealt with?[36]

The similarity between the rebels in Demerara and the rebels in England was obvious to radicals in Britain.

Quamina was "shot while trying to escape," while Jack was sentenced to death, but after an appeal for clemency by Sir John

Gladstone, was exiled to Saint Lucia, where he was sentenced to hard labor. Seventy-three rebels were tried by court martial, seventy of whom were found guilty. Of the guilty, twenty-one were executed, ten decapitated after being hanged. Their heads were put on poles, while the remainder were brutally flogged. Hundreds of others were murdered by soldiers during the uprising and in its immediate aftermath.

Historian Anya Jabour says of the whole attempt at amelioration:

> A new and hostile disease environment, coupled with extreme work loads and inadequate diet, put enslaved Africans and their descendants in the New World in a precarious position. The situation was compounded by miserliness and racism, which induced slave owners, doctors, and even slaves' advocates to overlook evidence of slave malnutrition and illness. Slaves were punished for complaining of poor health, exhibiting signs of illness and malnutrition, and for attempting to augment the scanty official care given them. As a result, proposed measures for improving slave health and achieving natural increase were ineffective. Racism and profit-seeking were key elements in the demographic debacle of Caribbean slavery.[37]

### Enslaved Women

Some of the proposals for amelioration were based on improving the treatment of enslaved women. This was not simply for altruistic reasons. After the prohibition of trafficking in enslaved Africans in 1807, reproduction of enslaved labor power required an increase in the birth rate. In the earlier period of colonial slavery, however, this had not been seen as cost-effective.

Historian Robin Blackburn has calculated the basic economics of slavery, starting from the estimated annual cost of maintaining an enslaved person at four or five pounds [$25]. If the cost of raising an enslaved child to the age of ten was only half of that, it would still amount to twenty-five pounds [$125], to which must be added the additional loss of the mother's time and output for a season and the interest to be paid on this unproductive expenditure over ten years. Add in the possibility of losing some or all of this investment through the risk of high infant mortality, and the total cost of raising an enslaved laborer to working age could be over forty pounds, while an adult enslaved African could be purchased for between thirty and thirty-five pounds [$150], and put to work immediately. The easier treatment required to reduce mortality would have equally reduced productivity and output. Since a British agricultural laborer earned twenty-five a year [$125] after three years, the slave owner would already be ten pounds [$50] in pocket, and his costs would be twenty pounds [$100] per year less for the remainder of the lifetime of the enslaved worker. This is the brutal calculation that made slavery so profitable.[38]

Barbara Bush, Professor of Imperial History at Sheffield Hallam University, wrote

> In the external work sphere, the woman's role differed only marginally from that of the male slave. . . . Because the woman was subjected to the same conditions as the male slave, she reacted to enslavement, punishment and coercion in similar ways, from everyday resistance to outright rebellion.[39]

Nineteenth-century poet and Maroon historian Robert Dallas argued, in 1803, that the most important class of laborer comprised "the most robust of both sexes," whose chief employment consisted of "preparing and planting the soil, cutting the canes, feeding the mill and aiding the manufacture of sugar and rum."[40] The comparative worth was reflected in the price of an enslaved woman, as Richard Ligon, writer and plantation owner, quoted thirty pounds for a male Negro and between twenty-five and twenty-seven pounds for a female.[41]

Trinidadian activist Rhoda Reddock, on the comparative worth: "This is interesting when one notes that job discrimination on the

## AMELIORATION, RESISTANCE, AND EMANCIPATION 123

basis of sex is often justified on the ground that women have lower physical strength and endurance."[42] While race and slavery historian Orlando Patterson comments:

> Slavery abolished any real social distribution between males and females. The woman was expected to work just as hard, she was as indecently exposed and was punished just as severely. In the eyes of the master she was equal to the man as long as her strength was the same as his.[43]

That spurious equality did not apply to skilled work, such as carpentry, while the drivers (enslaved workers in charge of a gang of their enslaved fellows) were almost universally men. This actually meant that there was a higher proportion of women than men doing the backbreaking fieldwork, preparing the soil for planting and cutting cane, as well as the dangerous work of feeding sugarcane into the mills.[44] Women were also subject to the same brutal punishments. However, apart from midwives, nurses, or housekeepers, the enslaved elite consisted almost entirely of men. Enslaved women would therefore have made up a significant proportion of the ordinary field hands.[45]

Throughout history, the subordination of women has centered around women's ability to reproduce human life. In addition to enslaving the children born on the Caribbean plantations, the Atlantic system of slavery exploited the reproductive labor of women in Africa by kidnapping their children to provide the supply of enslaved workers.[46] Moreover, a significant number of women were pregnant when they arrived in the Caribbean, having been raped by their enslavers in Africa while awaiting sale to the traffickers or else by the crew on the slave ship.[47]

The enslavers' attitude to the reproduction of labor falls roughly into two periods. The first, extending to the middle of the eighteenth century, relied on the women of Africa to reproduce the next generation of enslaved labor. Thereafter, as the ban on the slave trade became imminent, and then a reality, the enslavers moved toward using the children of their already enslaved women to reproduce the labor power they required.[48]

During the first period, extending to the middle of the eighteenth century, plantation owners assumed that regular purchases of African captives would be part of the requirements of running a plantation, and a cheaper option than raising children from birth. This approach relied on the women of Africa to reproduce the next generation of enslaved labor.[49] Blackburn notes that "Caribbean planters bought more male than female slaves because of their unwillingness to take on the expense of natural reproduction."[50] Professor and Haiti historian Jean Casimir wrote: "The existence of family groups and the presence of women were superfluous in a society that supplied itself with labor from beyond its borders."[51] Pregnant women were frequently made to work up to the last few weeks of pregnancy and were expected to return to work no later than three weeks after delivery.[52] Eighteenth-century planter and writer William Beckford noted that plantation owners did not provide better treatment for pregnant women and nursing mothers because "thereby so much work is lost in attendance on their infants."[53]

However, from the mid- to late-eighteenth century, with the actual timescale varying according to local circumstances, the enslavers, realizing that brutality and malnutrition were counterproductive, moved toward breeding new enslaved laborers by encouraging enslaved women to have children. There were also financial incentives for women who gave birth. For instance, at Drax Hall in Barbados, women were paid six shillings and three pence, which was worth one U.S. dollar and fifty cents at the time. This for an infant, worth eight pounds [$40] at birth.[54] In Saint Domingue in 1775, Stanislas Foache, owner of the Foache sugar plantation, instructed his overseers that both mother and midwife were to be compensated with money and fabric when the child was out of danger, but to be whipped if it died.[55]

Rhoda Reddock tells us: "Slave women of child-bearing age, now largely Creoles, were hardened in their anti-breeding attitudes, with the result that most of the schemes for increasing the population by greater reproduction failed."[56]

The modest changes in the material conditions of enslaved women's existence were not enough to change their attitudes. Thus, despite the enslavers' wish for increased reproduction, the enslaved women did not see it as in their interest to cooperate. It is easy to imagine the resentment women would feel at being turned into breeding machines. Sabina Park, an enslaved Jamaican woman, charged with the murder of her three-year-old child, said that "she had worked enough for 'bukra' already and that she would not be plagued to raise the child . . . to work for white people."[57]

Orlando Patterson defined this resistance as "natal alienation," the denial of an enslaved person's right to future and past, through ancestors and children.[58]

Childhood, for the enslaved, did not exist. From the age of four, enslaved girls as well as boys worked on the estate. According to Orlando Patterson, "In Rosehall Estate [Jamaica] girls started work at four and remained in the Hogmeat Gang (which consisted of young children employed in minor tasks such as collecting food for the hogs, weeding, and the like) until the age of nine."[59]

Legal practice in the British West Indian colonies derived its justification and practice from Roman slave law, in particular the concept that a child derived its status as enslaved or free from their mother. The sons or daughters of an enslaved woman were themselves enslaved, irrespective of the status of the father.[60] This legal concept enabled enslavers to father as many children as they pleased on their estates, while ensuring that the offspring of their liaisons, be they consensual or forced, had no claim to inheritance. Enslavers could therefore bequeath the bulk of their estates to family members back in Britain.[61]

Meanwhile, in Africa, the women whose sons and daughters were kidnapped, having made the social investment in bearing children, were denied the care in their old age that was customary in their societies. Addressing both the conditions of slavery and current migrant labor, author and feminist scholar Cindi Katz writes: "The social reproduction of a migrant workforce is carried out in its members' countries of origin. When they are employed elsewhere, this represents a direct transfer of wealth from generally poorer to richer countries."[62]

The enslavers failed to supply their enslaved laborers with sufficient food, preferring to encourage them to feed themselves from their gardens and provision grounds. In Jamaica, provision grounds were regulated by the Consolidated Slave Act of 1788, which provided that, except in crop time, the enslaved were to be allowed one day per fortnight, as well as Sundays and public holidays, to cultivate their plots. The whole enslaved family engaged in the cultivation of these provision grounds, while women also acted as market sellers or *higglers*, trading in whatever surplus was produced. The Sunday markets, dominated by women, became an important area of sociability, and gave enslaved people a small degree of independence. These markets were hated by evangelical abolitionists who would rather the enslaved laborers went to church on Sunday.[63]

Just as enslaved women were an integral part of the workforce, so they were also central to the opposition to enslavement, frequently playing an important role of encouraging a culture of resistance. Although the male chauvinism and white supremacy of contemporary chroniclers has meant that women's roles were often neglected,[64] women and men reacted to enslavement, punishment, and torture in similar ways, from everyday resistance to outright rebellion.[65]

Given that women's labor was as arduous as that of the men, it is hardly surprising that they were just as prone to absconding from the plantations, especially as such escapes were frequently provoked by a demand for an increase in the workload.[66] Indeed, the French historian Anne-Marie Bruleaux wrote:"Pregnant women as well as those carrying babies in their arms took to Marronage."[67] In fact, one of the most famous Maroon communities was commanded by a woman called Nanny. She led a community of Africans in Jamaica, called the Windward Maroons, who had escaped their enslavement. They fought a guerrilla war against the colonial authorities in the First Maroon War (1728–1740).[68]

Poisoning was a common form of individual resistance to slavery. Female enslaved domestic servants were able to use their positions to put poison in the food and drink of their enslavers with minimum of personal risk.[69]

Enslaved women also resisted in a manner similar to women involved in employed workers' struggles. They were verbally aggressive and were prepared to participate in physical confrontations with the authorities. Contemporary observers alluded to the verbal and physical aggressiveness of enslaved women, who were also frequently reported inciting their fellows to revolt.

> Barbara Bush tells us that an overseer from a neighboring estate had occasion to find fault with a female field hand belonging to a gang hired to perform a particular task. In response to his criticism, "she flew at him with the greatest fury," grasped him by the throat and cried to her fellow slaves, "Come here, let's Dunbar him!' (Dunbar was a white overseer killed during previous unrest among enslaved workers.) The suddenness of this attack "nearly accomplished her purpose" before the overseer's own slaves came to his assistance. The woman was executed.[70]

During the revolutionary wars in Saint Domingue and Guadeloupe, women played their part in the fighting. In Saint Domingue/Haiti, Marie-Jeanne, wife of General Louis Daure Lamartinière, "took her share in the defence."[71]

The records relating to armed revolt by the enslaved in the eighteenth century speak of the active involvement of all: male and female, young and old, plantation and urban.[72]

## THE BAPTIST WAR, JAMAICA 1831

Despite the talk from London of Amelioration, little had changed in the material conditions of the enslaved laborers in Jamaica.

What had changed, however, was their political organization. Using the Christian missions set up by the various missionary societies as organizing centers, networks of activists were formed. Although the European missionaries were careful to preach submission and respect for law and order, the enslaved workers, often using their own interpretations of the gospels, mixed with spiritual and cultural beliefs originating in Africa, developed into what became known as Native Baptists.[73]

The enslaved workers were well aware of the abolitionist movement in Britain but were inevitably overoptimistic about the speed with which emancipation would come. Many of the enslaved workers who had attended church had leaned how to read the Bible. This enabled them to learn, via the colonial newspapers to which the enslaved house servants had access, of the excited rantings in the Jamaican House of Assembly by the owners and managers against amelioration proposals from London (published shortly before the revolt); the enslaved workers believed that they had already been freed by Parliament, and that this was being kept secret by the colonial governor. As a result, there was a great expectancy and determination to extract the best conditions they could from the situation.

Sam Sharpe, a deacon of the Burchell Baptist Church in Montego Bay, as well as a recognized leader of the unofficial Native Baptists, led a group of enslaved laborers into a strike, demanding that they be paid for their labors. It was intended that this would be a peaceful work stoppage but, recognizing the brutality of the colonial authorities and the plantation management, the strikers formed an armed militia, the Black Regiment, to act in self-defense. Despite the initial success of the Black Regiment against the colonists' Western Interior Militia, their lack of military training and relatively few firearms resulted in a military victory by the colonial forces. The strike action, beginning on December 27, 1831, was at first quite successful. But it was not widespread or coordinated enough to succeed, allowing the authorities to smash the strikes on plantations one by one.

The reaction of the colonial government and reprisals by management were brutal. At least five hundred rebels were killed, with official figures showing 207 killed outright during the revolt, and 312 executed after. The real number massacred would inevitably have been much higher. Before the uprising, the planters and colonial authorities had been divided on their attitudes toward the Nonconformist missionaries from Britain, even though these were racialized as White. Some tolerated the missions as a way of sidetracking London talk of amelioration into Christian salvation; others were deeply suspicious and saw all Nonconformists as enemies of the system. The Baptist revolt united the planters in blaming the missionaries, and rabid white supremacist mobs, encouraged by the magistrates and planters, burned a number of Nonconformist chapels, attacking and imprisoning missionaries, who were then deported from the island.[74]

Although the parliamentary abolitionists back in London were placed on the back foot by these events, they came to see the necessity of blaming the brutality of enslavement for the uprising. Predictably, the sacking of Christian places of worship caused them more outrage than the torture and killing of rebels.[75] Nevertheless, the denial of religious liberty was a spur to the general abolitionist movement in Britain, encouraging greater antislavery activity, particularly among Baptist and Methodist congregations.[76]

Meanwhile, in Britain, there was an increasingly militant working-class opposition. This started with the Luddite revolt from 1811 to 1812, an urban movement in northern England opposed to job losses caused by mechanization of industry, followed by the Captain Swing movement in 1830, an agricultural laborers' campaign of sabotage aimed at preventing the introduction of threshing machines. These were followed by the widespread strikes in 1831, again centered in the north of England. Occurring coincidentally with the unrest in the Caribbean, the authorities were presented with the danger of fighting on two fronts. In general, the unrest of 1816 to 1832 helped both to destabilize and discredit slavery, and reconcile the slaveholders to emancipation. Rather than continue to resist abolition, the West Indian slave owners moved away from defending slavery toward demanding compensation for their loss of property.

## COMPENSATION AND COMPROMISE

When enslavement was finally abolished in the British Caribbean, the former slave owners were compensated to the tune of twenty million pounds, probably worth twenty-five billion pounds in today's money. This process was meticulously documented, and the compensation records provide a snapshot of the slave economy that gives us valuable data to assess the competing claims and the relationships between the various sectors of the British capitalist class.

The Centre for the Study of the Legacies of British Slavery has digitized the records of around 46,000 claimants of compensation and published them online. Of the 30,000 or so actual monetary awards, 83 percent of the compensation went to claimants of over 500 pounds, but these claims represented a mere 16 percent of the total number of claimants. Thus, less than five thousand enslavers, 20 percent of the total compensated, can be seen to have owned 80 percent of the enslaved workers.[77] Many of the smaller-scale owners of enslaved workers were women, often the widows of slave owners who were living in England and, it was argued at the time, the income derived from slave owning was the only financial support for many widows and orphans.[78] This argument shows a petit-bourgeois sense of entitlement; this relative comfort was predicated on the backbreaking toil of enslaved Africans, while working-class widows and orphans were cast into the workhouse.

The Reform Act of 1832, by introducing a limited increase in the size of the electorate and reducing the ability for local landowners to buy their seats in Parliament, severely reduced the number of MPs committed to the West Indian interest. Seeing that the loss of control of Parliament would inevitably lead to abolition of enslavement, West Indian slave owners moved toward seeking compensation, although some, especially resident owners, were still holding out and opposed emancipation.

Although there can be no doubt that prominent elite abolitionists such as Wilberforce and Thomas Clarkson were genuinely and deeply appalled by the violence and cruelty of slavery, they still firmly believed in the sanctity of property and were extremely reluctant to do anything that might undermine the capitalist system. Also, as a result of foreclosures on mortgages, London-based financiers came to hold interests in plantations. So we find that prominent abolitionists, such as the banker George Peters, were creditors of slave owners. In fact, committed abolitionists came to be included in the compensation scheme, such was the integrated nature of the London finance and credit system.[79]

The pro-slavery opinions of the royal family was another important factor that the abolitionist movement had to overcome. In the 1790s and early nineteenth century, Prince William, Duke of Clarence, later King William IV, emerged as a vocal defender of colonial slavery and a leading ally of the West India Committee in London, having served in the Royal Navy in the Caribbean, where he had been lavishly entertained by the leading local enslavers. Merchant, politician, and slave owner George Hibbert reported to a friend that "the Prince is most diametrically adverse to all views of the abolitionists whom he looks upon as equally enemies in the event to the monarchy and to the Peace of the Kingdom."[80]

In 1794 the duke personally presented a petition to the House of Lords on behalf of the Society of West Indian Planters and Merchants. He attended a Society meeting on February 14, 1805, where members declared "their sincerest gratitude to His Royal Highness for the distinguished and valuable services rendered to the West India Body by his judicious, indefatigable, zealous and able exertions displayed in various occasions in supporting their interests, particularly on every Question in Parliament relative to the Slave Trade."[81] An 1824 proclamation by King George IV asserted that the "Slave Population . . . will be undeserving of Our Protection if they shall fail to render entire Submission to the Laws, as well as dutiful Obedience to their Masters." As late as June 1833, there were troubling accounts of royal disapproval, all of which invoked the unwelcome prospect of the king withholding the Royal Assent (the legal necessity for the monarch to sign an Act of Parliament before it becomes law). "The King is no Abolitionist," noted the secretary of statesman Henry Brougham, who was Lord chancellor during the period of the debates about abolition. "He was much in the West Indies when in the Navy; [and] being a careless, superficial observer, he came home under the impression that the slaves were the happiest people in the world."[82]

The West Indian lobby exploited this royal support to the full. The initial scheme proposed by the government was to loan the plantation owners fifteen million pounds, but by shrewd negotiation and political maneuvering the West Indian interest managed to turn this into a nonrepayable grant of twenty million, and retained the services of their enslaved workforce for another four years, retitled as apprenticeship.[83] Their compensation was the equivalent of a ransom paid to kidnappers.

While this outraged many rank-and-file abolitionists, upper-class opponents of slavery clearly felt that the slave owners had engaged in a legitimate business, and that emancipation without compensation would threaten the basis of capitalist property relations. The establishment has boasted of its freedom-loving generosity ever since, probably believing its own propaganda.

Besides, the compensation was good business for Rothschild & Co., probably the biggest bank in the world. In 1835 the Rothschild Bank organized the finance involved in funding compensation by purchasing fifteen million pounds of British government bonds, known as gilts or 3 percent consols (consolidated stocks). These paid 3 percent interest in perpetuity and were not finally redeemed until 2015. This arrangement meant that, over the years, British taxpayers paid eighty-one million pounds in interest on this fifteen million original loan. To further sweeten the deal, Rothschild & Co. were permitted to purchase short-term stocks worth £101,875 [£135,200,000, $170,000,000] at a discount of 2 percent, giving the bank an immediate profit of £2,075 [£2,704,000, $3,450,000].[84] The final redemption value in 2015 was £218,388,715 ($277,353,668).[85]

This vastly increased national debt was paid off by taxation on items of everyday consumption. In this period, the majority of state revenue was raised by regressive taxation on items of basic consumption, which always hits the poor hardest.[86] Workers in Britain effectively compensated the slave owners, who were then able to invest their compensation money in new business ventures, which, in turn, increased the rate of exploitation of the working class in Britain.

The compensation records show that the contribution from British colonial slave ownership to industrialization did not cease with the abolition of the slave trade in 1807 or with emancipation in the 1830s.[87] In the earlier part of the nineteenth century, one in six of the richest, non-landowning people in Britain had derived a significant proportion of their wealth from the business of slavery.

Compensation money was an important factor in the change of land use in the Highlands and islands of Scotland, accompanied by enclosure and evictions, in a process known as the Highland Clearances. Research carried out by historians Iain MacKinnon and Andrew Mackillop on behalf of Community Land Scotland found that sixty-three estates in the north of Scotland were purchased by beneficiaries of slave-derived wealth. They argue that those linked to slavery brought some of the same arrogance, authoritarianism, and self-entitlement to bear on their newly acquired assets in Scotland.[88] For example, Colonel John Gordon of Cluny who claimed £15,056 [£18,650,000, $23,685,500] in compensation for 792 enslaved laborers on the island of Tobago.[89] He bought the Scottish islands of Benbebula, South Uist, and Barra in 1838, and went on to clear more than 2,900 people from the islands in the 1850s.

MacKinnon observed:

> It is now clear that returning wealth from Atlantic slavery had an important impact on landownership change in the West Highlands and Islands in the 19th century, and contributed

significantly to the development of extractive and ecologically damaging forms of land use.[90]

Many former slave owners went on to be important contributors to the transformation of the British economy between 1840 and 1870, while slave owners and their descendants were prominent among the directors of the Bank of England throughout the nineteenth century. The merchant banks that came to dominate the City of London and the British financial services industry developed from merchants active in the West Indian trade, who evolved into bankers, as they responded to the need for credit instruments to facilitate the flow of enslaved labor and tropical produce. Bills of exchange, which had a long history, became the most important such instrument for settling the commercial transactions of the time, as well as a way of increasing the money supply; in effect, they were an early form of paper money.[91]

The business of slavery needed the investment of vast sums of money. Once commodities such as sugar and cotton arrived in Britain, they were sold for cash, but the middle stages of commerce were fueled by bills of exchange. Banks also provided mortgages to buy land for plantations, and to buy or sell the enslaved laborers who worked on them. In this way, enslaved Africans were used as collateral in complex financial deals.[92]

Part of the long-term problem with slavery as a system, from the point of view of capitalist development, is that considerable amounts of capital are locked up in ownership of enslaved labor. Compensating former slave owners solved that by releasing the capital. A significant proportion of the slavery compensation money was reinvested in railways, canals, and steamship lines, essential to and profiting from manufacturing industry.[93] For example, the Bristol West Indian interest was prominent in financing the Great Western Railway. James MacQueen, pro-slavery polemicist and slave owner, invested heavily in the Royal Mail Steam Packet Company, of which nine out of the twelve directors were recipients of compensation.[94]

Compensation payments gave a boost to the financial services industry, and the Bank Charter Act of 1833 allowed joint-stock banks to open for the first time in London. In 1833 the finance house Baring Brothers had £250,000 [£363,100,000, $461,137,000] invested in mortgages on West Indian estates. The bank also invested heavily in U.S. cotton produced by enslaved labor, and had earned a one million U.S. dollars [$932,000,000, £733,858,267] commission for organizing the finance of the Louisiana Purchase, which vastly extended the scope of cotton slavery in the United States. Such was the nature of the compensation scheme that Barings, along with the majority of British commercial, financial, and manufacturing companies, gained rather than lost as a result of emancipation, as they were in a position to diversify their investments into new and profitable businesses.[95]

The compromise nature of emancipation can be seen in the full title of the act of Parliament of August 1833: "An Act for the abolition of slavery throughout the British colonies, for promoting the industry of the manumitted slaves and for compensating the persons hitherto entitled to the services of such slaves." This clearly indicates the priorities of the British Parliament, compensating the enslavers and ensuring the continued exploitation of the formerly enslaved.

The deportation of the Tolpuddle Martyrs, a group of agricultural laborers from Somerset in the west of England, who were arrested, convicted, and transported to Australia for the crime of forming a trade union in 1834 happened concurrently with the implementation of the 1833 Slave Emancipation Act. Coincidental as this appears at first sight, it can also be interpreted as being part and parcel of the reorganization of the British economy, necessitated by the emancipation of the enslaved workers in the Caribbean. This reorganization took place in the context of a particularly capitalist view of the concept of free labor.

Upper-class abolitionists extolled the virtue of free labor, but employers, then as now, saw the concept of free labor as an individual right, allowing workers to choose their employer, subject to the needs of the business, and to leave that employment as they wish or more likely, to be dismissed when their labor power is no longer required. This notion of free labor is hostile to collective rights such as those of trade unions: one worker leaving when they wish is fine; the entire workforce leaving at the same time and setting up a picket line is intolerable. Then as now, for a capitalist, individual human rights are allowed; collective civil rights are more problematic.

Moderate abolitionists believed in the superior productivity of free labor. But at the heart of the concept of free labor is a contradiction: although the reward of the payment of wages is supposed to make workers more productive and harder working than driving them by coercion and punishment, the pressures of capitalist competition force individual employers to reduce wages to the lowest level possible to allow workers to live, work, and reproduce the next generation of workers.

As a result of this need to keep wages as low as possible, Wilberforce and Clarkson could have won considerable working-class solidarity with the enslaved by reminding workers in Britain that slaves were denied even the pitiful level of wages earned by the nineteenth-century weaver. However, one can search in vain the speeches of Wilberforce and Clarkson looking for any indignation that enslaved workers must work without wages. This denial of wages to enslaved workers could have usefully related to the lived experience of employed workers in Britain but, while the Clapham Sect might have wanted working-class signatures on their antislavery petitions, they were as opposed to workers' self-activity in Britain as they were to revolts in the Caribbean, and fully supported the anti-trade union laws of the period.

To quote the Marxist historian A. L. Morton in his *A People's History of England*:

> These laws were the work of Pitt and of his sanctimonious friend Wilberforce, whose well known sympathy for the black slave never prevented him from being the foremost apologist and champion of every act of tyranny in England, from the

employment of Oliver the Spy or the illegal detention of poor prisoners in Cold Bath Fields gaol to the Peterloo massacre and the suspension of the habeas corpus.[96]

In his 1807 pamphlet, *A Letter on the Abolition of the Slave Trade*, Wilberforce wrote:

> It would be wrong to emancipate. To grant freedom to them immediately would be to insure not only their masters' ruin, but their own. They must first be trained and educated for freedom.

Meanwhile another prominent abolitionist, Zachary Macaulay, spoke of:

> preparing the slaves, gradually ... for the grand change of substituting a moral impulse of labor, for that of the whip.

Of course, the "moral impulse of labor" needed reinforcement, even in England, by laws such as the Vagrancy Act 1824, an act for the punishment of idle and disorderly persons, "rogues," and "vagabonds," and the introduction of workhouses and the Poor Law Amendment Act of 1834. It is no coincidence that the Slavery Abolition Act of 1833 was quickly followed by this new Poor Law, forcing people who had no means of support to enter the workhouse. This was a law to force proletarianization, even when the system could not provide work.

The dominance of sugar production in the British West Indies and the unsuitability of the islands for mass production of raw cotton meant that British textile manufacturers, once some of them had used profits from the sugar industry to start up their businesses, had no further interest in supporting the business of slavery. Thus, emancipation can be seen as part of a reorientation of British capitalism toward a manufacturing economy.

After emancipation, British capital continued to be active in the slave economy outside the British Empire. For example, the investment bank Kleinwort Benson started its corporate life brokering cotton, also dealing in Cuban sugar and cigars. Britain's growing manufacturing industry required raw cotton, and the cheapest and most abundant source was the enslaved laborers in the southern United States.

CHAPTER 7

# The Organized Working Class

The relationship of British big business with slavery did not stop with emancipation in 1838. Slavery continued in the United States, Brazil, and Cuba for many years thereafter. The dependence of British industrial capitalists on slave-grown cotton from the United States, coffee and sugar from Brazil, and copper from Cuba shows that their abolitionist principles had clear limits.

Those British business interests that had supported emancipation still needed raw cotton for their textile factories, and the London financial services industry needed investment opportunities. This explains the support that large sections of the British ruling class gave to the breakaway Confederate states during the U.S. Civil War. However, capitalism in Britain had, by now, produced a proletariat, a working class with its own political agenda. There was a serious dispute over the U.S. Civil War in Britain, which became a class struggle by proxy. The working-class movement rallied to support of the North and antislavery, despite enormous hardship, while the ruling class, with a few honorable exceptions, supported the secessionist rebels of the South because they wanted to maintain access to cheap raw cotton produced by enslaved labor.

This struggle elicited one of Karl Marx and Frederick Engels's major political interventions. They had been in exile in England since the defeat of the 1848 uprising in Germany that had been part of a wave of attempted revolutions that had swept across Europe in 1848–1849 affecting France, the Netherlands, Italy, the Austrian Empire, and the states of the German Confederation. While some important reforms were won, such as abolition of serfdom in Austria and Hungary, the revolts were quickly suppressed, tens of thousands of people were killed, and more were forced into exile. The defeat of these movements had shattered the self-confidence of the European workers' movement, so the increased political activity by the organized working class in Britain was particularly welcome to Marx and Engels, who saw in it a return to class consciousness. Many German exiles from the repression that followed the defeats of 1848 went to the United States, where they played an important role in the antislavery movement.

The debate as to whether chattel slavery was capitalist or somehow pre-capitalist is resurfacing in Marxist circles. A rereading of the contemporary writings of Marx and Engels demonstrates that they were quite clear that the business of slavery was very much part of the capitalist system. The end of the U.S. Civil War in 1865 coincided with the Morant Bay Rebellion in Jamaica, in which hundreds of people were killed by the British army following a protest about poverty and injustice. This showed that, despite no longer being enslaved, the workers of the British West Indies did not consider themselves truly free. Workers in Britain mobilized to denounce the repression and demand justice.

## Cotton Production

Less than one hundred years earlier, at the outbreak of the U.S. War of Independence, Rhode Island controlled two-thirds or more of the colonies' slave trade with Africa. When the trade resumed after the war ended in 1783, Rhode Island resumed its predominance, trafficking nearly fifty thousand more enslaved Africans in the next twenty years.[1]

Differences over slavery were left unresolved in the Declaration of Independence (1776) and the U.S. Constitution (1787), in part because the economic development of the northern states continued to be intertwined with the slavery-based South. In 1786 the Cabot brothers, having made their fortunes in the slave trade, established the first cotton mill in the Americas. The invention of the cotton gin by Eli Whitney in 1793, which mechanized the separation of cotton fiber and seed, made the mass production of cotton textiles practical. Total U.S. consumption of raw cotton increased from 2,500 U.S. tons in 1790, to 235,000 U.S. tons.[2]

Despite many northern textile mill owners purporting to abhor slavery, and some historians trying to separate the production of the finished product from the production of the raw material by forced labor, the profits of the whole process clearly depended on the unremunerated labor of the enslaved.[3] While technological change was responsible for the vastly increased productivity in the manufacture of cotton textiles, industrialization did nothing to lighten the workload of the enslaved laborers. Rather, it made matters worse, since workers were driven harder to keep up with the steam-driven processing of the raw cotton. Enslaved laborers worked under drivers in gangs that would build up a fierce momentum. Human resources techniques of the time, such as speed-up and measured task-working, enforced by the whip and other forms of torture, pushed cotton-picking productivity to increase by 400 percent between 1800 and 1860 in the United States.[4]

However, the economy of New England was not only dependent on the supply of cheap and plentiful raw cotton. The production of poor-quality clothing for the enslaved workers was vital to the continued operation of textile mills in the northern states during times of economic crisis.[5] Equally, capital investment by the New England banks became essential to the development of southern slave-based cotton agriculture, with mortgages frequently secured on the ownership of enslaved workers. By the middle of the nineteenth century, the two million enslaved workers represented one billion dollars in credit (six hundred and twenty-five trillion dollars in today's money).

The demand for cotton to supply the textile industries of England gave new life to the enslaved labor system. Plantation slavery, with its monocrop production, may have been a successful way of accumulating capital, but it was ecologically inefficient, as the soil was quickly exhausted.[6] Soil exhaustion meant that cotton plantations worked by enslaved labor had to expand, as the soil in the southern states became infertile through overuse. Marx and Engels consistently argued in their writings that large landholders were invariably more destructive in their relation to the earth than independent farmers. Engels wrote in *Anti-Dühring* that in North America, "The big landlords of the South, with their slaves and their rapacious tilling of the land, exhausted the soil until it could only grow firs."[7]

Indeed, in the context of the U.S. Civil War, it was not the continuation of slavery that drove the South to war, as the legislatures of the northern states would not have been particularly concerned if slavery had continued within its existing boundaries. Rather, it was the competition between North and South for the newly acquired lands of the West, from which the peoples of the Indigenous nations were being massacred and expelled. Soil exhaustion meant that cotton plantations worked by enslaved labor had to expand further west.

The northern bourgeoisie had long shown themselves perfectly content to coexist with southern slavery, provided that it stayed within the existing boundaries. However, they had other intentions for exploiting the West, based on cattle ranching and wheat cultivation by paid employees. The exhaustion of the soil in both the North and South resulted in increased competition for new farmlands in the West, particularly after the 1825 opening of the Erie Canal, connecting the Atlantic Ocean to the Great Lakes. Sections of the northern petite bourgeoisie and proletariat also had designs on obtaining cheap farmland in the West. The expansionist tendency by the enslavers of the South and the competition for land previously inhabited by the Indigenous nations were major factors in provoking the Civil War.[8] So, while slavery was at the heart of the differences between North and South, the reasons for the outbreak of war were more complicated than simple opposition to enslavement by northern Republicans.

Marx wrote:

> Finally, the number of actual slaveholders in the South of the Union does not amount to more than 300,000, a narrow oligarchy that is confronted with many millions of so-called poor whites, whose numbers have been constantly growing through concentration of landed property and whose condition is only to be compared with that of the Roman plebeians in the period of Rome's extreme decline. Only by acquisition and the prospect of acquisition of new territories, as well as by filibustering expeditions, is it possible to square the interests of these "poor whites" with those of the slaveholders, to give their restless thirst for action a harmless direction and to tame them with the prospect of one day becoming slaveholders themselves.
>
> A strict confinement of slavery within its old terrain, therefore, was bound according to economic law to lead to its gradual extinction, in the political sphere to annihilate the hegemony that the slave states exercised through the Senate, and finally to expose the slaveholding oligarchy within its own states to threatening perils from the "poor whites." In accordance with the principle that any further extension of slave territories was to be prohibited by law, the Republicans therefore attacked the rule of the slaveholders at its root. The Republican election victory was accordingly bound to lead to open struggle between North and South.[9]

### British Responses to the U.S. Civil War

When the Civil War finally broke out in 1861, Marx and Engels supported the North wholeheartedly. Their dispatches in the *New-York Daily Tribune* and Vienna's *Die Presse* informed readers on both sides of the Atlantic of the numerous pro-North meetings that English workers held in opposition to the Confederate sympathies of the British government and press.

At the time of the "Trent Affair," when the U.S. Navy seized two Confederate envoys from a British Royal Mail steamer and war between Britain and the United States threatened, Marx wrote in the *Daily Tribune*:

> It ought never to be forgotten in the United States that at least the working classes of England, from the commencement to the termination of the difficulty [the Trent Affair], have never forsaken them. To them it was due that, despite the poisonous stimulants daily administered by a venal and reckless press, not one single public war meeting could be held in the United Kingdom during all the period that peace trembled in the balance.[10]

During the Civil War, from 1861 to 1865, British textile-industry owners, finance capital, and aristocracy argued for armed intervention on the side of the slave owners. The working-class and socialist movements in Britain, despite the hardships caused by the cotton famine, stood in solidarity with the antislavery struggle represented by the northern states, and formed part of a mass movement against British intervention.[11]

Cotton, produced by enslaved labor in the southern states of the United States, had fueled Britain's industrialization which, in turn, led to the further expansion of slavery.[12] In 1860 over 80 percent of the raw cotton used in Britain came from the southern United States, the majority of whose cotton export went to Britain. Throughout the Civil War, Britain's Lancashire cotton industry suffered from a severe shortage of raw cotton, a result the blockade of southern ports by the northern navy. When the blockade began to hinder the arrival of supplies of cotton, some of the larger manufacturers and traders actually managed to profit from it, since their stocks of the raw material commanded a higher price than before. The employers, for their part, used the reduced ability of the textile workers to defend their jobs to expand unemployment further with increased mechanization. Karl Marx writes of "galloping improvements in machinery," which made "the 'temporary' misery inflicted on the workpeople by the cotton-crisis" permanent.[13] Despite a strike, both wage cuts and short-time working were introduced in 1861. By 1863, half the cotton workers in England were unemployed, and many of the rest on short-time working.[14]

The southern breakaway Confederate States of America hoped that the cotton famine would push the British and French governments into supporting their secession, secure diplomatic recognition, and provoke military intervention. In December 1861, Marx wrote in the *New-York Daily Tribune*:

> The wish uppermost in the minds of the slavocracy . . . was always to plunge the United States into a war with England. The first step of England as soon as hostilities broke out would be to recognize the Southern Confederacy, and the second to terminate the blockade.[15]

Indeed, the greater part of the British ruling class were supporters of the Confederacy. The British Chancellor of the Exchequer, William Gladstone, favored British intervention to reestablish the trade in cotton.[16] Gladstone was the son of the slave owner Sir John Gladstone, who had received £106,769 [£132,200,000, $168,000,000] in compensation for the 2,508 enslaved people he had title to in the Caribbean. Foreign Secretary Lord Russell put forward proposals ranging from mediation—effectively, diplomatic recognition of the Confederacy—to military intervention in favor of the South. Samuel Wilberforce, Bishop of Oxford and son of antislavery campaigner William Wilberforce, also supported the South. The British and Foreign Anti-Slavery Society refused to take sides in the war, though one of its founders, Lord

Brougham, denounced the Union's war effort as dangerous and unjust, and called the Emancipation Proclamation unprincipled and irresponsible.[17]

Much of the British ruling class also supported the South from fear and hatred of any extension of democracy. The *Morning Post* warned of a northern victory, saying, "Who can doubt that Democracy will be more arrogant, more aggressive, more leveling and vulgarizing, if that were possible, than ever before."[18] Liverpool merchants were eager to restart their imports of slave-grown cotton, and agitated for armed intervention on behalf of the South. Two warships, the *Alabama* and the *Florida*, were built for the Confederate Navy at Birkenhead, and the British government did nothing to prevent their departure, despite contravening the Foreign Enlistment Act. And, of course, the Manchester textile-industry employers were staunch supporters of the Confederacy, eager as they were to regain their supply of raw cotton. These upper-class opinions received the complete support of the major newspapers, particularly the *Times*, the *Economist*, and the *Manchester Guardian*. Marx wrote:

> At the present moment, English interference in America has accordingly become a knife-and-fork question for the working class. Moreover, no means of inflaming its wrath against the United States is scorned by its "natural superiors." The sole great and widely circulating workers' organ still existing, *Reynolds's Newspaper*, has been purchased expressly in order that for six months it might reiterate weekly in raging diatribes the ceterum censeo of English intervention.[19]

and:

> Most of the London weekly papers are mere echoes of the daily press, therefore overwhelmingly warlike. The Observer is in the ministry's pay. The Saturday Review strives for esprit and believes it has attained it by affecting a cynical elevation above "humanitarian" prejudices. To show "esprit," the corrupt lawyers,

parsons and schoolmasters that write this paper have smirked their approbation of the slaveholders since the outbreak of the American Civil War. Naturally, they subsequently blew the war-trumpet with The Times. They are already drawing up plans of campaign against the United States displaying a hair-raising ignorance.[20]

Yet while the textile bosses, finance capital, and the aristocracy argued for armed intervention on the side of the slave owners, the majority of the working class in Britain, despite the hardships caused by the cotton famine, stood in solidarity with the Union struggle, thereby enabling Marx and Engels to play a part in a mass movement against British intervention.

In the second half of 1862, a series of pro-Union working-class rallies were attended by thousands of people in Lancashire and Yorkshire, adopting antislavery resolutions and denouncing any sort of British intervention in support of the Confederacy. At a meeting attended by six thousand workers in the Free Trade Hall in Manchester on December 31, 1862, the following resolution was carried:

> Why should the Lancashire laborers sympathize with the laborers in the Southern States? Why should they not, like the economists, argue that the slavery of Alabama is a part of the complex labor system by which they live, and wish it to go on? Why not assume the languid indifference of the upper classes as to the result of the great struggle? Perhaps it is . . . because, possessing little more than our common humanity, [we] prize that above artificial distinctions of class and color . . . whatever others think is to be said for the slave owner, in [our] eyes his offense is the greatest man can commit against man, the sum and parent of all villainies.[21]

An African American, William Jackson, who had previously been enslaved by Confederate president Jefferson Davis, addressed the meeting to great applause. Out of this meeting the Union and Emancipation Society was formed, and it went on to organize nearly 350 meetings over the next three years. This campaign was part of a general revival in militancy and political engagement among workers in Britain. As one of Karl Marx's friends, Edward Beesly, who had helped to organize the first large mass meeting in St. James's Hall in London, put it:

> We are met here tonight, we say it openly, not merely as friends of Emancipation, but as friends of Reform. This is the first time, I believe, that the Trades' Unionists of London have met together to pronounce on a political question ... but I am sure it will not be the last.[22]

On March 26, 1863, Marx attended a large meeting of trade unionists at St. James's Hall. Henry Adams, son of the U.S. ambassador to Great Britain, also attended the meeting and reported that some three thousand people were present, all of whom were, "with the exception of a few invited guests, members of the working classes."[23]

It was in this atmosphere that the International Workingmen's Association (IWA) was formed at a large international meeting in Covent Garden in Central London, attended by delegates from Britain, France, Ireland, Poland, and Germany. Marx wrote the inaugural address, which included reference to the U.S. Civil War:

> If the emancipation of the working classes requires their fraternal concurrence, how are they to fulfill that great mission with a foreign policy in pursuit of criminal designs, playing upon national prejudices, and squandering in piratical wars the people's blood and treasure? It was not the wisdom of the ruling classes, but the heroic resistance to their criminal folly by the working classes of England that saved the West of Europe from plunging headlong into an infamous crusade for the perpetuation and propagation of slavery on the other side of the Atlantic.[24]

The International Workingmen's Association instructed Marx to send a message of congratulations to Abraham Lincoln, on his reelection in 1864. Marx's address, after pointing out the loyal support given to the United States by the workers of Europe, spoke of "an earnest sign of the epoch to come that it fell to the lot of Abraham Lincoln, the single-minded son of the working class, to lead his country through the matchless struggle for the rescue of an enchained race and the reconstruction of a social world." [25]

For Marx and Engels, the resistance by the European workers' movement to British and French intervention on the side of the Confederacy demonstrated the possibility of giving organizational form to the revolutionary socialist politics that had been so lacking since the defeat of the 1848 revolutionary upsurge.[26] As Marxist theoretician Karl Korsch put it:

> We can see the revived revolutionary enthusiasm of the 1860s. At last, after fifteen years of demoralization and lack of participation by the masses, the revival of the working class was visible all at once in England, France, Germany and Italy.[27]

The Civil War was still continuing, and the International Workingmen's Association made solidarity with the struggle against slavery in the United States one of its main focuses. The link was made explicit by the chair of a pro-Union meeting in Manchester, who argued that the International was fighting for "enfranchising black labor in America and . . . enfranchising white labor in England."

Karl Marx, in *Capital*, was keen to stress the importance of antislavery for the struggle to improve working conditions for all workers:

> After the abolition of slavery, a radical transformation in the existing relations of capital and landed property is on the agenda.[28]

and furthermore:

But out of the death of slavery a new life at once arose. The first fruit of the Civil War was the eight hours' agitation. . . . The General Congress of Labor held at Baltimore in August 1866 declared: "The first and great necessity of the present, to free the labor of this country from capitalistic slavery, is the passing of a law by which eight hours shall be the normal working day in all the states of the American Union. We are resolved to put forth all our strength until this glorious result is attained."[29]

The abolition of slavery would not only benefit enslaved people, it would also benefit the White workers. By weakening their identification with their own ruling classes, the abolition of slavery would encourage united working-class self-activity. Marx recognized that solidarity across national borders strengthened working-class movements; he opposed all forms of nationalism and working-people's identification with the ruling classes of their nation.[30]

The working men have no country. We cannot take from them what they have not got. Working Men of All Countries, Unite![31]

## Marxism and the Political Economy of Slavery

There are two misconceptions about Marx and Engels's attitude to slavery. The first is that slavery, particularly the cash-crop production of the southern United States and the Caribbean, was pre-capitalist or semifeudal. This supposedly Marxist view is best expressed by Eugene Genovese and Charles Post.[32] The other, most influentially argued by Edward Said, is that Marx and Engels were "Eurocentrists," solely concerned with the emancipation of European and White U.S. workers.[33] The truth or otherwise of these accusations can be clarified by reading their own writings.

Marx and Engels's views on slavery changed significantly over time, amended in the light of international events and their interaction with the mass movements of their day. As Engels put it in 1887, "Our theory is a theory of evolution, not a dogma to be learned by heart."[34]

Karl Marx's first mention of slavery is in *The Poverty of Philosophy*, published in 1847, a year before the Europe-wide uprisings of 1848 that so transformed the thinking of both Marx and Engels. This book is, despite its title, fundamentally a work of economic analysis, in which Marx argues the centrality of slavery to capitalist economic development:

> Direct slavery is just as much the pivot of bourgeois industry as machinery, credits, etc. Without slavery you have no cotton; without cotton you have no modern industry.

One particular statement in this work is sometimes used to claim that Marx was prepared to support slavery because it was essential to the development of capitalism and thus was somehow progressive:

> Without slavery North America, the most progressive of countries, would be transformed into a patriarchal country. Wipe North America off the map of the world, and you will have anarchy—the complete decay of modern commerce and civilization.[35]

This is to take the paragraph completely out of context. In fact, in this sentence Marx is attacking French socialist philosopher Proudhon, by parodying his approach to political economy. In a letter to Russian literary critic Pavel Vasilyevich Annenkov criticizing Proudhon's book, *Système des contradictions économiques, ou Philosophie de la misère*, Marx uses almost the same words, followed by, "After these reflections on slavery, what will the good Mr Proudhon do? He will seek the synthesis of liberty and slavery, the true golden mean, in other words the balance between slavery and liberty."[36]

Marx did not use the word "progressive," in the sense used by many later socialists and communists, as a way of avoiding accusations of class collaboration when justifying alliances with bourgeois or petit-bourgeois movements. When Marx speaks of the achievement of the ten-hour day, he does not see it as progress, but rather "the victory of the economy of the laboring class over the economy of the bourgeoisie." The only "progressive" aspect of capitalism is that it has produced its own potential grave digger, the organized working class.

Thus, in the letter from the International Workingmen's Association to Abraham Lincoln, Marx writes that slavery was "an obstacle to progress and to the development of power for the working class."[37] He was frequently scathing in his contempt for people who called themselves progressives, but who were mainly concerned with advancing their own position. On July 6, 1848, in the *Neue Rheinische Zeitung*, the German radical newspaper he edited, Marx criticized the work of a recent U.S. antislavery convention on the grounds that the "delegates and speakers loosed all sorts of shafts against the planter and his system but took no practical steps toward its abolition."

Marx's critique of bourgeois abolitionists continued in 1853, in an article attacking the Duchess of Sutherland for her hypocrisy in condemning slavery in the United States, while her family had made its fortune in expropriating the Scottish peasantry during the highland clearances.[38] Marx here takes a hard class line, the start of his linking emancipation of the enslaved to the general emancipation of the working class:

> The enemy of British Wage-Slavery has a right to condemn Negro-Slavery; a Duchess of Sutherland, a Duke of Atholl, a Manchester Cotton-lord—never![39]

This does not mean that Marx would not work alongside capitalists on single-issue campaigns; just that he would not compromise his principles to do so. Thus, he worked alongside John Bright, a Birmingham industrialist, in the campaign against British support for the Confederacy, but without holding back on his criticisms of capitalism.

Through his relationship with the Chartist radical and labor poet Ernest Jones, Marx realized the need to oppose slavery and colonialism as part of the struggle against capitalism. Chartism was a working-class movement for political reform in the United Kingdom that took its name from the People's Charter of 1838, which was a list of demands that would grant the vote to all men over twenty-one. Campaigning in London for political reform had taught Jones that the battle for the Charter was interwoven with abolitionism and anti-colonialism, and that the working class was global and multiracial. But the defeat in 1848 and 1849 and the political apathy that followed made Jones believe that the revolution would not start in Europe, but would come out of the oppressed colonies.

Jones was editor of the *People's Paper*, which became the main Chartist journal. Marx contributed twenty-five articles, some of them reprinted from the *Tribune*. The first issue of the *People's Paper* declared its anti-colonialism, with this appeal to the workers: "We have looked, and very properly, at the interests of European democracy; be it ours to look at our colonial struggles." Liberation from British rule in the colonies, in other words, was the lever for proletarian liberation in the capitalist heartland.[40]

Jones wrote a series of articles, published in May 1853 in the *People's Paper*, that denounced British rule in India as a legalized, direct plunder of the Indigenous population. He referred to India as the "Ireland of the East," where decades of "British barbarism," as he labeled British rule, did not result in progress but dire misery. Jones linked the exploitation of British workers to the colonial oppression of the Indian population, reiterating that an independent India was crucial to the class struggle at home.

In his article of August 8, 1853, "The Future Results of British Rule in India," Marx condemned British rule in India as an example of "the inherent barbarism of bourgeois civilization," couching his contempt in terms consistent with the anti-imperialism of the

Chartist movement: "The profound hypocrisy and inherent barbarism of bourgeois civilization, lies unveiled before our eyes, turning from its home, where it assumes respectable form, to the colonies, where it goes naked."[41] In the same article, he argued that the liberation of India could come either from a working-class uprising in Britain, or from a movement of self-emancipation led by the Indians themselves. This was a major shift in Marx's thinking. For the first time, he recognized that colonial peoples had the capacity for revolutionary social change, a position that he now shared with Jones. "India is now our best ally," Marx wrote to Engels. The anti-colonial uprising in India in 1857 caused Marx to revise his position and integrate colonialism into his materialist conception of history.[42]

It was, however, the actual struggle of the enslaved that really began to excite Marx's interest and revealed their revolutionary possibilities. Following news of the failed uprising in the United States led by John Brown in 1859, he wrote to Frederick Engels:

In my view, the most momentous thing happening in the world today is the slave movement—on the one hand, in America, started by the death of Brown, and in Russia, on the other. . . . I have just seen in the Tribune that there's been another slave revolt in Missouri, which was put down, needless to say. But the signal has now been given.[43]

Marx and Engels would not have known it, but among John Brown's closest supporters there were several veterans of the 1848 revolutions in Europe, and two of Brown's close friends, Richard Hinton and James Redpath, came from families that had been active in the British Chartist movement. Hinton would go on to command one of the first African-American regiments, the First Kansas Colored Volunteers and later became one of the leaders of the U.S. section of the International Workingmen's Association.[44]

Many veterans of the German revolutions of 1848 had made their way to the United States following the defeat. Viewed from

Europe, the United States might have appeared more progressive, but on confronting the power of the slave owners, many of the "Forty-eighters" became involved in the antislavery campaign and served as active recruiters and soldiers for the Union in the Civil War. They quickly came to see the danger posed by the "Slave Power," the disproportionate and corrupt influence wielded by rich slave owners who had seized political control of their own states in an attempt to force the federal government to expand and protect slavery. This awareness of the slavocracy changed the attitudes of many German immigrants in the United States and fed back into the development of Marx and Engels's thinking.[45]

Marx's correspondence with German American communists, particularly his old friend and comrade from the 1840s, Joseph Weydemeyer, was an important factor in the development of Marx's politics. Weydemeyer was a Prussian military officer and socialist who emigrated to the United States to escape the consequences of his participation in the failed revolution of 1848. He became an important activist in the early North American workers' movement and was a leading advocate of abolitionism and racial equality. Weydermeyer's economic analysis of slavery, tariffs, and industrialization was written after extensive correspondence with Marx and Engels. He lectured throughout the western states on the question of slavery, arguing that opposition to chattel slavery was not just a defense of free labor but was also implicitly an attack on private property.[46] He was very influential in winning the German American community to support the election of Lincoln and gaining their solid commitment to the Union and antislavery.

The German American socialist veterans of 1848 helped put this into practice, at least on the Missouri front. Missouri was a slave state but had a large and radical German-speaking population in St. Louis. When the Democratic state governor, Claiborne Fox Jackson, tried to use the state militia to take Missouri into the Confederacy, he was frustrated by the recruitment of five regiments of Home Guards, four of which were German-speaking. These Home Guards formed an important part of the Union forces that drove Governor Jackson and his pro-Confederate militia out of St. Louis. Missouri was an important theater of war and forty thousand men from the state joined the Confederate Army, many of them taking part in guerrilla operations. One hundred and ten thousand Missourians served in the Union Army as the state stayed in the Union. Weydermeyer himself became a colonel in the Union Army and led the fight against the Confederate guerrillas on the Missouri battlefield.[47]

Given that Marx's initial interest in the issue of slavery was aroused by the prospect of a slave rebellion following John Brown's raid on Harpers Ferry, he consistently urged the use of the formerly enslaved as soldiers, well before it became Union policy:

> A single Negro regiment would have a remarkable effect on Southern nerves. . . . A war of this kind must be conducted on revolutionary lines while the Yankees have thus far been trying to conduct it constitutionally.[48]

Marx and Engels saw the struggle by the Union against the Confederacy as a revolution, but a revolution from above, led by Abraham Lincoln and Republican generals such as Grant, Sherman, and Frèmont. Given that their sources were abolitionist newspapers and correspondence with radical abolitionists and his old German-American comrades, this analysis is hardly surprising. Marx frequently urged the Union to wage the war by revolutionary means, by the use of Black troops, or by encouraging an uprising by the enslaved, while criticizing Lincoln's apparent timidity. As Marx wrote in a private letter to his uncle in May 1861:

> But in the long run, of course, the North will win, for in case of necessity it can play the last card, that of a slave revolution.

Missouri German-language newspapers brought revolutionary anti-capitalist politics to the wider German-speaking population, attacking slavery as a class system of private property. For instance,

St. Louis's *Westliche Post* observed that the rebellion depended on the labor of the enslaved, and advised its readers that "the more one encourages slaves to escape from the South, the more one weakens the rebellion and the sooner one defeats it." Moreover, the enslaved were not simply capital whose expropriation would undermine the slaveholding ruling class, but they could also serve as soldiers in the Union forces. As the first German-language newspaper in St. Louis, Missouri, *Anzeiger des Westens,* put it: "No people has ever been lifted up to freedom. Freedom is not something that is given—it has to be taken." The "best preparation" for freedom, it continued, "has always been a revolution or a war." Slavery, then, would end when "it is the rebel masters who run away from their slaves rather than the other way around."[49]

Despite the objections of more conservative and conventional Union officers, the fortified camp of the St. Louis Home Guard at Rolla, for a time commanded by Franz Sigel, the former minister of war of the 1848 Baden Revolutionary Republic, became a center for enslaved workers escaping slavery, where they were welcomed, protected, and, if the men wished, given a uniform and musket. Thus, in September and October 1861, these became the first African Americans to fight in the Union Army.[50] The rest had to wait until the Emancipation Proclamation of January 1, 1863, when President Lincoln finally announced that African American men would be accepted into the U.S. Army and Navy. By the end of the Civil War, roughly 179,000 African Americans had served as soldiers in the Union Army, and another 19,000 in the Navy. Nearly 40,000 of them died during the war.

Recognition of the full contribution of the enslaved population of the South to their own emancipation would have to wait over seventy years for W. E. B. Du Bois's *Black Reconstruction*, wherein Du Bois speaks of the desertion of hundreds of thousands of enslaved laborers from plantations to the Union Army as a "General Strike."[51]

Karl Marx wrote about the human consequences of chattel slavery:

The slave-owner buys his laborer as he buys his horse. If he loses his slave, he loses capital that can only be restored by new outlay in the slave-mart. But the rice-grounds of Georgia, or the swamps of the Mississippi may be fatally injurious to the human constitution; but the waste of human life which the cultivation of these districts necessitates is not so great that it cannot be repaired from the teaming preserves of Virginia and Kentucky. Considerations of economy, moreover, which, under a natural system, afford some security for humane treatment by identifying the master's interest with the slaves, when once trading in slaves is practiced, become reasons for racking to the uttermost the toil of the slave; for, when his place can at once be supplied from foreign preserves, the duration of his life becomes a matter of less moment than its productiveness while it lasts. It is accordingly a maxim of slave management, in slave-importing countries, that the most effective economy is that which takes out of the human chattel in the shortest space of time the utmost amount of exertion it is capable of putting forth. It is in tropical culture, where annual profits of often equal for the whole capital of plantations, that Negro life is most recklessly sacrificed.[52]

Marx adds that this is not a distinctive feature of slavery, but also applies to workers in England. He cites as examples the low life expectancy of potters, bakers, and workers in the cotton industry.[53]

Marx divides the working class into two types of slavery, the indirect slavery of the wage-working proletariat, and the direct slavery of forced labor. In considering the relationship between the enslaved person and their labor power, Marx wrote:

The slave did not sell his labor power to the slave owner, any more than the ox sells his labor to the farmer. The slave, together with his labor power, was sold to his owner once and for all. He is a commodity that can pass from the hand of one owner to that of another. He himself is a commodity, but his labor power is not his commodity. . . . The free laborer, on the other hand, sells his very self, and that by fractions.... The laborer belongs neither to an owner nor to the soil, but eight, 10, 12, 15 hours of his daily life belong to whomsoever buys them.[54]

Although Marxists such as Robert Brenner have insisted that slavery is somehow pre-capitalist, this has been adequately refuted in recent years by Walter Johnson, Edward Baptist, and Sven Beckert, who have built on the work of C. L. R. James and Eric Williams. Robin Blackburn is clear that, at the time of the Civil War, "Marx was focused on destroying true chattel slavery, which he knew to be a critical component of the reigning capitalist order." He viewed the conflict between the North and South as a contest between "two species of capitalism—one allowing slavery the other not."[55]

Marxist historian Jairus Banaji argues that "it is accumulation or the 'drive for surplus-value' that defines capitalism, not the presence or absence of paid employment."[56]

When Marx defined how surplus value[57] was generated by the employment of paid labor, he was using a simplified, ideal scenario to explain how one aspect of capitalism worked. He wrote *Capital* and his other works of political economy to explain how the system worked, not to shoehorn reality into his preconceived ideas.

Marx was indeed quite clear that the chattel slavery of his day was essentially part of the capitalist mode of production, and that the international market served to transform all forms of labor into commodity production:

> Where commercial speculations figure from the start and production is intended for the world market, the capitalist mode of production exists, although only in a formal sense, since the slavery of Negroes precludes free wage labor, which is the basis of capitalist production. But the business in which slaves are used is conducted by capitalists....[58]

As soon as people, whose production still moves within the

lower forms of slave labor, courvee labor, etc., are drawn into the whirlpool of an international market dominated by the capitalistic mode of production, the sale of their products for export becoming their principal interest, the civilized horrors of over-work are grafted on the barbaric horrors of slavery.... In proportion, as the export of cotton became of vital interest to these states, the over-working of the Negro and sometimes the using up of his life in 7 years of labor became a factor in a calculated and calculating system. It was no longer a question of obtaining from him a certain quantity of useful products. It was now a question of production of surplus labor itself.[59]

So, the slave owner is a capitalist, and the slave-based economy produces profit for these capitalists:

The price paid for a slave is nothing but the anticipated and capitalized surplus value or profit, which is to be ground out of him.[60]

The capitalist buys the labor power of the enslaved worker, not from those workers themselves, but from their kidnappers. In a sense they are therefore receivers of stolen goods.

Industrial relations lecturer Thierry Drapeau argues that the relationship between capital and wage labor, often expressed as the wage earners' supposed right to freely dispose of their labor power under capitalism, did not begin with proletarianization but resulted from a political struggle waged by the workers themselves.[61] As Karl Marx put it, the "starting-point of the development that gave rise both to the wage laborer and to the capitalist was the enslavement of the worker. The advance made consisted in a change in the form of this servitude."[62]

Marx's involvement in the campaign against slavery in the United States led him to reorganize the writing of *Capital*.[63] As Belgian Marxist economist Ernest Mandel indicates, Marx integrated "the development of the class struggle between capital and labor into his analysis of the production of surplus-value."⁶⁴ Marx argued that the fight against slavery as part of the class struggle was as important as the role slavery played in the development of capitalism:

> While the cotton industry introduced child-slavery into England, in the United States it gave the impulse for the transformation of the earlier, more or less patriarchal slavery into a system of commercial exploitation. In fact, the veiled slavery of the wage laborers in Europe needed the unqualified slavery of the New World as its pedestal.⁶⁵

Marx and Engels held that the secessionist counterrevolution had to be crushed in order to emancipate U.S. society from the domination of the southern slaveholding oligarchy. The support that they gave to the North during the Civil War came from their conviction that the abolition of slavery was necessary to the development of an independent working-class movement in America. "Labor cannot emancipate itself in a white skin where in the black it is branded."⁶⁶ So long as slavery "disfigured a part of the republic," industry could not flourish, and the development of an independent labor movement was not possible.

It has been argued that this formulation demonstrates that Marx and Engels "wrote as if the fight against slavery was primarily a white working-class struggle, with Black workers and soldiers playing a vital, but only supporting, role."⁶⁷

The paragraph often offered as evidence is in the letter that Marx, on behalf of the International Workingmen's Association, wrote to Abraham Lincoln to congratulate him on his reelection:

> While the workingmen, the true political powers of the North, allowed slavery to defile their own republic, while before the Negro, mastered and sold without his concurrence, they boasted it the highest prerogative of the white-skinned laborer to sell himself and choose his own master, they were unable to attain

the true freedom of labor, or to support their European brethren in their struggle for emancipation; but this barrier to progress has been swept off by the red sea of civil war.[68]

This paragraph purportedly shows Marx's Eurocentrism, and his view of White workers as the revolutionary vanguard.[69] But this interpretation ignores the context of the letter. Marx and Engels were deeply involved in the campaign to win European and White U.S. workers to support the abolition of slavery, so many of their arguments are framed in such a way as to win over White workers to the cause of abolition, and to urge solidarity across racial lines. If White laborers could see how they themselves were threatened by slavery, they would have a stake in its abolition. Besides seeing the abolition of slavery as a step toward the emancipation of all workers, Marx pointed out the horrific alternative for northern workers if the Confederacy won the war: "The slave system would infect the whole Union. In the northern states, where Negro slavery is unworkable in practice, the White working class would be gradually depressed to the level of helotry."[70] As the Industrial Workers of the World (IWW) would later write on their banners: "An Injury to One Is an Injury to All."

Marx's Civil War writings demonstrate that he was not exclusively focused on the emancipation of the White working class; rather, Marx saw the destruction of capitalism as a means to achieve complete human emancipation. The vital role played by enslaved labor in the capitalist economy made it a good place to start the revolutionary process.[71] But we also see the human solidarity in Marx, who, though far from being a moralist, nevertheless saw the war to end slavery as one that "must enlist the warmest sympathies of every man, not a confessed ruffian, on its side."[72]

The renegade former Marxist, historian of slavery Eugene Genovese criticizes "the retreat of Marx, Engels, and too many Marxists into liberalism" when it came to the Civil War. Genovese, who argues that slavery was pre-capitalist because capitalism was defined by its dependence on wage labor, and that slaveholders were to be admired because they were "class conscious, socially responsible, and personally honorable; they selflessly fulfilled their duties and did what their class and society required from them."[73] This assertion led him to state that Marx's "burning hatred of slavery and commitment to the Union cause interfered with his judgment."[74] Genovese mistakes internationalist solidarity for liberalism, but in his headlong flight from Marxism to conservative, Catholic reaction, he did not pause to stop at liberalism on the way. Meanwhile, the importance of internationalism in the development of Marx's politics is particularly relevant in the context of the response of the Lancashire textile workers to the U.S. Civil War.

Despite accusations to the contrary, Marx did not downplay the terrible capitalist exploitation of colonial societies, or the necessity for social revolt by Indigenous populations. He not only condemned colonialism from the standpoint of those who suffered from it, but he also said that capitalist penetration was providing the material preconditions, that, when coupled with social revolution, opened the way to socialism.[75] This was progress, in the sense of making a revolution possible.

However, he became increasingly concerned about the role of international exploitation in creating a permanent structural relation of dependency of poor nations on rich nations, and the effect of this exploitation on working-class internationalism. Ireland, Marx observed, was sending its surplus, derived largely from agricultural production, to England, where it was used to expand industrial production.

By the end of the 1850s, there was a shift in emphasis in the writings of Marx and Engels toward the defense of Indigenous, anti-colonial struggles, recognizing the importance of non-capitalist modes of production. This was, in part, influenced by the wars of anti-colonial resistance waged by the Indigenous populations, particularly the Algerian revolt against French settler colonialism, led by Emir Abdelkader in the 1830s and 1840s; the Taiping Rebellion of 1850–1864; the Indian Mutiny of 1857–1859; the nationalist struggle in Ireland led by the Fenians in the 1860s and after; and the Zulu War against the British in 1879. Writing on each of these uprisings, Marx and Engels were to take the side of the Indigenous people.

## Morant Bay

In 1865 a rebellion by formerly enslaved workers occurred in Morant Bay in Jamaica.

Marx wrote to Engels in 1865, regarding these events:

> The Jamaican business is typical of the utter turpitude of the "True Englishman." These fellows are as bad as the Russians in every respect. . . . The Irish affair and the Jamaica butcheries were all that was needed after the American war to complete the unmasking of English hypocrisy![76]

The Morant Bay Rebellion began on October 11, 1865, with a protest march to the courthouse in Morant Bay by hundreds of people led by Paul Bogle, a Baptist preacher of African heritage. Some were armed with sticks and stones. The volunteer militia shot and killed seven men. In response, the protesters attacked and burned the courthouse and nearby buildings killing twenty-five people in the process.

The revolt was put down with the utmost brutality, on the instructions of Governor Edward Eyre. British imperial soldiers and militia killed 439 African Jamaicans directly, and arrested 354, many of whom were later executed. Among the victims of this repression was George William Gordon, a political opponent of Eyre who had nothing to do with the uprising.[77] Gordon was born in Jamaica to a Scottish planter and an enslaved woman, thus he was born enslaved, but his father freed him at the age of ten. By the mid-1860s, he had emerged as a radical politician and a critic of the colonial government, especially Governor Eyre. Gordon was tried under martial law and quickly hanged.

Back in England, there was a campaign to have Eyre prosecuted, involving leading figures who included John Bright, John Stuart Mill, Charles Darwin, Thomas Henry Huxley, and many of the leading liberals and radicals of the day. However, writer and philosopher John Ruskin was one of the leading speakers in the defense of Governor Eyre, working alongside such racists as Thomas Carlyle and Charles Dickens.[78] Contributors to the Eyre Defense Fund included seventy-one peers, six bishops, twenty MPs, forty generals, twenty-six admirals, and four hundred Anglican clergymen.[79]

The dispute was also, in part, a continuation of the economic and political divisions between the more liberal and reformist industrialists, personified by Quaker statesman John Bright, and the more reactionary landed interest and their Tory allies, led by Thomas Carlyle and John Ruskin. Carlyle was particularly venomous toward the African inhabitants of the West Indies, continuing his rants about the "Lazy Negro."[80]

Meanwhile, the trade union journal *The Bee-Hive* displayed the same contempt for the Jamaican plantation owners as they showed for the British landed gentry, and reversed Carlyle's accusation of idleness:

> The emancipation of the blacks left all the land in the possession of the whites, a lazy, vicious, bankrupt class, filled with hatred for their late slaves; too proud to work, though not ashamed to beg in a genteel way.[81]

The Colonial Office in London was clearly on the same side of the argument as Carlyle and Ruskin. In 1865, in what was probably a contributing factor in the rebellion, the Colonial Office had replied to "An Humble Petition of the Poor People of Jamaica and the Parish of St Ann's" with "The Queen's Advice."[82] This reply advised the petitioners that the prosperity of Jamaica depended "upon their working for wages, not uncertainly or capriciously, but steadily and continuously, at the times when their labor is wanted, and for so long as it is wanted."

This attitude was taken to task by *Reynold's News*:

> When the Negroes obtained their nominal freedom, they very naturally preferred to work for themselves. They desired to be their own masters.... But, because they have done this—because they declined to work for the white planters as slavishly and cheaply as when they were slaves—they have been denounced as lazy, sensual, and insolent creatures, unfit for freedom and incapable of sustained industry.[83]

Ruskin denounced the hypocrisy of the liberal bourgeoisie who, he claimed, were making Eyre a scapegoat to draw attention away from their own connivance in the murder by neglect of British workingmen as a result of the dreadful conditions under which they worked and lived. Yet there was enormous support for the prosecution of Eyre among that very working class that Ruskin purported to defend. When Ruskin spoke at a banquet in Southampton alongside Lord Cardigan, probably the most reactionary man in England, to welcome the return from Jamaica of Edward Eyre, the hall was surrounded by what was described as a "howling mob of ruffians." Meanwhile, other opponents of Eyre were holding a predominantly working-class protest elsewhere in Southampton. A demonstration in London of ten thousand protesters, again mainly working class, later burned an effigy of Eyre on Clerkenwell Green.[84]

Today, Ruskin is generally viewed positively and considered to have been socially progressive but, just in case one might think that Ruskin's defense of Governor Eyre is out of character, let us remember that he also supported the South in the U.S. Civil War. This was at a time when support for the North and the Emancipation Proclamation was widespread in the British working class, particularly among Lancashire textile workers, even though they were suffering greatly from the Cotton Famine.

CHAPTER 8

# Imperial Reconfiguration

Profits from the business of slavery had been central in the construction of the British Empire but, in the mid-nineteenth century, the center of empire was shifting toward the East. Just as capitalism was reorganizing in Britain, and the most profitable sector of the economy was moving from agriculture to manufacturing, so India became central to British imperial exploitation and expropriation. For example, Sir John Gladstone, with the ending of enslavement, sold most of his West Indian landholdings, and transferred his investments to sugar production in Bengal.[1] Similarly, on a wider scale, the loss of British industry's principal raw cotton provider in the south of the United States sent British imperialism to seek new providers in India, Brazil, and, most importantly, Egypt.[2]

But the plantation oligarchy's measures to control labor did not end in 1838. The following hundred years saw attempts to introduce new human resource regimes in the West Indies that would ensure a supply of cheap labor. These included legal restrictions such as the Master and Servant Acts, Vagrancy Laws, workhouses and prohibitions on emigration, combined with measures to control land ownership and thereby prevent the development of small-scale farming by the descendants of the previously enslaved workers. The emancipated workers did not submit easily, and there was a century of resistance, culminating, in the 1930s, in a Caribbean-wide rebellion, which is credited with leading the way to eventual decolonization.

### Free Labor, Free Trade

The ideology of free labor had its counterpart in free trade. With the population of northern India already reduced to poverty and hunger by the extractions of the East India Company, a crop failure caused by drought in 1837 tipped the balance into famine. The East India Company, championing their ideology of free trade, refused to force the merchants, who were hoarding grain, to sell at prices the ordinary people could afford, claiming that the market was the best mechanism. As a result, 800,000 people died of starvation. There were many similar famines during the British imperial rule of India, culminating in the Bengal famine of 1943, during which one million people died of starvation and disease.[3]

Many slaveholders were also shareholders in the East India Company. The year 1833 was significant not only because of the passing of the law emancipating the enslaved in the Caribbean, but it was also the year in which the East India Company was given a new charter, which terminated the company's commercial role and compensated the shareholders with a guaranteed annual return of 10.5 percent on their investment. This return was funded from increased rents that the Indian farmers were required to pay on their own land. They had to pay for their own oppression and exploitation.[4]

Another implementation of free trade was in opium, which the Royal Navy forced on China in the Opium Wars (1839–1842 and 1856–1860). In the 1830s and 1840s, textiles worth 12 million pounds [£17,290,000,000, $21,958,300,000] a year were exported to India, and tea from China, worth 20 million pounds [£28,820,000,000, $36,601,400,000], was imported back to Britain, the tax on which provided 10 percent of total government revenue. To balance the trade, opium was exported from India to China. When the emperor of China, conscious of the devastating effect that opium addiction was having on his subjects, banned the trade, the Royal Navy and the new steamships of the East India Company attacked China and forced the free trade in narcotics. Thus, fossil-fuel-driven steam power enabled the use of violence to enforce the interests of British capitalism.

Slavery compensation money was also used to help finance the colonization of Australia and New Zealand. Former slave owners transferred their investments in enslaved human beings in the Caribbean to sheep and cattle in the Antipodes, on land they had stolen from the Indigenous population.[5] Land sales were restricted to the already rich, to ensure a supply of labor from poor White immigrants, whose immigration was funded by the land sales.

The African trade had been central to Europe's economic growth, most importantly through the slave trade. This led to a thwarting of the development of African societies through the lost labor potential resulting from the enslavement of so many fit and healthy people. The range of exports to Europe from Africa likewise narrowed to focus on just a few commodities, while imports were typically in the form of nonproductive luxury items and weapons. Neither process led to the development of productive capacity in Africa. As historian and revolutionary Walter Rodney put it, this system of trade produced "a loss of development opportunity, and this is of the greatest importance.... The lines of economic activity attached to foreign trade were either destructive, as slavery was, or at best purely extractive."[6]

Against this historical backdrop, the final quarter of the nineteenth century saw a "Scramble for Africa," as the colonial carve-up of the continent between European imperialist powers became known. Thus, by 1900, virtually the entire African continent was partitioned between the European powers, with colonies covering over 90 percent of its territory. Through warfare, torture, and deception, European rulers subdivided the continent into nations whose new borders served only the imperialists and had no logic based on local language, culture, religion, or geography. The subjugation of the African continent through forced labor and territorial conquest provided an immense accumulation of wealth for the capitalists in the imperialist countries.[7]

The plunder was enormous. Marx wrote: "The treasures captured outside Europe by undisguised looting, enslavement and murder, flowed back to the mother-country." The colonial system "proclaimed the making of profit as the ultimate and sole purpose of mankind."[8]

### Reorganization of Labor

The British government may have ended direct enslavement in the West Indies, but it had no wish to dismantle the plantation system. James Stephen (1789–1859), under secretary of state for the colonies, wrote in 1836:

> It will be necessary to prevent the occupation of any Crown lands by persons not possessing title to them, and to fix such a price upon all Crown land as may place them out of the reach of persons without capital.[9]

The period between 1834 and 1838, during which time slavery was renamed as apprenticeship, not only gave the plantation owners another four years of unpaid labor, it also gave them time to prepare a new human resource regime that would ensure that, thereafter, they would have a supply of cheap labor that would maintain their profits. The key to this was to make sure that little or no land was available for the emancipated, formerly enslaved workers to gain the economic independence that small-scale farming might have given them.

Having used the enclosures of common land in England and the highland clearances in Scotland to proletarianize or pauperize the majority of country people in Britain, the ruling class was hardly likely to allow the formerly enslaved laborers to live by independent farming in the Caribbean. In an attempt to ensure an adequate supply of cheap labor for the plantations, the colonial authorities adopted measures to prevent these laborers from acquiring enough land on which to survive without working for the landlords.

This landless freedom was deliberately designed to maintain the status quo of White supremacy, with the plantation oligarchy maintaining their economic and political control. Workers of African descent had little option but to labor in the cane fields at near starvation wages, while the lack of land enabled the oligarchy to maintain political control, as the property qualification for voting ensured that there were only 1,322 electors in Barbados, a mere 5 percent of the population.[10]

The Barbados colonial legislature passed the Master and Servant Act of 1838, which restricted the right to strike and other collective activity by workers that might have increased wages. The emancipated workers faced having to pay rent, which was frequently deducted from their miserable wages, while their proletarian status was reinforced by penal laws against vagrancy and debt.[11] Furthermore, various laws were passed to ensure that emigration was not practically possible. In preparation for this new system, a police force had been created in 1835. Meanwhile, the main tax base on the island was shifted from a land tax to duties on imported food, thereby moving the tax burden from the employers to the workers.

To this repressive legislation, the landowners in Barbados added an additional twist, introducing a system of tenantry whereby small plots of land were granted on contract to the laborers on a plantation in return for regular work on the estate owners' fields. This involved workers in a form of debt peonage, with the rent for these provision grounds and the accompanying dwellings concealed in the reduced wages. Drax Hall Estate, ever in the forefront of political and economic changes in Barbados, built some new housing to reinforce the landlord/tenant relationship, which they were hoping would replace the enslaver/enslaved relationship that had preceded it. Part of the response from previously enslaved people was to create the Chattel House, a wooden construction that could be quickly dismantled and re-erected elsewhere when its owners found other employment.[12]

But the overcrowding was dire, as a contemporary witness recounts:

> Who has ever entered one of these wretched homes, those almost loathsome scenes of human existence, without being shocked at the misery and extreme degradation in every corner of the dwelling. In a wooden hut, not twenty feet by ten, with the bare, unleveled earth for a flooring, you not uncommonly find families of eight, ten twelve in number, of every age and sex crowded and huddled together more like the beasts that perish than members of a Christian household.[13]

During the days of enslavement, the slave owners had been obliged to maintain unproductive aged and infirm persons. But, with the move to paid employment, they were no longer required to do so. The new regime allowed for a structural adjustment, as unproductive persons were driven from the estates and only the able-bodied were retained. As a result, plantations in Barbados considerably increased their production of sugar, while employing 25 percent fewer workers.[14]

Wage rates became dependent on the international market price of sugar. When the British Parliament passed the Sugar Duties Act of 1846, which removed the protective tariffs from imported sugar, thereby considerably reducing the price of sugar in Britain, the employers saved their profits by cutting wages in Barbados by 50 percent. Meanwhile, food prices on the island increased dramatically.

There was a decline in the quantity and quality of foods consumed by the workers as they became responsible for the provision of their own subsistence. They needed to earn enough money to buy provisions or to rent enough land to provide for their own subsistence, both of which proved unattainable. The majority lived on the old diet of rice, salt fish, yams, potatoes, breadfruit, cornmeal pap, and biscuits, which was not only deficient in vitamins and minerals, but did not even provide a sufficient calorific intake for the heavy manual labor they performed. Even the drinking water was unwholesome.[15]

Malnutrition was widespread. In 1858 the Reverend Edward Pinder wrote:

> I have seen repeatedly children wasting away from starvation, when sickness has prevented their parents from earning subsistence for them by their daily labor. I have known instances where old laborers, who have worked all their lives on one estate or another, have at last ended their days without food, shelter, or clothing, in some out-building of our properties, either in the stock-house or in the stock-hole.[16]

Mechanization increased specialization, in particular skills of production. Women were relegated to fieldwork, whereas some men moved into more skilled occupations. The majority of men still worked in the cane fields, but the opportunity for advancement, which was denied women, opened up divisions between male and female workers, helping the development of male-chauvinist attitudes. Following emancipation, women were only paid half as much as men for the same work tasks, and the employers' ideological offensive relegated women's role in society to the reproduction of labor as housewife, rather than as proletarians in their own right, a new form of divide and conquer.[17]

The plantation oligarchy remained opposed to education, as they wished to maintain an abundance of child labor, and feared the increased resistance that might arise from an educated working class. Despite the widespread and often-expressed desire for education for their children, the high cost of school fees meant that most workers had to choose between education and food.

Meanwhile, emigration from Barbados was effectively banned, and any protest was met by eviction, the demolition of houses, and destruction of provision grounds.

### Resistance

The workers did not take this assault lying down. The first Master and Servant Act passed by the Barbados legislature in 1838 was met with strikes, which started on August 2, just one day after legal emancipation. These strikes were accompanied by a campaign of arson, burning cane fields and the fuel used to power the sugar-processing machinery. The Colonial Office in London realized that the situation was untenable and struck down that law. The subsequent 1840 act was somewhat less draconian, but still produced ten days of strike action, particularly strong in Saint George Parish, the site of Drax Hall. These strikes were broken by the police and soldiers, with hundreds of arrests.[18]

Thereafter, strikes still took place, but they were difficult to sustain because of the threat of eviction and arrest. So, as workers the world over will frequently do in such circumstances, they turned to sabotage. There was a long tradition of the enslaved laborers setting fire to cane fields as a form of resistance, and as a way of bringing their grievances forcefully to the attention of management without the risk of individual victimization. This continued in the 1840s and 1850s, as the emancipated workers expressed their discontent with their wages and working conditions, as well as their generally oppressed and subordinate role in society.[19]

Samuel Jackman Prescod was editor of *The Liberal*, a Barbados newspaper that spoke up for the rights of the formerly enslaved working class. In 1843 Prescod became the first man of known African heritage to be elected to the Barbados House of Representatives. In 1840 he founded the Colonial Union of Coloured Classes, which campaigned "to put the two races upon a complete footing of equality, so that the black man and the mulatto man may occupy the same position in civil society with the white man."[20] This organization formed workplace cells that provided an organizational vehicle for the workers on the plantations. These groups were able to conduct negotiations with the employers, the police, and courts and were, in effect, the forerunner of the later trade union movement in Barbados. There were further revolts in 1854, 1863, 1872, 1876, and 1895.

The main achievement of these revolts was in pushing the imperial government to send a royal commission from London in 1897, enabling workers' representatives to make impassioned appeals for land redistribution. The royal commission did support the idea of "settling the labouring population on small plots of land as peasant proprietors." Although this land distribution was slowly put into effect on some islands, particularly on Dominica and Saint Vincent, little progress was made in Barbados, given the solid control of the legislature by the plantocracy.[21] Indeed, rioting and widespread arson broke out again in 1898, including the assassination of A. J. Pile, the speaker of the House of Assembly.

### The Riot Is the Ballot Box of the Poor

In the absence of any form of meaningful parliamentary representation anywhere in the British West Indies, rioting and arson were the only ways of drawing working-class grievances to the attention of the authorities.[22] The 1930s would see that concept applied throughout the British West Indies, when the British colonies in the Caribbean witnessed a series of strikes and riots that came to be known as the Labour Rebellions.[23] These certainly laid the foundations for decolonization and national independence in most of the British West Indies; what is more open to question, however, is the basis of that independence.

The colonial authorities succeeded in safely incorporating most of the trade union leadership by rewarding respectable behavior by posts in pre-independence governments and granting them recognition by honors, decorations, and medals such as the Order of the British Empire.²⁴ In most of the independent nations of the Caribbean, these trade union leaders went on to be the new political rulers. But, given that the economic structure of the ex-colonies remained unchanged, they ruled on behalf of the same business interests that had previously dominated the colonial economy. It is not surprising, therefore, that the ordinary members of trade unions found themselves economically little better off than they were in colonial times, giving a hollow ring to economist Arthur Lewis's confident prediction in 1939 that independence "will make of the West Indies of the future a country where the common man may lead a cultured life in freedom and prosperity."²⁵

Independence and the creation of postcolonial nation-states in the former British West Indies was contingent on accepting the global capitalist paradigm, with its inherent male chauvinism. Addressing the rights and liberation of women was pushed into second place. One or two token women were allowed a seat at the top table, but the radical women's movement was marginalized. This is not only true of twentieth-century independence: even in revolutionary Haiti, women were denied the vote.²⁶

Hilary Beckles summarized the relationship between male chauvinism, racism, colonialism, and capitalism by explaining that colonizers arrived in the Americas carrying

> commercial capitalism; the ideology of racism which at that time was not clearly articulated, but which rooted itself in the Caribbean; the social ideology of patriarchy which assumed the superior political and intellectual capacity of men over women; an intolerant Christian theology which defined other religions as primitive subtypes; an expansionist imperialist consciousness that focused on total territorial acquisition; and a rationalist philosophy that promoted the notion of materialism as the way forward for mankind.²⁷

Angela Davis, in her landmark essay "Reflections on the Black Woman's Role in the Community of Slaves," wrote:

> The black woman in her true historical contours must be resurrected. We, the black women of today, must accept the full weight of a legacy wrought in blood by our mothers in chains. Our fight, while identical in spirit, reflects different conditions and thus implies different paths of struggle. But as heirs to a tradition of supreme perseverance and heroic resistance, we must hasten to take our place wherever our people are forging on towards freedom.[28]

## RACE AND CLASS

The enormous profits made by the business of slavery enabled the endowment of colleges and universities that have repaid this generosity by producing tendentious justifications for racism. Anthropologists and Social Darwinists have given White Supremacy a scientific gloss. Populist politicians were able to play to the gallery by spouting rubbish about how the enslaved in the Caribbean were not treated as badly as workers in Britain. Elite abolitionists, who would do nothing to campaign for the rights of the laboring poor in Britain, and supported repressive anti-union legislation, helped discredit antiracism. Schools, cheap newspapers, comics and other young people's literature, music hall comedians, and other popular entertainment served to reinforce racist stereotypes.

Institutionalized racism[29] is an important part of the mechanism of government in Europe and the United States. During the time of slavery, giving small privileges to workers racialized as White had proved an effective means of dividing employed workers of European heritage from enslaved Africans in the Caribbean. In colonies, the small number of Europeans were needed by the plantation oligarchy as foremen, drivers, bookkeepers, and militia soldiers in order to discipline and enforce the enslaved labor system and extract the maximum surplus value from the enslaved workers. In the White settler colonies, such as Australia, Canada, and South Africa, the settlers needed little encouragement to see themselves as superior to the Indigenous population, who they stole the land from, and then exploited or exterminated.

However, in Britain, the majority of workers were of European heritage. These were the people that the capitalist class wished to exploit, so giving them privileges that cost money defeated the object of the exercise. Nevertheless, the ruling oligarchy had seen how the principle of divide-and-rule could effectively reduce the ability of the working class to resist such exploitation. Racism proved an effective tool in the armory of the ruling class. This is not to suggest that racism was a deliberate conspiracy by a cynical bourgeoisie—having presided over a system based on the enslavement of Africans in the West Indies for two hundred years they clearly believed their own propaganda.

Propagandists for colonialism and slavery claimed that Black people had been put on Earth expressly to work for White people, especially in the tropics. This view, advocated by Thomas Carlyle and Anthony Trollope, was summed up thus in 1865, in *The Spectator*: "The Negroes are made on purpose to serve the whites." James Hunt, founder of the Anthropological Society of London, claimed that Black people were closer to monkeys than to Europeans, intellectually inferior, and needed to be civilized and controlled by White people.[30] Advocates of these politically useful theories were much more likely to get funding for research and promotional preference within academic institutions. This gave a spurious respectability to racism.

The racist offensive was successfully linked with appeals to nationalism and nativism. Many British workers, particularly the skilled workers sometimes referred to as the aristocracy of labour, became convinced that their standard of living depended on their employment, which in turn depended on trade with the colonies.[31] The fact that they were only employed as long as their employer could make a profit from their labor, and that they were merely getting crumbs from the table of imperialism was lost in the claims of a common national interest. Nowhere in the history of the British Empire did the British trade unions or Labour Party take an unequivocal stand for the self-determination of the colonies against their own government.[32] In 1924, Sydney Olivier, a leading member of the Labour Party who became secretary of state for India in the first Labour government, wrote:

> There can be no reasonable question of locking up these sources of wealth because certain barbarous tribes, as a result of the migration of centuries, are found in this day and age sparsely inhabiting the countries which can produce them.[33]

Nevertheless, there would always be a minority of workers in Britain who could see that their class interests lay in unity between workers of different ethnicities, and that imperialism operated for the profit of the same capitalists who exploited them. During the campaign for the abolition of slavery, more workers in Britain signed petitions against enslavement than signed the People's Charter of 1838, which was about securing their own rights.[34] The solidarity of the Lancashire textile workers with the Union in the U.S. Civil War is perhaps the high point of British working-class internationalism.

Today, privatization has resulted in racial discrimination being increasingly based in the outsourcing of many essential jobs. Black and immigrant workers are more likely to be in the outsourced sector, with lower pay, fewer employment rights, worse conditions, and as a result indirect race discrimination. Their struggles for equality and union recognition have begun to change trade unionism in Britain.[35] As a result of this and consistent campaigning by antiracists, the more obscene manifestations of public racism have been considerably toned down, although far from eliminated.

When looking for evidence of structural racism in Britain, one has to look no further than the 2018 Windrush scandal, where people who were born in the British West Indies, migrated to Britain and thought they were British citizens, suddenly found themselves deprived of all rights, even health care, and were frequently deported to countries they had left fifty years ago because they had failed to get the required paperwork, which was now no longer obtainable. It is indeed shocking, if unsurprising, that one of the principal groups targeted by the Home Office's Hostile Environment policy are the descendants of the enslaved Africans trafficked to the Caribbean with the full support of the British state. They would not even be in the Caribbean, were it not for the slave trade organized by British big business. This is the basis of the claim for reparations for African enslavement.

# Conclusion

The debate over the contribution of slavery to modern capitalism cannot be confined to narrow considerations of profit and loss or to a single national economy. Atlantic slavery was inextricably interwoven with the markets, commodification, capital growth, credit, and the raw materials that were required for the expansion of capitalism in Europe and North America. West Indian merchants became the merchant bankers who were important to the growth of the City of London. The modern insurance industry had its roots in the maritime insurance of the triangular trade. Important infrastructure projects such as canals, docks, and railways were financed out of the profits of slavery and the compensation received after abolition. But from the point of view of the enslaved worker, this is of little moment.

Economically speaking, the major difference between slavery and paid employment is the lack of wages paid to the enslaved. Let us do a calculation for the amount of unpaid wages owed in the case of Barbados alone:

- Take the available figures for numbers of enslaved laborers between 1617 and 1838.

- Calculate the average number for each period under consideration.
- Multiply this figure by the number of years in that period.
- Multiply by £15, the average annual wage of a British agricultural worker for the years 1650 to 1780, or by £25, the average annual wage for the period 1780–1850.
- This gives a total of £211,113,465 [£564,200,000,000, $716,534,000,000].[1]

Similarly, for Jamaica we have a figure of £612,794,965 [£1,722,000,000,000, $2,276,613,150,000].

Applying this calculation to the whole of the former British West Indies produces a figure of £1,222,781,000, which is worth approximately two thousand, five hundred billion pounds sterling in today's money [$3,200,000,000,000].

Reparations for enslavement are proposed as an international means to at least mitigate the aftermath and consequences of enslavement. In the context of Britain's foreign policy, this means developing a society-wide awareness of colonialism and its consequences. Education is central to this process.[2]

Education has played and still plays a central role in the transmission of societal values, as well as knowledge. Unfortunately, the UK education system has been central to maintaining British institutional racism through the periods of colonization, enslavement, empire building, and postwar immigration. European colonizing explorers were ignorant of what they would find when they went on their so-called voyages of discovery. However, they set forth with plans to increase their wealth not just through trade, but also through exploiting and expropriating whatever and whomever they found in the lands they later claimed. Moreover, the European venturers already had theories of class, civilization, gender, savagery, entitlement, and ownership that they exported as part of their colonizing. A major omission in history education is the British Empire itself.

Guardian journalists Anna Leach, Antonio Voce, and Ashley Kirk write:

> In contrast, there are 21 modules on British history that make little to no reference to the Empire. . . . The erasure of Black history in Britain is an intentional feature of racism that can be traced back to Enoch Powell, whose search for a precolonial White England discards 400 years of British history and skips back to before the Elizabethans.[3]

The links between racism, politics, education policy, and what is and is not taught in schools can be traced further back to the post–Second World War period.[4]

On the one hand, the neglect in teaching about the history of the British Empire spills over into the neglect of teaching about its end, even as the end was happening. On the other hand, the consequence of leaving out colonial history in postwar British schooling has had a knock-on, or domino, effect on the persistence of both widespread racism and the institutional discrimination experienced by children of Caribbean, African, and Asian heritage.[5]

We need to question the comfortable and self-congratulatory view of abolition and emancipation summed up by the inscription on William Wilberforce's monument in Westminster Abbey, which claims that Wilberforce "removed from England the guilt of the African slave trade." The idea of slavery as a national sin, for which we are all responsible, conveniently absolves the enslavers who made huge profits from this crime against humanity.

Profits from British trafficking and the unpaid labor of enslaved workers contributed significantly to the accumulation of capital in England and, conversely, contributed to the underdevelopment of member states of the Caribbean community. Profits made from sugar and other tropical products, as well as the supply of cheap raw materials such as cotton to European and North American manufacturers, helped finance the Industrial Revolution. These profits went, directly or indirectly, to the manufacturers and other suppliers in the trafficking of enslaved Africans, to the shipping industry, to the construction of infrastructure such as canals and railways—but above all, to the financial services industry. The origin of many of today's banks and insurance companies can be traced back directly to enterprises that had their first growth through their financing of trafficking and enslavement. It would therefore seem reasonable that these modern corporations should refund the unpaid wages from which their predecessors profited so handsomely. It is for the descendants of the enslaved to determine the form such reparations should take.

As well as the return of unpaid wages, the worldwide reparations movement demands redress for the former enslaved Africans and their descendants for the denial of their culture and history, the human rights abuses they suffered, including but not limited to murder, rape, flogging, branding, denial of freedom of movement, freedom to worship, freedom to own land, the right to education, and for the severe psychological damage to enslaved people and their descendants, continued long after 1838 by systemic racism and racial discrimination.

In the Americas, Indigenous genocide is frequently added to the demand for reparations. There has been some debate about whether the term "genocide" is appropriate, or whether it would be better to speak of ethnic cleansing, which the press often uses as a lesser charge than genocide. Although there is a legal difference in the definition of the terms, both are nevertheless internationally considered crimes against humanity and war crimes.[6] Despite the genocidal policies of European colonial settlers, there are still 9,666,058 persons identified as Indigenous in the United States, with another 1,807,250 in Canada, while there are a quarter of a million Garifuna in Central America.[7]

Common stereotypes of the Indigenous peoples of North America are highly influenced by their portrayal in film and television, ranging from the bloodthirsty barbarian to the noble savage. There has been a tendency to lump together the cultures of the wide variety of Indigenous nations inhabiting the region, despite their vastly different customs, social structures, and political economies. Only the Indigenous living on the Great Plains of North America ever lived in tipis; only First Nations and Indigenous peoples of the Pacific Northwest Coast erected totem poles. Both of these are a small proportion of the over 900 Indigenous national groups based on territory now part of the United States as well as the 634 First Nations across Canada.[8]

The call for reparations for enslavement and Indigenous genocide, made by many governments across the Caribbean, appeals, in a broader sense, to the correcting of a wrong. In the case of trafficking and enslavement, with its persistent legacies, this means implementing measures of compensation at different levels, including the call for apology, accountability, and recognition, as well as collective investments of money and resources to address the structural inequalities and racial discrimination that people of African heritage continue to suffer. Besides financial transfers, claims for reparations demand support for commemorative activities, the erection of memorials, returning artifacts, days of remembrance, and institutions such as museums that contribute to decolonizing the history of enslavement and its legacies.

Campaigns for the removal of the statues of enslavers are a public part of this education process. When the people of Bristol pitched the statue of merchant and slave trader Edward Colston into the river, the story of how he made his money was heard the world over. This was a fitting culmination of a campaign that many people in Bristol had been waging for years. Mark Steeds and Roger Hill's finely researched book *From Wulfstan to Colston* had provided the historical information, and the statue's headlong dive into Bristol Harbour completed the history lesson.

Official history ignores completely the fact that the enslaved did not sit passively and await saviors from on high to deliver. They fought on the beaches of Africa; they mutinied on the slave ships; they deserted to form free, independent communities in the hills of the Caribbean colonies; they engaged in day-to-day resistance such as strikes and go-slows, as well as, given the slightest opening, engaging in full-scale rebellions. This history needs to be more widely known.

Equally hidden from history is the role that employed workers in Britain played in bringing down the structures of slavery. Workers, particularly trade unionists in Yorkshire and Lancashire, have a proud history of internationalism and opposition to slavery and racism, from the antislavery petitioning campaigns of the late eighteenth and early nineteenth centuries through their solidarity with the antislavery forces in the U.S. Civil War, to the more recent support for anti-apartheid in South Africa.

Upper-class abolitionists such as William Wilberforce tried to restrict the campaign against slavery to a single-issue campaign, while working-class activists of the time saw it as part of the wider campaign against corruption and class privilege, as well as for reform of the whole system and a fight for democratic rights.

We frequently read that slavery brought prosperity to Britain. The UK Parliament website maintains:

> The slave trade benefited many parts of British life and its economy, from the businessmen, financiers and landowners who ran and profited from the trade, to businesses, workers and consumers.
>
> The rewards of the transatlantic slave system were everywhere. From the urban fabric of slave ports, to the grand homes of those made wealthy, to the jobs created in industrial cities, to the coffee and tobacco shops dotting British cities.[9]

There is, however, little discussion about what that meant for the overwhelming majority of the population of Britain. There is a general lack of a class analysis of the situation. This book has tried to address that gap by examining some of those who gained from the business of slavery, with examples of major businessmen, bankers, and commodity traders, as well as landowners and enslavers. Their fabulous wealth contrasted starkly with the overwhelming majority of the population of Britain who lived in abject poverty. Trickle-down economics was no more a reality in the eighteenth and nineteenth centuries than it is today. The descriptions contained in *London Labour and the London Poor* by Henry Mayhew, or Frederick Engels's *The Condition of the Working-Class in England* portray most workers and poor farmers earning just about enough to survive, a subsistence income that barely guaranteed the reproduction of their labor power.[10]

It might be argued that workers gained employment on the back of the profits made by the enslavers. This argument assumes that employment is beneficial to a worker. Of course, when the alternative is unemployment, the employed worker is obviously better off than the unemployed. But this ignores the exploitation at the root of the relationship between management and labor. Employers employ workers to make a profit by extracting surplus value from their labor power. The threat of unemployment, with its resulting poverty, houselessness, and starvation, is a form of coercion that leaves the worker no other alternative than to seek employment. The concept of capitalist management claiming that it has the "right to manage," itself derived from the practice of slavery, leaves workers with no say in what is produced once they have sold their labor power to the employer.

What determines wages, the monetary expression of the cost to the employer of purchasing labor power? According to Karl Marx:

> The mere bodily existence of the worker is sufficient, the cost of his production is limited almost exclusively to the commodities necessary for keeping him in working condition. The price of his work will therefore be determined by the price of the necessary means of subsistence. . . . The cost of production of simple labour-power must include the cost of propagation, by means of which the race of workers is enabled to multiply itself, and to replace worn-out workers with new ones. . . . Thus, the cost of production of simple labour-power amounts to the cost of the existence and propagation of the worker. The price of this cost

of existence and propagation constitutes wages. The wages thus determined are called the minimum of wages.[11]

The investment of the profits of the business of slavery in industry and infrastructure enabled the capitalist class to better exploit the workers they employed, but brought scant benefit to those workers, other than to raise them slightly from the ranks of the utterly destitute.

True, some workers were able to form an "aristocracy of labor" by manipulating skill shortages, restricting entry to their trade, militant trade union activity, or political activism. But these were temporary improvements in living standards that the employers overcame by either technological innovations or state repression. In any case, if the slightly better-off skilled workers in Britain had not been paid wages above the level of subsistence, their modest excess would not have been returned to the enslaved workers of the Caribbean. Imperialism gives no refunds.

Any improvement above the socially necessary minimum wage required to reproduce labor power is partly a result of the class struggle, and partly an effort to provide an internal market to sell the commodities, and thereby for the capitalist to realize a profit. Today, workers in Western Europe and North America have a generally higher standard of living than workers in the Third World. This is not a privilege but can be seen as the minimum acceptable standard that should be available to all workers worldwide. In addition to notions of international solidarity, workers in Western Europe and North America have an economic self-interest in assisting workers in the Third World in their struggles for equal rights and an increased standard of living. Otherwise, they risk seeing their standards dragged down.

The business of slavery, a unique combination of exploitation and expropriation, was intertwined with banking, insurance, commodity trading, the textile industry, the food industry, construction, transport and infrastructure, agriculture, and conspicuous consumption by the wealthy. It polluted British politics for over two hundred years and was the cause of war, inter-imperialist rivalry, Indigenous genocide, and the murderous suppression of the civil rights of the enslaved. Even when enslavement was finally abolished in the British West Indies, British big business continued to profit from slave-based production of cotton, coffee, sugar, and copper.

Racism, which the profiteers of the business of slavery used as a justification for enslavement, has left a legacy that continues to have a detrimental effect on society. The institutional racism of the police, stop-and-search, the unemployment figures for young Black people, the endless discrimination and petty humiliations of everyday life, the Windrush scandal—all these factors and more have their origins in the wealth and power that the ruling class gained from the business of slavery.

Throughout its history, the Caribbean has been denied participation in Europe's industrialization process, confined to the role of producer and exporter of raw materials. The African-descended population in the Caribbean has the highest incidence in the world of chronic diseases in the forms of hypertension and Type 2 diabetes. The history of enslavement has inflicted massive psychological trauma upon African descendant populations.

Correcting these wrongs will cost money. This means implementing measures of compensation at different levels, including the call for apology and recognition, but also for collective investments that would address the structural inequalities and racial discrimination that people of African heritage still suffer, both in Europe and North America, as well as in the Caribbean, in terms of accessing education, health systems, income, housing, and labor markets, to name just a few.

The British bourgeoisie profited from Caribbean sugar slavery, from North American slave-picked cotton, from the colonization of Africa and Asia, from the expropriation of the English peasants from their common land, and from the genocide of Indigenous nations. They used that capital to develop a fossil fuel–based economy that is now the major factor in global warming, and threatens human existence in general and the Caribbean in particular.

Part of the demand for reparations is that European and North American big business, in addition to compensating the unpaid wages denied to the enslaved laborers, should fund the repair of the ecology of the Caribbean islands, and reverse the fossil fuel-driven economy that is causing global warming.

Similarly, the deforestation of the Caribbean islands to produce sugar, along with the soil exhaustion resulting from monocrop, export-based agriculture, has severely damaged the possibilities for sustainable development. Deforestation of the region has also adversely affected weather patterns, making the general effects of global warming more severe. Deforestation, pollution of the air from coal burning and of the water from industrial and human waste were already problematic in the sixteenth century, but have now spread into Africa, Asia, and the Americas. The natural world has always been treated as a free gift for capitalism.[12]

The more dominant global capital has become, the more rampant the growth of $CO_2$ emissions. As Andreas Malm says, "The decisive capitalist victory in the long twentieth-century struggle with labour was crowned by the post-2000 rush towards catastrophic global warming."[13] And Rex Tillerson, CEO of ExxonMobil, said in March 2013: "My philosophy is to make money. If I can drill and make money, then that's what I want to do."[14]

Presently, the Caribbean islands face one of the worst threats in the planet of flooding from sea-level rises and increasingly violent hurricanes. At the same time, Caribbean victims of climate change are denied the right to migrate out of the threatened region, while industrial production is moved from the metropolitan countries to the Third World in order to profit from lower wage rates.

The last hundred years have seen a dramatic hardening of borders and restrictions on the free movement of labor, while free movement of capital and free trade have become the norm worldwide, making it easy for corporations to move production to ever-cheaper locations, and to dump their pollution on the Third World. Corporations operate across borders, while regulations and workers are contained by them.[15] Oil and mineral extraction, as well as pollution, is done by corporations unbounded by borders and protected by free trade, so the real control of the environment currently rests with those corporations.

The 2018 hurricanes Irma and Maria signaled the emergence of a new climate pattern in the Caribbean. At no point in the historical records dating back to the 1880s have two Category 5 storms struck the eastern Caribbean in a single year. The Caribbean is experiencing repeated and prolonged droughts, an increase in the number of very hot days, intense rainfall events causing repeated localized flooding, and rising sea levels.[16]

Caribbean economies are built on industries and sectors that are extremely sensitive to climate variations, such as tourism and agriculture. The ferocity of Irma and Maria brought devastation of catastrophic proportions. Without global action, it is predicted that by the end of the current century the Caribbean region will warm a further 2–3°C over the 1°C already seen in the last century. Annual rainfall amounts will decrease by up to 40 percent, posing a significant challenge to already water-stressed islands. Projections also show sea levels rising by one or two meters. There will be more of the strongest tropical Atlantic hurricanes. The region's climate will be altered beyond recognition.

The Caribbean islands are minor emitters of greenhouse gases, but the future viability of the region depends on collective global action to reduce greenhouse gas emissions. It is for this reason that the Caribbean and other small island and developing states have argued for a limit to global warming of 1.5°C.

The slogan "1.5°C to Stay Alive!" was adopted by the Caribbean Community Climate Change Centre. A world warmed by no more than 1.5°C is one in which existing Caribbean societies have a future. The emissions reductions that have been voluntarily agreed through the United Nations have been predicted to lead to warming of 2.7–3.7°C.[17]

The failure of efforts by the United Nations to deal with climate change can partly be attributed to the domination of these discussions by the former colonialist powers, those which, as the major historical and current polluters, are mainly responsible for the state of the climate. At the behest of the major polluters, the United Nations currently lacks a mechanism to hold countries to any commitments that they might make on climate change, as these are only voluntary. In light of this, the credibility of the UN-led process for securing the future of the Caribbean is completely compromised. The globally unequal distribution of wealth that leaves many Caribbean countries without the resources necessary to respond adequately to climate change is a consequence of the legacies of imperialism, slavery, and colonialism, combined with contemporary forms of neoliberal capitalism.

Now the same logic of unlimited economic growth and unchecked global inequality that are the motor of climate change are extended to the conditions accompanying proposed solutions. Here the distribution of financial support depends on potential returns for wealthy investors. Financing is utilized as a mechanism to further extend the pursuit of the business opportunities and potential investment, the latest form of neocolonialism.[18] So-called green capitalism is nearly always just an advertising agent's way of whitewashing the same old polluting industry, while the term "just transition" has frequently been hijacked by some governments to disguise what should really be called "structural adjustment."

The UN approach to climate change has prevented discussion of alternative approaches, which might not be in the interests of global capitalism. The call for 1.5°C requires an end to highly resource-intensive models of capitalist development and the obsession with capital accumulation. If we examine the conditions attached to the meager funding that has been begrudgingly promised to vulnerable countries, we see how the interests of big business are prioritized at the expense of Caribbean societies.

Mia Mottley, prime minister of Barbados, speaking at COP 27 United Nations Climate Change Conference in Sharm el-Sheikh in November 2022, said:

We were the ones whose blood, sweat and tears financed the

Industrial Revolution. Are we now to face double jeopardy by having to pay the cost as a result of those greenhouse gases from the Industrial Revolution? That is fundamentally unfair.[19]

Stopping climate change, opposing racism, and seeking reparations for slavery are social justice issues. An apology, if it is to mean anything, must be more than the regret and remorse expressed by criminals in the hope of a lighter sentence after they have been found guilty. It must involve real and appropriate action.

David Comissiong, Barbados's ambassador to CARICOM, an intergovernmental Caribbean organization, says of the Drax family:

> You can't simply walk away from the scene of the crime. They have a responsibility now to make some effort to help repair the damage. We are establishing a fund into which families, corporations and establishments like universities that were implicated in some way in the crime of enslavement can pay.[20]

Barbados MP and Special Envoy on Reparations and Economic Enfranchisement Trevor Prescod is demanding that Sir Richard Drax return Drax Hall Plantation to the people of Barbados. He said:

> Our people suffered a lot as a result of improper nourishment during the period of slavery and some of the major diseases that we have had to go through today derive from malnutrition and all types of challenges that we faced as a people. Some of the diseases that we face apart from the foods and so on were diseases that came because of the interaction between African people and the Europeans. However, the 21st century must be the century where we call for justice against slavery and for Reparations. There must be a compensatory approach to assist these people who are still living in mass poverty, illiteracy, poor public health, and whose development is being blocked because of the legacy of slavery.[21]

## FURTHER READING

We need to start with a recognition of Eric Williams, who wrote *Capitalism and Slavery* (New York: André Deutsch, 1944). Ever since his book was published, there have been furious arguments over the connection between slavery and capitalism, with many historians attempting to prove that slavery did not contribute greatly to the development of modern capitalism.

For an assessment of the whole debate on the Williams thesis, see Barbara Solow and Stanley Engerman, *British Capitalism and Caribbean Slavery: The Legacy of Eric Williams* (Cambridge: Cambridge University Press, 1987). Joseph Inikori in *Africans and the Industrial Revolution in England* (Cambridge: Cambridge University Press, 2002) provides support for Williams, whereas Seymour Drescher, *Econocide: British Slavery in the Era of Abolition* (Pittsburgh: University of Pittsburgh Press, 1977) presents an alternative case. More recently, Stephan Heblich, Stephen Redding, and Hans-Joachim Voth, *Slavery and the British Industrial Revolution* (Cambridge, MA: National Bureau of Economic Research, Working Paper 30451, 2022), Erika Brodnock and Johannes Lenhard, *Better Venture: Improving Diversity, Innovation, and Profitability in Venture Capital and Startups* (San Francisco: Holloway, 2023) have contributed to the discussion on the relationship between capitalism and slavery.

If you are looking for a book that contests the bourgeois economists on their own terms, I recommend Maxine Berg and Pat Hudson, *Slavery Capitalism and the Industrial Revolution* (Cambridge: Polity Press, 2023).

The other classic work on the history of slavery is Robin Blackburn, *The Making of New World Slavery: From the Baroque to the Modern*,

*1492–1800* (London: Verso Books, 1997). Blackburn's narrative, contained in his five volumes on slavery, is uncontested as the basis for all subsequent writing.

The life stories of individuals who profited from the business of slavery provide the narrative for Matthew Parker, *The Sugar Barons: Family, Corruption, Empire, and War in the West Indies* (London: Hutchinson, 2011), and a useful account of a single family, the Hibberts, is contained in Katie Donington, *The Bonds of Family: Slavery, Commerce and Culture in the British Atlantic World* (Manchester, UK: Manchester University Press, 2019).

The Hibberts were important participants in the building of the West India Dock in London, the finance of which is described by Nick Draper, "The City of London and Slavery: Evidence from the First Dock Companies, 1795–1800" (*Economic History Review*, vol. 61, no. 2, 2008), and the history of the dock from the point of view of the dockworkers is told in Peter Linebaugh, *The London Hanged: Crime and Civil Society in the Eighteenth Century* (London: Verso Books, 2006). This book also deals with the origins of the London police and the relationship of the police with the West Indian trade.

The history of the Royal African Company is comprehensively covered by William Pettigrew, *Freedom's Debt: The Royal African Company and the Politics of the Atlantic Slave Trade, 1672–1752* (Chapel Hill: University of North Carolina Press, 2013). For the East India Company, see Nick Robins, *The Corporation That Changed the World: How the East India Company Shaped the Modern Multinational* (London: Pluto Press, 2012).

Lorenzo Greene's *The Negro in Colonial New England, 1620–1776* (New York: Columbia University Press, 1942), as Betty Wood observed, still "remains the only book-length study of the colonial era" involving African Americans and slavery. See Betty Wood, *The Origins of American Slavery: Freedom and Bondage in the English Colonies* (New York: Hill & Wang, 1997). Eric Kimball's PhD dissertation, "An Essential Link in a Vast Chain: New England and the West Indies, 1700–1775" (Pittsburgh: University of Pittsburgh, 2009), examines New England's involvement in the business of slavery in great detail; a more journalistic view is provided by Anne Farrow, Joel Lang, and Jenifer Frank, *Complicity: How the North Promoted, Prolonged, and Profited from Slavery* (New York: Ballantine, 2006). For the development of cotton production in the southern United States, see Dale Tomich, *New Frontiers of Slavery* (Albany, NY: SUNY Press, 2016).

Katharine Gerbner's *Christian Slavery: Conversion and Race in the Protestant Atlantic World* (Philadelphia: University of Pennsylvania Press, 2018) is probably the definitive text on its subject, although on the specific question of Nonconformist missionaries, see Mary Turner, *Slaves and Missionaries: The Disintegration of Jamaican Slave Society, 1787–1834* (Kingston, Jamaica: University of the West Indies, 1998).

For studies of the specific condition of enslaved women, Barbara Bush, *Slave Women in Caribbean Society, 1650–1832* (Bloomington: Indiana University Press, 1990) and Hilary Beckles, *Natural Rebels: A Social History of Enslaved Black Women in Barbados* (London: Zed Books, 1989) are classics, and Diana Paton's "Gender History, Global History, and Atlantic Slavery: On Racial Capitalism and Social Reproduction" (*American Historical Review*, vol. 127, no. 2, June 2022) reflects recent research.

The relationship between slavery and management science is dealt with theoretically by Bill Cooke, *The Denial of Slavery in Management Studies* (Manchester, UK: University of Manchester, 2002) and, in detail but with reference to the southern states of the United States, Sven Beckert and Seth Rockman, *Slavery's Capitalism, A New History of American Economic Development* (Philadelphia: University of Pennsylvania Press, 2016). This book also contains valuable material for the discussion about whether plantation slavery was capitalist or precapitalist, although a recent publication on this topic takes an alternative view: Nick Nesbitt, *The Price of Slavery: Capitalism and Revolution in the Caribbean* (Charlottesville: University of Virginia Press, 2022).

Robin Blackburn, *An Unfinished Revolution: Karl Marx and Abraham Lincoln* (Verso Books, 2011) is a good introduction to the debate about Marx and slavery. Karl Marx, *Capital, A Critique of Political Economy*, volume 1 (First English edition of 1887) and the subsequent two volumes edited by Engels are, despite their forbidding reputation, surprisingly accessible. The works of Marx and Engels quoted in the text can all be found online at the Marxist Internet Archive.[1]

There has been recent debate on the relationship between the British country house and slavery. Madge Dresser and Andrew Hann, *Slavery and the British Country House* (Swindon: English Heritage, 2013), Stephanie Barczewski, *Country Houses and the British Empire, 1700–1930* (Manchester, UK: Manchester University Press, 2017), and Caroline Dakers (ed.), *Fonthill Recovered: A Cultural History* (London: UCL Press, 2018) all make useful contributions. Dakers's book also contains a useful account of the life of William Beckford and serves as a counter to a much less critical study, Perry Gauci, *William Beckford: First Prime Minister of the London Empire* (New Haven: Yale University Press, 2013).

Few writers make the connection between the enclosures and slavery. One who does is Corinne Fowler, *Green Unpleasant Land* (Leeds: Peepal Tree Press, 2021). Simon Fairlie, "A Short History of Enclosure in Britain" (*The Land*, no. 7, Summer 2009), provides a simple introduction to the enclosures from the perspective of the dispossessed, a theme continued by Peter Linebaugh in *Stop, Thief!: The Commons, Enclosures, and Resistance* (Oakland, CA: PM Press, 2014). See Ian Angus, *The War Against the Commons: Dispossession and Resistance in the Making of Capitalism* (New York: Monthly Review Press, 2023) for a historical account of poor people's self-defense strategies in the face of the privatization of common land.

The parliamentary politics surrounding the abolition of slavery are well covered by Michael Taylor, *The Interest: How the British Establishment Resisted the Abolition of Slavery* (London: Bodley Head, 2020). The contribution of the enslaved laborers in the Caribbean to their own emancipation is dealt with by Mary Turner, *From Chattel Slaves to Wage Slaves: The Dynamics of Labour Bargaining in the Americas* (Kingston, Jamaica: Ian Randle, 1995), Thomas Harding,

*White Debt: The Demerara Uprising and Britain's Legacy of Slavery* (London: Weidenfeld & Nicolson, 2022), Emilia Viotti da Costa, *Crowns of Glory, Tears of Blood: The Demerara Slave Rebellion of 1823* (New York: Oxford University Press, 1997), Tom Zoellner, *Island on Fire: The Revolt That Ended Slavery in the British Empire* (New York: Harvard University Press, 2020), and Richard Hart, *Slaves Who Abolished Slavery* (Kingston, Jamaica: University of West Indies Press, 2002).

Gelien Matthews, in *Caribbean Slave Revolts and the British Abolitionist Movement* (Baton Rouge: Louisiana State University Press, 2012), considers the relationship between the abolitionist movements in Britain and the West Indies.

For some recent writing on the Maroons, see Jean Besson, *Transformations of Freedom in the Land of the Maroons: Creolization in the Cockpits* (Kingston, Jamaica: Ian Randle, 2016).

Katie Donington, Nicholas Draper, Catherine Hall, Rachel Lang, and Keith McClelland (eds.), in *Legacies of British Slave-Ownership: Colonial Slavery and the Formation of Victorian Britain* (Cambridge: Cambridge University Press, 2014), provide great detail on the topic, expanding on the groundbreaking work of Nicholas Draper, *The Price of Emancipation: Slave-Ownership, Compensation and British Society at the End of Slavery* (Cambridge: Cambridge University Press, 2010).

Alan Lester, Kate Boehme, and Peter Mitchell, in *Ruling the World: Freedom, Civilisation and Liberalism in the Nineteenth-Century British Empire* (Cambridge: Cambridge University Press, 2021), provide a valuable overview of the changes that took place across the British Empire during the nineteenth century.

For a view of the changes to the management of labor in the Caribbean after emancipation, see Hilary Beckles, *Great House Rules: Landless Emancipation and Workers' Protest in Barbados 1838–1938* (Kingston, Jamaica: Ian Randle, 2004). Beckles deals in general terms with the resistance of the emancipated laborers, but for the details of the resistance, see Henderson Carter, *Labour Pains: Resistance and Protest in Barbados, 1838–1904* (Kingston, Jamaica: Ian Randle, 2012). A Caribbean-wide view of workers' resistance in the 1930s can be found in Nigel Bolland, *On The March: Labour Rebellions in the British Caribbean, 1934–39* (Martlesham, UK: James Currey, 1995).

There are two aspects of the legacy of slavery: the environmental and the social consequences. Andreas Malm, *Fossil Capital: The Rise of Steam Power and the Roots of Global Warming* (London: Verso Books, 2020), links the industrial revolution to global warming. The effect of slave-based agriculture on the soil is dealt with by David Silkenat, *Scars on the Land: An Environmental History of Slavery in the American South* (New York: Oxford University Press, 2022), which, while concentrating on the United States, provides valuable parallels for the Caribbean.

Generally, on the environmental crisis, we have the work of John Bellamy Foster and Brett Clark, *The Robbery of Nature: Capitalism and the Ecological Rift* (New York: Monthly Review Press, 2020), John Bellamy Foster, Brett Clark, and Richard York, *The Ecological Rift: Capitalism's War on the Earth* (New York: Monthly Review Press, 2010), and specifically for the Caribbean, Leon Sealey-Huggins, "1.5°C to Stay Alive: Climate Change, Imperialism and Justice for the Caribbean" (*Third World Quarterly*, vol. 38, no.11, 2017).

James Walvin has written a devastating attack on the health implications of sugar consumption, linking today's worldwide obesity epidemic with the origins of the slavery-based sugar industry: *Sugar: The World Corrupted: From Slavery to Obesity* (London: Robinson, 2017).

For the social consequences and the culture wars debate, Robert Bevan's *Monumental Lies: Culture Wars and the Truth About the Past* (New York: Verso Books, 2022) deals with the issue of the way in which the past is remembered. Theodore Allen, in *The Invention of the White Race* (London: Verso Books, 1997), explains the development of white supremacy, and Angela Saini, in *Superior, the Return of Race Science* (London: 4th Estate, 2020), brings the study of scientific racism up to date.

Finally, on the question of reparations for African enslavement, the official case is given by the Chair of the CARICOM Reparations Committee, Hilary Beckles, in *Britain's Black Debt: Reparations* for Caribbean Slavery and Native Genocide, (Kingston, Jamaica: University of the West Indies Press, 2013).

Nothing published to date deals with the question of reparations from a class-based perspective.

## SELECTED BIBLIOGRAPHY

Allen, Theodore, *The Invention of the White Race* (London: Verso, 1997).
Baptist, Edward, *The Half Has Never Been Told* (New York: Basic Books, 2015).
Barczewski, Stephanie, *Country Houses and the British Empire, 1700–1930* (Manchester, UK: Manchester University Press, 2017).
Beckert, Sven, *Empire of Cotton: A Global History* (New York: Vintage, 2014).
Beckert, Sven, and Seth Rockman, *Slavery's Capitalism, A New History of American Economic Development* (Philadelphia: University of Pennsylvania Press, 2016).
Beckles, Hilary, *Natural Rebels: A Social History of Enslaved Black Women in Barbados* (London: Zed Books, 1989).
Beckles, Hilary, *Great House Rules: Landless Emancipation and Workers' Protest in Barbados, 1838–1938* (Kingston, Jamaica: Ian Randle, 2004).
Beckles, Hilary, *How Britain Underdeveloped the Caribbean* (Kingston, Jamaica: University of the West Indies Press, 2021).
Berg, Maxine, and Pat Hudson, *Slavery, Capitalism and the Industrial Revolution* (Cambridge: Polity Press 2023).
Blackburn, Robin, *The Making of New World Slavery: From the Baroque to the Modern 1492–1800* (London: Verso Books, 1997).
Blackburn, Robin, *An Unfinished Revolution: Karl Marx and Abraham Lincoln* (London: Verso Books, 2011).
Bolland, Nigel, *On The March: Labour Rebellions in the British Caribbean, 1934–39* (London: James Currey, 1995).
Brodnock, Erika, and Johannes Lenhard, *Better Venture: Improving Diversity, Innovation, and Profitability in Venture Capital and Startups* (San Francisco: Holloway, 2023).
Calder, Angus, *Revolutionary Empire: Rise of the English-Speaking Empire from the Fifteenth Century to the 1780s* (London: Pimlico, 1998).
Carter, Henderson, *Labour Pains: Resistance and Protest in Barbados, 1838–1904* (Kingston, Jamaica: Ian Randle, 2012).
Cooke, Bill, *The Denial of Slavery in Management Studies* (Manchester, UK: University of Manchester 2002).
Dakers, Caroline (ed.), *Fonthill Recovered: A Cultural History* (London: UCL Press, 2018).

# SELECTED BIBLIOGRAPHY

Davis, Mike, *Late Victorian Holocausts* (London: Verso Books, 2017).

Desmond, Adrian, and James Richard Moore, *Darwin's Sacred Cause: How a Hatred of Slavery Shaped Darwin's Views on Human Evolution* (New York: Houghton Mifflin Harcourt, 2009).

Donington, Katie, *The Bonds of Family: Slavery, Commerce and Culture in the British Atlantic World* (Manchester, UK: Manchester University Press, 2019).

Donington, Katie, Nicholas Draper, Catherine Hall, Rachel Lang, and Keith McClelland (eds.), *Legacies of British Slave-ownership: Colonial Slavery and the Formation of Victorian Britain* (Cambridge: Cambridge University Press, 2014).

Draper, Nicholas, *The Price of Emancipation: Slave-Ownership, Compensation and British Society at the End of Slavery* (Cambridge: Cambridge University Press, 2010).

Drescher, Seymour, *Capitalism and Antislavery: British Mobilization in Comparative Perspective* (London: Macmillan, 1986).

Du Bois, W. E. B., *Black Reconstruction: An essay toward a history of the part which black folk played in the attempt to reconstruct democracy in America* (New York: Harcourt, Brace and Co., 1935).

Dresser, Madge, and Andrew Hann, *Slavery and the British Country House* (Swindon, UK: English Heritage, 2013).

Dunn, Richard, *Sugar and Slaves: The Rise of the Planter Class in the English West Indies, 1624–1713* (Chapel Hill: Omohundro Institute and University of North Carolina Press, 2012).

Empson, Martin, *Land and Labour: Marxism, Ecology and Human History* (London: Bookmarks, 2014).

Engels, Friedrich, *The Condition of the Working Class in England* (London: Panther, 1969).

Evans, Chris, *Slave Wales: The Welsh and Atlantic Slavery, 1660–1850* (Cardiff: University of Wales Press, 2010).

Farrow, Anne, Joel Lang, and Jenifer Frank, *Complicity: How the North Promoted, Prolonged, and Profited from Slavery* (New York: Ballantine, 2008).

Fogel, Robert, and Stanley Engerman, *Time on the Cross: the Economics of American Negro Slavery* (New York: W. W. Norton, 1974).

Fowler, Corinne, *Green Unpleasant Land* (Leeds. UK: Peepal Tree Press, 2021).

Foot, Paul, *Immigration and Race in British Politics* (Harmonsdworth, UK: Penguin, 1965).

Foster, John Bellamy, *Marx's Ecology: Materialism and Nature* (New York: Monthly Review Press, 2000).

Foster, John Bellamy, *The Return of Nature: Socialism and Ecology* (New York: Monthly Review Press, 2020).

Foster, John Bellamy, and Brett Clark, *The Robbery of Nature: Capitalism and the Ecological Rift* (New York: Monthly Review Press, 2020).

Foster, John Bellamy, Brett Clark, and Richard York, *The Ecological Rift: Capitalism's War on the Earth* (New York: Monthly Review Press, 2010).
Fryer, Peter, *Black People in the British Empire* (London: Pluto, 1988).
Fuentes, Marisa, and Deborah Gray White (eds.), *Scarlet and Black: Slavery and Dispossession in Rutgers History* (New Brunswick, NJ: Rutgers University Press, 2016).
Gerbner, Katharine, *Christian Slavery: Conversion and Race in the Protestant Atlantic World* (Philadelphia: University of Pennsylvania Press, 2018).
Greene, Lorenzo, *The Negro in Colonial New England, 1620–1776* (New York: Columbia University Press, 1942).
Griffin, Carl, *Protest, Politics and Work in Rural England, 1700–1850* (Basingstoke, UK: Palgrave Macmillan, 2014).
Hart, Richard, *Slaves Who Abolished Slavery* (Kingston, Jamaica: University of West Indies Press, 2002).
Hart, Richard, *From Occupation to Independence: A History of the Peoples of the English-Speaking Caribbean Region* (London: Pluto, 1998).
Heblich, Stephan, Stephen Redding, and Hans-Joachim Voth, *Slavery and the British Industrial Revolution* (Cambridge, MA: National Bureau of Economic Research, Working Paper 30451, 2022).
Heuman, Gad, *The Killing Time: The Morant Bay Rebellion in Jamaica* (London: Macmillan, 1994).
Huxtable, Sally-Anne, Corinne Fowler, Christo Kefalas, and Emma Slocombe, *Interim Report on the Connections between Colonialism and Properties Now in the Care of the National Trust, Including Links with Historic Slavery* (Swindon, UK: National Trust, September 2020).
Inikori, Joseph, *Africans and the Industrial Revolution in England* (Cambridge: Cambridge University Press, 2002).
Jones, Reece, *Violent Borders, Refugees and the Right to Move* (London: Verso Books, 2017).
Kimball, Eric, "An Essential Link in a Vast Chain: New England and the West Indies," 1700–1775 (PhD diss., Pittsburgh: University of Pittsburgh, 2009).
Lester, Alan, Kate Boehme, and Peter Mitchell, *Ruling the World: Freedom, Civilisation and Liberalism in the Nineteenth-Century British Empire* (Cambridge: Cambridge University Press, 2021).
Linebaugh, Peter, *The London Hanged: Crime and Civil Society in the Eighteenth Century* (London: Verso Books, 2006).
Linebaugh, Peter, *Stop, Thief!: The Commons, Enclosures, and Resistance* (Oakland, CA: PM Press, 2014).
Malm, Andreas, *Fossil Capital: The Rise of Steam Power and the Roots of Global Warming* (London: Verso Books, 2020).

Marks, Susan, *A False Tree of Liberty: Human Rights in Radical Thought* (New York: Oxford University Press, 2019).

Marx, Karl, *Capital, A Critique of Political Economy* (First English edition of 1887, Marxist Internet Archive[2]).

Matthews, Gelien, *Caribbean Slave Revolts and the British Abolitionist Movement* (Baton Rouge: Louisiana State University Press, 2012).

Mintz, Sidney, *Sweetness and Power* (New York: Viking-Penguin, 1985).

Morley, Neville, *The Roman Empire: Roots of Imperialism* (London: Pluto Press, 2010),

Mullen, Stephen, and Simon Newman, *Slavery, Abolition and the University of Glasgow Report and Recommendations of the University of Glasgow History of Slavery Steering Committee* (Glasgow: University of Glasgow, 2018).

Parker, Matthew, *The Sugar Barons: Family, Corruption, Empire, and War in the West Indies* (London: Hutchinson, 2011).

Pawley, Dawn, *Drug War Capitalism* (Oakland, CA: AK Press, 2015).

Perera, Jessica, *The London Clearances: Race, Housing and Policing* (London: Institute of Race Relations, 2019).

Petley, Christer, and J. McAleer (eds.), *The Royal Navy and the British Atlantic World, c. 1750–1820* (London: Palgrave Macmillan 2016).

Pettigrew, William, *Freedom's Debt: The Royal African Company and the Politics of the Atlantic Slave Trade, 1672–1752* (Chapel Hill: University of North Carolina Press, 2013).

Rediker, Marcus, *The Slave Ship: A Human History* (New York: Viking, 2007).

Rediker, Marcus, and Peter Linebaugh, *The Many-Headed Hydra: Sailors, Slaves, Commoners and the Hidden History of the Revolutionary Atlantic* (Boston: Beacon Press, 2013).

Robins, Nick, *The Corporation That Changed the World: How the East India Company Shaped the Modern Multinational* (London: Pluto Press, 2012).

Rodney, Walter, *How Europe Underdeveloped Africa* (London: Bogle-L'Ouverture Publications, 1972).

Saini, Angela, *Superior, the Return of Race Science* (London: 4th Estate, 2020).

Saville, John, *The Consolidation of the Capitalist State, 1800–1850* (London: Pluto Press, 1994).

Sealey-Huggins, Leon, "1.5°C to Stay Alive: Climate Change, Imperialism, and Justice for the Caribbean" (*Third World Quarterly*, vol. 38, no.11, 2017).

Sivanandan, A., "From Resistance to Rebellion: Asian and Afro-Caribbean Struggles in Britain" (*Race and Class*, vol. 23, no. 2–3, 1981).

Steeds, Mark, and Roger Ball, *From Wulfstan to Colston: Severing the Sinews of Slavery in Bristol* (Bristol: Bristol Radical History Group, 2020).

Taylor, Michael, *The Interest: How the British Establishment Resisted the Abolition of Slavery* (London: Bodley Head, 2020).
Thomas, Hugh, *The Slave Trade: The Story of the Atlantic Slave Trade 1440–1870* (New York: Simon & Schuster, 1997).
Thompson, E. P., *The Making of the English Working Class* (London: Pelican, 1975).
Thompson, E. P., *Whigs and Hunters: The Origin of the Black Act* (London: Penguin Books, 1990).
Tomich, Dale, *New Frontiers of Slavery* (Albany, NY: SUNY Press, 2016).
Turner, Mary, *From Chattel Slaves to Wage Slaves: The Dynamics of Labour Bargaining in the Americas* (Kingston, Jamaica: Ian Randle, 1995).
Viotti da Costa, Emilia, *Crowns of Glory, Tears of Blood: The Demerara Slave Rebellion of 1823* (New York: Oxford University Press, 1997).
Vitale, Alex, *The End of Policing* (London: Verso Books, 2017).
Walia, Harsha, *Undoing Border Imperialism* (Oakland, CA: AK Press, 2013).
Walvin, James, *Sugar: The World Corrupted: From Slavery to Obesity* (London: Robinson, 2017).
Williams, Eric, *Capitalism and Slavery* (London: Penguin Classics, 2022).
Zoellner, Tom, *Island on Fire: The Revolt That Ended Slavery in the British Empire* (Cambridge, MA: Harvard University Press, 2020).

# Notes

### Introduction: The Political Economy of Enslavement in the British Empire

1. Kenneth Kiple, *The Caribbean Slave: A Biological History* (Cambridge: Cambridge University Press, 2002), 65.
2. Simon Newman, *A New World of Labor: The Development of Plantation Slavery in the British Atlantic* (Philadelphia: University of Pennsylvania Press, 2013), 203.
3. Barbara Bush-Slimani, "Hard Labour: Women, Childbirth and Resistance in British Caribbean Slave Societies," *History Workshop Journal*, no. 36 (1993): 86.
4. Dr. Collins, *Practical Rules for the Management and Medical Treatment of Negro Slaves in the Sugar Colonies* (London: Vernor and Hood, 1803), 35, quoted in Barbara Bush, "African Caribbean Slave Mothers and Children: Traumas of Dislocation and Enslavement Across the Atlantic World," *Caribbean Quarterly*, vol. 56, no. 1/2 (2010): 69–94.
5. Both Article 16 of the Universal Declaration of Human Rights and Article 23 of the International Covenant on Civil and Political Rights provide the basis for the right to family life as a fundamental human right.
6. Bob Milward, *Marxian Political Economy: Theory, History, and Contemporary Relevance* (London: Palgrave 2000).
7. If you are looking for a book that contests the bourgeois economists on their own terms, I recommend Maxine Berg and Pat Hudson, *Slavery Capitalism and the Industrial Revolution* (Oxford: Polity Press, 2023).
8. Karl Marx, *Capital, A Critique of Political Economy* (First English

edition of 1887, Marxist Internet Archive) 918, https://www.marxists.org/archive/marx/works/1867-c1/.
9. Henry Heller, *The Birth of Capitalism* (London: Pluto Press, 2011), 169.
10. Patrick O'Brien and Stanley L. Engerman, "Exports and the growth of the British Economy from the Glorious Revolution to the Peace of Amiens," in *Slavery and the Rise of the Atlantic System*, ed. Barbara Solow (Cambridge, MA: Harvard University Press, 1991), 177–209.
11. E. P. Thompson, *The Making of the English Working Class* (London: Pelican, 1968); Roger Anstey, Christine Bolt, and Seymour Drescher, *Anti-Slavery, Religion, and Reform: Essays in Memory of Roger Anstey* (Folkestone. UK: W. Dawson, 1980); James Walvin, "The Impact of Slavery on British Radical Politics: 1787–1838," *Annals of the New York Academy of Sciences*, no. 292 (1977).
12. Katharine Gerbner, *Christian Slavery: Conversion and Race in the Protestant Atlantic World* (Philadelphia: University of Pennsylvania Press, 2018); Theodore Allen, *The Invention of the White Race* (London: Verso Books, 1997); Angela Saini, *Superior: The Return of Race Science* (London: 4th Estate, 2020).
13. Robert Bevan, *Monumental Lies: Culture Wars and the Truth About the Past* (London: Verso Books, 2022), 29.
14. Michael Taylor, *The Interest: How the British Establishment Resisted the Abolition of Slavery* (London: Bodley Head, 2020).
15. Mary Turner, *From Chattel Slaves to Wage Slaves: The Dynamics of Labour Bargaining in the Americas* (Kingston, Jamaica: Ian Randle Publishers, 1995); Emília Viotti da Costa, *Crowns of Glory, Tears of Blood: The Demerara Slave Rebellion of 1823* (New York: Oxford University Press, 1997); Tom Zoellner, *Island on Fire: The Revolt That Ended Slavery in the British Empire* (Cambridge, MA: Harvard University Press, 2020); Thomas Harding, *White Debt: The Demerara Uprising and Britain's Legacy of Slavery* (London: Weidenfeld & Nicolson, 2022); Richard Hart, *Slaves Who Abolished Slavery* (Kingston, Jamaica: University of West Indies Press, 2002); Gelien Matthews, *Caribbean Slave Revolts and the British Abolitionist Movement* (Baton Rouge: Louisiana State University Press, 2012).
16. Alan Lester, Kate Boehme, and Peter Mitchell, *Ruling the World: Freedom, Civilisation and Liberalism in the Nineteenth-Century British Empire* (Cambridge: Cambridge University Press, 2021); Hilary Beckles, *Great House Rules: Landless Emancipation and Workers' Protest in Barbados 1838–1938* (Kingston, Jamaica: Ian Randle, 2004).
17. John Bellamy Foster, Brett Clark, and Hannah Holleman, "Capitalism and Robbery: The Expropriation of Land, Labor, and Corporeal Life," *Monthly Review*, vol. 7, no.1 (December 2019).

18. Henderson Carter, *Labour Pains: Resistance and Protest in Barbados, 1838–1904* (Kingston, Jamaica: Ian Randle Publishers, 2012); Nigel Bolland, *On The March: Labour Rebellions in the British Caribbean, 1934–39* (London: James Currey, 1995).
19. Stephen Mullen, "James Watt and Slavery in Scotland," *History Workshop* (August 17, 2020), https://www.historyworkshop.org.uk/slavery/james-watt-and-slavery-in-scotland/; Stephen Mullen and Simon Newman, *Slavery, Abolition and the University of Glasgow Report and Recommendations of the University of Glasgow History of Slavery Steering Committee* (Glasgow: University of Glasgow, 2018), 21.
20. Andreas Malm, *Fossil Capital: The Rise of Steam Power and the Roots of Global Warming* (London: Verso Books, 2020); Leon Sealey-Huggins, "1.5°C to Stay Alive: Climate change, imperialism and justice for the Caribbean," *Third World Quarterly*, vol. 38, no.11 (2017).
21. David Silkenat, *Scars on the Land: An Environmental History of Slavery in the American South* (New York: Oxford University Press, 2022); John Bellamy Foster and Brett Clark, *The Robbery of Nature: Capitalism and the Ecological Rift* (New York: New York University Press, 2020).
22. Robert Bevan, *Monumental Lies, Culture Wars and the Truth About the Past* (London: Verso Books, 2022), deals with the issue of memorialization.
23. Hilary Beckles, *Britain's Black Debt: Reparations for Caribbean Slavery and Native Genocide* (Kingston, Jamaica: University Press of the West Indies, 2013).
24. "EU agrees to loss and damage fund to help poor countries amid climate disasters," *The Guardian*, November 18, 2022; "IPCC report's verdict on climate crimes of humanity: guilty as hell," *The Guardian*, August 9, 2021; IPCC Sixth Assessment Report, *Climate Change 2021: The Physical Science Basis* (Intergovernmental Panel on Climate Change, August 2021), https://www.ipcc.ch/report/ar6/wg1/.
25. Paul Lashmar and Jonathan Smith, "Barbados plans to make Tory MP pay reparations for family's slave past," *Guardian*, November 26, 2022.
26. MeasuringWorth Foundation, https://www.measuringworth.com/index.php.
27. Samuel H. Williamson and Louis Cain," Defining Measures of Worth: Most are better than the CPI," https://www.measuringworth.com/defining_measures_of_worth.php.
28. https://www.archives.gov/research/catalog/lcdrg/appendix/enslaved-person.

## 1. The Early Days

1. I would like to thank Les Kennedy and the participants in the Tolpuddle

Radical History School 2022 for their help with this section, as well as with chapters 3 and 5.
2. Martin Empson, *Land and Labour: Marxism, Ecology and Human History* (London: Bookmarks, 2014), 69–70; Roxanne Dunbar-Ortiz, *An Indigenous Peoples' History of the United States* (Boston: Beacon Press, 2014), 49.
3. Paul Kelton, *Epidemics and Enslavement: Biological Catastrophe in the Native Southeast, 1492–1715* (Lincoln: University of Nebraska Press, 2009), xviii.
4. Louis Bergeron, "Reforestation helped trigger Little Ice Age, researchers say," *Stanford Report*, December 17, 2008.
5. P. F. Campbell, *Some Early Barbadian History* (St. Michael, Barbados: Caribbean Graphics & Letchworth, 1993), 13–14, 99.
6. Trans-Atlantic Slave Database, https://www.slavevoyages.org/voyage/database.
7. Matthew Parker, *The Sugar Barons: Family, Corruption, Empire, and War in the West Indies* (London: Hutchinson, 2011), 65–67.
8. Richard Dunn, *Sugar and Slaves: The Rise of the Planter Class in the English West Indies 1624–1713* (Chapel Hill: University of North Carolina Press, 2000), 73.
9. Jerome Handler, "Slave revolts and conspiracies in seventeenth-century Barbados," *New West Indian Guide* (January 1982): 5–42.
10. Catherine Hall, "Gendering Property, Racing Capital," *History Workshop Journal*, vol. 78, no. 1 (Autumn 2014): 22–38.
11. Theodore Allen, *The Invention of the White Race* (London: Verso Books, 1997), vol. 2, chap. 13.
12. Peter Fryer, *Black People in the British Empire* (London: Pluto, 1988), 65–66.
13. Theodore Allen, *Class Struggle and the Origin of Racial Slavery: The Invention of the White Race* (Boston: New England Free Press, 1976), 28.
14. Steve Cushion, *Sir Robert Geffrye and the Business of Slavery* (London: Bookmarks, 2022). I gratefully acknowledge the help of the Hackney, East London branch of the antiracist organization Stand Up to Racism,
15. A Liveryman was a full-voting member with the right to participate in elections.
16. *The Ironmongers' Company*, https://www.ironmongers.org/dining-and-celebrations.
17. Charles Welch, "Robert Geffrey," *Dictionary of National Biography*, vol. 10 (London: Elder Smith & Co, 1887).
18. Chris Evans and Göran Rydén, "'Voyage Iron': An Atlantic Slave Trade Currency, Its European Origins, and West African Impact," *Past & Present*, vol. 239, no. 1 (May 2018): 41–70.

19. Robin Blackburn, *The Making of New World Slavery: From the Baroque to the Modern 1492-1800* (London: Verso Books, 1997), 524, 542; Joseph Inikori, *Africans and the Industrial Revolution in England* (Cambridge: Cambridge University Press, 2002), 118, 100.
20. Kenneth Davies, *The Royal African Company* (London: Longmans, 1957), chap. 1.
21. William Pettigrew, *Freedom's Debt: The Royal African Company and the Politics of the Atlantic Slave Trade, 1672-1752* (Chapel Hill: University of North Carolina Press, 2013), 30.
22. The calculation used in this book to relate monetary values of the past to today's equivalent is the relative income measure, which measures an amount of income or wealth relative to per capita gross domestic product (GDP). When compared to other incomes or wealth, it shows the economic status or relative prestige value the owners of this income or wealth have because of their rank in the income distribution. More details are obtainable from the MeasuringWorth Foundation: https://www.measuringworth.com/index.php.
23. Mark Steeds and Roger Ball, *From Wulfstan to Colston: Severing the Sinews of Slavery in Bristol* (Bristol: Bristol Radical History Group, 2020), 49-53.
24. Charles Killinger, *The Royal African Company Slave Trade to Virginia, 1689-1713* (MA diss., College of William & Mary, 1969), 17.
25. Pettigrew, *Freedom's Debt*, 52-58.
26. Angus Calder, *Revolutionary Empire: Rise of the English-Speaking Empire from the Fifteenth Century to the 1780s* (London: Pimlico, 1998), 241-50.
27. Penelope Hunting, *Riot and Revolution: Sir Robert Geffrye 1613-1704* (London: Geffrye Museum, 2013), 79-86.
28. RB Allen, *European Slave Trading in the Indian Ocean, 1500-1850* (Athens: Ohio University Press, 2015), 1.
29. Susan Rosenthal, "Philanthropy: The Capitalist Art of Deception," *Socialist Review* no. 402 (April-May 2015).
30. Frederick Engels, *The Condition of the Working Class in England* (London: Panther, 1969), 185.
31. Neil Burton, *The Geffrye Almshouses* (London: Inner London Education Authority, 1979), 14.

## 2. The British Atlantic Empire

1. Selwyn Carrington, "The American Revolution and the British West Indies' Economy," *Journal of Interdisciplinary History*, vol. 17, no. 4 (1987): 823-50.
2. G. E. Thomas, "Puritans, Indians, and the Concept of Race," *New England Quarterly*, vol. 48, no. 1 (1975): 21.

3. Danny Reilly and Steve Cushion, *Telling the Mayflower Story: Thanksgiving or Land Grabbing, Massacres and Slavery* (London: Socialist History Society, 2018) 14-15.
4. John Winthrop, *Winthrop's Journal: "History of New England,"* 1630–1649 (New York: Scribner's, 1908), 260.
5. Anne Farrow, Joel Lang, and Jenifer Frank, *Complicity: How the North Promoted, Prolonged, and Profited from Slavery* (New York: Ballantine, 2008), 77; Lorenzo Greene, "Slave-Holding New England and Its Awakening," *Journal of Negro History*, vol. 13, no. 4 (1928): 513.
6. Lorenzo Greene, *The Negro in Colonial New England, 1620–1776* (New York: Columbia University Press, 1942), 75.
7. Ulrich Phillips, *American Negro Slavery: A Survey of the Supply, Employment and Control of Negro Labor as Determined by the Plantation Régime* (New York: Appleton, 1918), 101.
8. Herbert Klein, *The Middle Passage: Comparative Studies in the Atlantic Slave Trade* (Princeton: Princeton University Press, 1978), 133–34.
9. Maxine Berg and Pat Hudson, *Slavery, Capitalism and the Industrial Revolution* (London: Polity Press, 2023), 27.
10. Ian Angus, "The Fishing Revolution and the Origins of Capitalism," *Monthly Review*, vol. 74, no. 10 (March 2023): 1–26, https://monthlyreview.org/2023/03/01/the-fishing-revolution-and-the-origins-of-capitalism.
11. Greene, *The Negro in Colonial New England*, 30–31.
12. Ronald Bailey, "The Slave(ry) Trade and the Development of Capitalism in the United States: The Textile Industry in New England," *Social Science History*, vol. 14, no. 3 (1990): 385.
13. Greene, "Slave-Holding New England and Its Awakening," 496–98.
14. Greene, *The Negro in Colonial New England*, 68–69.
15. *Petition from the Massachusetts House of Representatives to the House of Commons*, November 3, 1764, https://avalon.law.yale.edu/18th_century/petition_mass_1764.asp.
16. Bailey, "The Slave(ry) Trade and the Development of Capitalism in the United States," 374.
17. Richard Gott, *Britain's Empire* (London: Verso Books, 2011), 37.
18. Peter Wood, *Black Majority: Negroes in Colonial South Carolina from 1670 Through the Stono Rebellion* (New York: W. W. Norton, 1974), chap. 1.
19. Alan Gallay, *The Indian Slave Trade: The Rise of the English Empire in the American South 1670–1717* (New Haven: Yale University Press, 2002), 8.
20. Ibid., 299; Gary Clayton Anderson, *Ethnic Cleansing and the Indian: The Crime That Should Haunt America* (Norman: University of Oklahoma Press, 2015), 53.

21. Ibid., chap. 12.
22. John Grenier, *The First Way of War: American War Making on the Frontier, 1607–1814* (Cambridge: Cambridge University Press, 2005), 44–45.
23. Verner Crane, *The Southern Frontier, 1670–1732* (Ann Arbor: University of Michigan Press, 1956), 75–78.
24. Anderson, *Ethnic Cleansing and the Indian*, chap. 12.
25. In 1712, North and South Carolina were officially divided.
26. Paul Kelton, *Epidemics and Enslavement: Biological Catastrophe in the Native Southeast, 1492–1715* (Lincoln: University of Nebraska Press, 2009), xviii. Anderson, *Ethnic Cleansing and the Indian*, chap. 12.
27. This section on the Kalinago people is drawn from Tessa Murphy, *The Creole Archipelago: Race and Borders in the Colonial Caribbean* (Philadelphia: University of Pennsylvania Press, 2021).
28. There were two Treaties of Paris, 1763 and 1783.
29. Alfred W. Crosby, *The Columbian Exchange: Biological and Cultural Consequences of 1492* (Westport, CT: Greenwood Press 1972); Jared Diamond, *Guns, Germs, and Steel: The Fates of Human Societies* (New York: W. W. Norton, 1997); Linda A Newson, "The Demographic Collapse of Native Peoples of the Americas, 1492–1650," in *The Meeting of Two Worlds: Europe and the Americas 1492–1650* (1993), 247–88.
30. Roxanne Dunbar-Ortiz, *An Indigenous Peoples' History of the United States* (Boston: Beacon Press, 2014), 49.

### 3. Plantation Management

1. Peter Thompson, "Henry Drax's Instructions on the Management of a Seventeenth-Century Barbadian Sugar Plantation," *William and Mary Quarterly*, vol. 66, no. 3 (2009), 565–604.
2. Ken Owen, *Teaching Through Primary Sources: Henry Drax's Plantation Instructions* (2014), https://earlyamericanists.com/2014/01/14/teaching-through-primary-sources-henry-draxs-plantation-instructions/.
3. Frederick Engels, *The Part Played by Labour in the Transition from Ape to Man* (Moscow: Progress Publishers, 1934), https://www.marxists.org/archive/marx/works/1883/don/ch09.htm. Engels is referring to Spanish Catholic practices here, but while the religious and ideological approaches were different, the political economy and brutality of enslavement in Cuba was much the same as in the Protestant British West Indies.
4. David Watts, *Man's Influence on the Vegetation of Barbados, 1627 to 1800* (Hull: University of Hull Publications, 1966) 45.
5. Thompson, "Henry Drax's Instructions," 565–604.

6. *The Junto: A Group Blog on Early American History*, https://earlyamericanists.com/2014/01/14/teaching-through-primary-sources-henry-draxs-plantation-instructions/.
7. Bill Cooke, "The Denial of Slavery in Management Studies," *Journal of Management Studies* (Manchester, UK: University of Manchester, November 6, 2003), 21, 23.
8. Karl Marx, *Capital, A Critique of Political Economy* (1887), chap. 10, section 5, https://www.marxists.org/archive/marx/works/1867-c1/ch10.htm#S5. The quotations from Marx and Engels are to be found in the online Marxist Internet Archive and therefore are not given page numbers.
9. Geoffrey Nuttall, *The Holy Spirit in Puritan Faith and Experience* (Chicago: University of Chicago Press, 1992), 157.
10. Caitlin Rosenthal, "Slavery's Scientific Management, Masters and Managers," in *Slavery's Capitalism, A New History of American Economic Development*, ed. Sven Beckert and Seth Rockman (Philadelphia: University of Pennsylvania Press, 2016), 79.
11. Sébastien Rioux, "Slavery, Capitalism, and Imperialism," in *The Oxford Handbook of Economic Imperialism*, ed. Zak Cope and Immanuel Ness (Oxford: Oxford University Press, 2022), 8–9.
12. David Brion Davis, *The Problem of Slavery in the Age of Emancipation* (New York: Alfred A. Knopf, 2014), 358.
13. Edward Baptist, *The Half Has Never Been Told* (New York: Basic Books, 2015), 164, 332, 426.
14. Technically speaking, the Church of Scotland, which is Presbyterian rather than Anglican, is the official church in Scotland, but in practice it was the Church of England that represented state religion in the British West Indies.
15. Noel Titus, "Concurrence without Compliance: SPG and the Barbadian Plantations 1710–1834," in *Three Centuries of Mission: The United Society for the Propagation of the Gospel 1701–2000*, eds. Daniel O'Connor et al. (London: Bloomsbury Publishing, 2010) 250.
16. Travis Glasson, *Mastering Christianity: Missionary Anglicanism and Slavery in the Atlantic World* (Oxford: Oxford University Press, 2012), 143–44.
17. Janice McLean-Farrell and Michael Anderson Clarke. "Missions in Contested Places/Spaces: The SPG, Slavery, and Codrington College, Barbados," *Mission Studies*, vol. 38, no, 3 (2021): 330–34.
18. Katharine Gerbner, *Christian Slavery: Conversion and Race in the Protestant Atlantic World* (Philadelphia: University of Pennsylvania Press, 2018), 2.
19. William Edmundson, *A Journal of the Life, Travels, Sufferings, and Labour of Love in the Work of the Ministry* (London: M. Hinde, 1774), 78.

20. Thomas Drake, *Quakers and Slavery in America* (New Haven: Yale University Press, 1950), 4–6; Edward B. Rugemer. "The Development of Mastery and Race in the Comprehensive Slave Codes of the Greater Caribbean During the Seventeenth Century," *William and Mary Quarterly*, vol. 70, no. 3 (2013), 429–58.
21. Richard Hall, *Acts, Passed in the Island of Barbados. From 1643, to 1762* (London: Printed for Richard Hall, 1764), 4–5, 63–64.
22. Edmundson, *A Journal of the Life, Travels, Sufferings, and Labour of Love in the Work of the Ministry*, 78.
23. Jenny Shaw, *Everyday Life in the Early English Caribbean: Irish, Africans, and the Construction of Difference* (Athens: University of Georgia Press, 2013), 7.
24. William Frost, "George Fox's Ambiguous Anti-Slavery Legacy," in *New Light on George Fox, 1624–1691*, ed. Michael Mullett (York: William Sessions, 1994) 82–84.
25. Gerbner, *Christian Slavery Conversion and Race in the Protestant Atlantic World*, 125.
26. Ibid., 134.
27. Lilian McNaught, *The 1816 Barbados Slave Revolt* (MA thesis, University of Exeter, 2017), 63.
28. Barbados House of Assembly, *The Report from a Select Committee of the House of Assembly*, 29, (Barbados Legislature, 1818), in David Lambert, *White Creole Culture, Politics and Identity during the Age of Abolition* (Cambridge: Cambridge University Press, 2005), 122–126.
29. Adam Hochschild, *Bury the Chains: The British Struggle to Abolish Slavery* (London: Pan, 2006), 219.
30. Robert Jackson, "Codrington at All Souls: 'Retain + Explain' = Vandalise and Vilify," *History Reclaimed* July 11, 2022, https://historyreclaimed.co.uk/codrington-at-all-souls-retain-explain-vandalise-and-vilify/.
31. McLean-Farrell and Clarke, "Missions in Contested Places/Spaces," 330, 344.

### 4. Law and Order

1. Sean Moore, "Exorcising the Ghosts of Racial Capitalism from the South Sea Bubble: Pent-up Racist Liquidity and the Recent Four-Year Stock Surge," *Eighteenth-Century Studies*, vol. 54, no. 1 (2020): 1.
2. John Carswell, *The South Sea Bubble* (London: Cresset Press, 1960), 48–52.
3. Helen Paul, *Politicians and Public Reaction to the South Sea Bubble: Preaching to the Converted?* (Discussion Papers in Economics and Econometrics, University of Southampton, 2009), 2.
4. Helen Paul, *The South Sea Company's Slaving Activities* (Discussion

Papers in Economics and Econometrics, University of Southampton, 2009), 2.
5. Hugh Thomas, *The Slave Trade: The Story of the Atlantic Slave Trade 1440–1870* (New York: Simon & Schuster, 1997), 339.
6. Victoria Gardner Sorsby, *British Trade with Spanish America Under the Asiento 1713–1740* (PhD diss., University of London, 1975).
7. Moore, "Exorcising the Ghosts of Racial Capitalism from the South Sea Bubble," 2.
8. John Trenchard, *A Comparison between the Proposals of the Bank and the South-Sea Company* (London: J. Roberts, 1720), 18.
9. Andrew Odlyzko, "Isaac Newton, Daniel Defoe and the Dynamics of Financial Bubbles," *Financial History*, no. 124 (Winter 2018): 18–21.
10. Peter Temin and Hans-Joachim Voth, "Riding the South Sea Bubble," *American Economic Review*, vol. 94, no. 5 (2004): 1654–68.
11. W. A. Speck and Matthew Kilburn, "Promoters of the South Sea Bubble (act. 1720)," *Oxford Dictionary of National Biography* (Oxford: Oxford University Press, 2007), https://www.oxforddnb.com/view/10.1093/ref:odnb/9780198614128.001.0001/odnb-9780198614128-e-92793.
12. Harvard Library, "Curiosity Collections, The South Sea Bubble, 1720," https://curiosity.lib.harvard.edu/south-sea-bubble/feature/the-crash.
13. Moore, "Exorcising the Ghosts of Racial Capitalism from the South Sea Bubble," 2.
14. Sorsby, *British Trade with Spanish America Under the Asiento*, 277.
15. Stephanie Barczewski, *Country Houses and the British Empire, 1700–1930* (Manchester, UK: Manchester University Press, 2017), chapter 3.
16. Nick Hayes, *The Book of Trespass, Crossing the Lines that Divide Us* (London: Bloomsbury, 2020), 125–26.
17. The National Trust, "Addressing our histories of colonialism and historic slavery" (16 September 2020), https://www.nationaltrust.org.uk/features/addressing-the-histories-of-slavery-and-colonialism-at-the-national-trust.
18. Gerald Horne, *The Counter Revolution of 1836: Texas Slavery & Jim Crow and the Roots of U.S. Fascism* (New York: International Publishers, 2022).
19. Timothy Rooks, *The Social and Political Contexts Which Led to the Building of Harewood House* (Berlin: Grossbritannien-Zentrum, n.d.).
20. Karl Marx, "The Expropriation of the Agricultural Population," *Capital*, vol. 1, chap. 27, https://www.marxists.org/archive/marx/works/1867-c1/ch27.htm.
21. Imogen Tyler, "Enclosures and the Making of the Modern World," *Sociological Review, Connected Sociologies Curriculum Project* (May 27, 2021), https://thesociologicalreview.org/projects/connected-sociologies/curriculum/mmw/enclosures-and-state-formation/.

22. Simon Fairlie, "A Short History of Enclosure in Britain," *The Land*, vol. 7 (Summer 2009); Peter Linebaugh, *Stop, Thief: The Commons, Enclosures, and Resistance* (Oakland, CA: PM Press, 2014).
23. Karl Marx, "So-Called Primitive Accumulation," *Capital*, vol.1, part 8, https://www.marxists.org/archive/marx/works/1867-c1/ch26.htm.
24. J. V. Beckett, "The Pattern of Landownership in England and Wales, 1660–1880," *Economic History Review*, vol. 37, no. 1 (February 1984): 1–22.
25. Peter Linebaugh, *The Magna Carta Manifesto: Liberties and Commons for All*. (Oakland, CA: University of California Press, 2008), 46–93.
26. Karl Marx. *Capital* vol. 1, chap. 27, https://www.marxists.org/archive/marx/works/1867-c1/ch27.htm
27. Iain MacKinnon and Andrew Mackillop, *Plantation Slavery and Land Ownership in the West Highlands and Islands: Legacies and Lessons* (Coventry University, Community Land Scotland, 2020), 13, https://pure.coventry.ac.uk/ws/portalfiles/portal/54426539/Plantation_slavery_and_landownership_in_the_west_Highlands_and_Islands_legacies_and_lessons.pdf.
28. Corinne Fowler, *Green Unpleasant Land* (Leeds, UK: Peepal Tree Press, 2021), 44.
29. *Historic England*, https://historicengland.org.uk/listing/the-list/list-entry/1000713.
30. J. R. Wordie, "The Chronology of English Enclosure, 1500–1914," *Economic History Review*, vol. 36, no. 4 (1983): 494–95.
31. Wendy McElroy, *The Enclosure Acts and the Industrial Revolution* (Fairfax, UK: Future of Freedom Foundation, 2012); J. M. Neeson, *Commoners: Common Right, Enclosure and Social Change in England, 1700–1820* (Cambridge: Cambridge University Press, 1996).
32. E. P. Thompson, *The Making of the English Working Class* (London: Pelican, 1975), 223–24.
33. Michael Turner, *Enclosures in Britain 1750–1830* (London: Macmillan, 1984), 21;
John Chapman, "The Extent and Nature of Parliamentary Enclosure," *Agricultural History Review*, Vol. 35 (1987) 25, 28.
34. Thomas Rudge, quoted in Neeson, *Commoners*, 30.
35. John Arbuthnot, quoted in Keith Snell, *Annals of the Labouring Poor: Social Change and Agrarian England 1660–1900* (Cambridge: Cambridge University Press, 1987), 173.
36. Susan Marks, *A False Tree of Liberty: Human Rights in Radical Thought* (Oxford: Oxford University Press, 2019), 155–61.
37. Utsa Patnaik and Sam Moyo, *The Agrarian Question in the Neoliberal Era: Primitive Accumulation and the Peasantry*, (Cape Town: Pambazuka Press, 2011), 25.

38. Ian Angus, *The War Against the Commons: Dispossession and Resistance in the Making of Capitalism* (New York, Monthly Review Press, 2023), 169.
39. John Nef, *Rise of the British Coal Industry*, vol. 1 (London: Routledge, 1966), 342–43, 310.
40. Karl Marx, "Wages of Labor," in *The Economic and Philosophical Manuscripts* (Paris 1844), https://www.marxists.org/archive/marx/works/1844/epm/1st.htm#s1.
41. Christopher Hill, *Liberty Against the Law : Some Seventeenth-Century Controversies* (New York: Penguin Books, 1996), 66.
42. Angus, *The War Against the Commons*, 46.
43. Brian Manning, "A Voice for the Poor," *International Socialism*, vol. 2, no.72 (September 1996): 96.
44. E. P. Thompson, *Whigs and Hunters: The Origin of the Black Act* (London: Penguin Books, 1990), 217.
45. Ibid., 147–213.
46. Nicholas Radburn, "Guinea Factors, Slave Sales, and the Profits of the Transatlantic Slave Trade in Late Eighteenth-Century Jamaica: The Case of John Tailyour," *William and Mary Quarterly*, vol. 72, no. 2 (2015): 243.
47. Nick Draper, "The City of London and Slavery: Evidence from the First Dock Companies, 1795–1800," *Economic History Review*, vol. 61, no. 2 (2008): 433, 460.
48. Ibid., 435, 458–59.
49. Walter M. Stern, "The First London Dock Boom and the Growth of the West India Docks," *Economica*, vol. 19, no. 73 (1952): 59–77.
50. See, for example, P. Colquhoun, *A Treatise on the Commerce and Police of the River Thames* (1800), https://play.google.com/books/reader?id=sx49OgFD4uAC&pg=GBS.PA2&hl=en_GB.
51. Peter Linebaugh, *The London Hanged: Crime and Civil Society in the Eighteenth Century* (London: Verso Books, 2006), chap. 12.
52. Jill Lepore, "The Invention of the Police," *The New Yorker* (July 13, 2020).
53. Derica Shields, "No Escape from Empire: Cameron Rowland at London's ICA," *Frieze* 91 (2020).
54. *An Act for the Governing of Negroes*, Barbados, 1688, in William Rawlin, *The laws of Barbados collected in one volume by William Rawlin, of the Middle-Temple, London, Esquire, and now clerk of the Assembly of the said island* (London: Printed for William Rawlin, 1699).
55. Gary Clayton Anderson, *The Conquest of Texas: Ethnic Cleansing in the Promised Land, 1820–1875* (Norman: University of Oklahoma Press, 2005).
56. Alex Vitale, *The End of Policing* (London: Verso Books, 2017), chap. 2.
57. Peter Daniel, "The Governor Eyre Controversy," *New Blackfriars*, vol. 50, no. 591 (1969): 575–76.

58. "The British Atrocities in Jamaica," *Reynold's News*, November 26, 1865. This and the following newspaper quotation from Priyamvada Gopal, *Insurgent Empire: Anticolonial Resistance and British Dissent* (London: Verso Books, 2020), chap. 2.
59. "The Negro Revolt in Jamaica," *Reynold's News*, November 12, 1865.
60. Jessica Perera, *The London Clearances: Race, Housing and Policing* (London: Institute of Race Relations, 2019).

## 5. Finance and Industry

1. Chris Evans, *Slave Wales: The Welsh and Atlantic Slavery, 1660–1850* (Cardiff: University of Wales Press, 2010), 69–72.
2. Catherine Hall, "The Politics of History: A Global Family Story," *ISHA Newsletter*, vol. 6, no. 1 (December 2017).
3. The National Trust, "History of Penrhyn Castle and Garden," https://www.nationaltrust.org.uk/penrhyn-castle/features/a-brief-history-of-penrhyn-castle.
4. Trades Union Congress, "The great Penrhyn quarry strike: Capturing the public imagination," TUC150, https://tuc150.tuc.org.uk/stories/the-great-penrhyn-quarry-strike/.
5. The National Trust, "Penrhyn Castle and slave trade history," https://www.nationaltrust.org.uk/penrhyn-castle/features/penrhyn-castle-and-the-transatlantic-slave-trade.
6. The National Trust, "The Great Penrhyn Quarry Strike," https://www.nationaltrust.org.uk/penrhyn-castle/features/penrhyn-castle-and-the-great-penrhyn-quarry-strike-1900-03.
7. Mark Harvey, "Slavery, Indenture and the Development of British Industrial Capitalism," *History Workshop Journal*, vol. 88 (Autumn 2019): 66–88.
8. Sidney Mintz, *Sweetness and Power* (New York: Viking-Penguin, 1985), chap. 3.
9. James Walvin, *Sugar: The World Corrupted from Slavery to Obesity* (London: Robinson, 2017), chap. 14.
10. Karl Marx, *Capital*, vol. 1, chap. 26, https://www.marxists.org/archive/marx/works/1867-c1/ch26.htm.
11. Karl Marx. "Genesis of the Industrial Capitalist," *Capital*, vol. 1, chap. 31, https://www.marxists.org/archive/marx/works/1867-c1/ch31.htm.
12. Robin Blackburn, *The Making of New World Slavery: From the Baroque to the Modern 1492–1800* (London: Verso Books, 1997), 524, 542.
13. Joseph E. Inikori, *Africans and the Industrial Revolution in England* (Cambridge: Cambridge University Press, 2002), 100, 118.
14. Henry Heller, *The Birth of Capitalism* (London: Pluto Press, 2011), 169.
15. Patrick K. O'Brien and Stanley L. Engerman, "Exports and the growth

of the British economy from the Glorious Revolution to the Peace of Amiens," in *Slavery and the Rise of the Atlantic System*, ed. Barbara Solow (Cambridge: Cambridge University Press, 1994).
16. Robin Blackburn, "The Scope of Accumulation and the Reach of Moral Perception: Slavery, Market Revolution and Atlantic Capitalism," in *Emancipation and the Remaking of the British Imperial World*, ed. Catherine Hall, Nicholas Draper, and Keith McClelland (Manchester, UK: Manchester University Press, 2014), 31.
17. Karl Marx, *Capital*, vol. 1, chap. 28, https://www.marxists.org/archive/marx/works/1867-c1/ch28.htm.
18. Blackburn, *The Making of New World Slavery*, 541–48.
19. Ian Angus, "The meaning of 'So-Called Primitive Accumulation,'" *Climate & Capitalism*, September 5, 2022, https://climateandcapitalism.com/2022/09/05/so-called-primitive-accumulation/. Rosa Luxemburg catalogs the way in which expropriation and extra-economic coercion of labor continued under colonialism, and David Harvey argues that the process continues to this day, and uses the term "Accumulation by Dispossession." Rosa Luxemburg, *The Accumulation of Capital* https://www.marxists.org/archive/luxemburg/1913/accum-ulation-capital/.
20. Donald Jones, *Bristol's Sugar Trade and Refining Industry* (Bristol: Bristol Branch of the Historical Association, Bristol University,1996), 2.
21. John Evans, *A Chronological Outline of the History of Bristol and the Stranger's Guide through Its Streets and Neighbourhood* (Bristol: Office of the "Bristol Observer," 1824).
22. William Miles, Profile and Legacies Summary, *Centre for the Study of the Legacies of British Slavery*, https://www.ucl.ac.uk/lbs/person/view/2146639021.
23. Philip John Miles, *Profile and Legacies Summary, Centre for the Study of the Legacies of British Slavery*, https://www.ucl.ac.uk/lbs/person/view/19118.
24. Stephen Mullen and Simon Newman, *Slavery, Abolition and the University of Glasgow: Report and Recommendations of the University of Glasgow History of Slavery Steering Committee* (Glasgow: University of Glasgow, 2018), 23.
25. Andreas Malm, "The Origins of Fossil Capital: From Water to Steam in the British Cotton Industry," *Historical Materialism*, vol. 21 (2013): 15–68. The full argument can be read in Malm's book *Fossil Capital: The Rise of Steam Power and the Roots of Global Warming* (London: Verso Books, 2016).
26. Walter Scott, *Familial Letters of Sir Walter Scott in Two Volumes*, vol. 2 (Boston: Houghton Mifflin, 1894), quoted in Malm, *Fossil Capital*, 52.

27. Mick Jenkins, *General Strike of 1842* (London: Lawrence & Wishart, 1980), chap 7.
28. Barbara Solow, "Capitalism and Slavery in the Exceedingly Long Run," *Journal of Interdisciplinary History*, vol.17, no. 4 (1987): 731.
29. Katie Donington, "Transforming Capital: Slavery, Family, Commerce and the Making of the Hibbert Family," in *Legacies of British Slave Ownership: Colonial Slavery and the Formation of Victorian Britain*, ed. Catherine Hall, Nicholas Draper, Keith McClelland, Katie Donington, and Rachel Lang (Cambridge: Cambridge University Press, 2014), 203–49.
30. Joseph Inikori, "The Import of Firearms into West Africa 1750–1807: A Quantitative Analysis," *Journal of African History*, vol. 18, no. 3 (1977): 339–68; William Richards, "The Import of Firearms into West Africa in the Eighteenth Century," *Journal of African History*, vol. 21, no. 1 (1980): 43–59.
31. Emma George Ross, *The Age of Iron in West Africa* (New York: Metropolitan Museum of Art, 2002), https://www.metmuseum.org/toah/hd/iron/hd_iron.htm.
32. Jenny Bulstrode, "Black metallurgists and the making of the industrial revolution," *History and Technology*, vol. 39, no.1 (2023): 1–41.
33. Evans, *Slave Wales*, 33–38.
34. Nuala Zahedieh, "Eric Williams and William Forbes: Copper, colonial markets, and commercial capitalism," *Economic History Review*, vol. 74, no. 3 (August 2021): 784–808.
35. Evans, *Slave Wales*, 117–21.
36. Hall et al., *Legacies of British Slave Ownership*, 98.
37. Guy Faulconbridge, "Some Facts About London's Role in Insuring the Slave Trade," *Insurance Journal* (June 19, 2020), https://www.insurancejournal.com/news/international/2020/06/19/572859.htm.
38. Inikori, *Africans and the Industrial Revolution in England*, 313–61; Anita Rupprecht, "Excessive Memories: Slavery, Insurance and Resistance," *History Workshop Journal*, vol. 64 (Autumn 2007): 12,15, 21.
39. Michael Tadman, *Speculators and Slaves: Masters, Traders, and Slaves in the Old South* (Madison: University of Wisconsin Press, 1996); Robert Fogel and Stanley Engerman, *Time on the Cross: The Economics of American Negro Slavery* (New York: W. W. Norton, 1974).
40. Brodnock and Lenhard, *Better Venture: Improving Diversity, Innovation, and Profitability in Venture Capital and Startups*, chap. 8.

### 6. Amelioration, Resistance, and Emancipation

1. Epigraph: Eric Williams, *Capitalism & Slavery* (London: Penguin Classics 2022), 211.

2. Seymour Drescher, *Econocide: British Slavery in the Era of Abolition* (Pittsburgh, PA: University of Pittsburgh Press, 1977).
3. Katie Donington, Nicholas Draper, Catherine Hall, Rachel Lang, and Keith McClelland, eds., *Legacies of British Slave-Ownership: Colonial Slavery and the Formation of Victorian Britain* (Cambridge: Cambridge University Press, 2014), 33.
4. Angelina Gillian Osborne, *Power and Persuasion: The London West India Committee, 1783-1833* (PhD diss., University of Hull, 2014).
5. Nicholas Draper, "The City of London and Slavery: Evidence from the First Docks Companies, 1785–1800," *Economic History Review*, vol. 61, no. 2 (2008).
6. John Gilmore, "West India Interest," in *Oxford Companion to Black British History* (Oxford: Oxford University Press, 2007).
7. Nick Robins, *The Corporation That Changed the World: How the East India Company Shaped the Modern Multinational* (London: Pluto Press, 2012).
8. John Saville, *The Consolidation of the Capitalist State, 1800–1850* (London: Pluto Press, 1994), 8; Donington et al., *Legacies of British Slave-Ownership*, 50.
9. Zach Sell, *Trouble of the World: Slavery and Empire in the Age of Capital* (Chapel Hill: University of North Carolina Press, 2021), 30–32.
10. Peter Linebaugh and Marcus Rediker, *The Many-Headed Hydra* (London: Verso Books, 2000), 19.
11. Iain McCalman, ed., *Horrors of Slavery and Other Writings by Robert Wedderburn* (Princeton, NJ: Markus Wiener Publishers, 1991).
12. Olaudah Equiano, *The Interesting Narrative of the Life of Olaudah Equiano, or Gustavus Vassa, the African* (London, 1794), https://en.wikisource.org/wiki/The_Interesting_Narrative_of_the_Life_of_Olaudah_Equiano,_or_Gustavus_Vassa,_the_African.
13. Roger Anstey, Christine Bolt, and Seymour Drescher, *Anti-slavery, Religion, and Reform: Essays in Memory of Roger Anstey* (Folkestone, UK: W. Dawson, 1980), 153.
14. James Walvin, "The Impact of Slavery on British Radical Politics: 1787–1838," *Annals of the New York Academy of Sciences*, vol. 292 (1977): 344–50.
15. D. S. Gadian, "Class Consciousness in Oldham and Other North-West Industrial Towns 1830–1850," *Historical Journal*, vol. 21, no. 1 (1978): 161–72; Arthur Scherr, "'Sambos' and 'Black Cut-Throats': Peter Porcupine on Slavery and Race in the 1790's," *American Periodicals* 13 (2003): 3–30.
16. Seymour Drescher, *Capitalism and Antislavery: British Mobilization in Comparative Perspective* (London: Macmillan, 1986), 151.

17. Aline Helg, *Plus Jamais Esclaves! De l'insoumission à la révolte, le grand récit d'une émancipation 1492-1838* (Paris: La Découverte 2016), 66-77.
18. Richard Hart, *Caribbean Workers' Struggles* (London: Bogle L'Ouverture, 2012), 26.
19. *The Report from a Select Committee of the House of Assembly Appointed to Inquire into the Origins, Cause, and Progress of the Late Insurrection-April 1816* (Barbados Legislature, 1818), in David Lambert, *White Creole Culture, Politics and Identity during the Age of Abolition* (Cambridge: Cambridge University Press, 2005), 122-126
20. *An Account of the late Negro Insurrection which took place in the Island of Barbados on Easter Sunday, April 14, 1816*, cited in Hilary McDonald Beckles, "The Slave-Drivers' War: Bussa and the 1816 Barbados Slave Rebellion," *Boletín de Estudios Latinoamericanos y Del Caribe*, no. 39 (1985): 87.
21. Beckles, "The Slave-Drivers' War," 85-110.
22. Mary Turner, "The Baptist War and Abolition," *Jamaica Historical Review*, vol. 13 (1982): 31-41; Emília Viotti da Costa, *Crowns of Glory, Tears of Blood: The Demerara Slave Rebellion of 1823* (New York: Oxford University Press, 1997); Tom Zoellner, *Island on Fire: The Revolt That Ended Slavery in the British Empire* (Cambridge, MA: Harvard University Press, 2020).
23. Richard Sheridan, "The Condition of the Slaves on the Sugar Plantations of Sir John Gladstone in the Colony of Demerara, 1812-49," *NWIG: New West Indian Guide / Nieuwe West-Indische Gids*, vol. 76, no. 3/4 (2002): 47.
24. Trevor Burnard and Kit Candlin, "Sir John Gladstone and the Debate over the Amelioration of Slavery in the British West Indies in the 1820s," *Journal of British Studies*, vol. 57, no. 4 (2018): 760-82.
25. Michael Taylor,. *The Interest: How the British Establishment Resisted the Abolition of Slavery* (London : Bodley Head, 2020), 61.
26. Mary Turner, *Slaves and Missionaries: The Disintegration of Jamaican Slave Society, 1787-1834* (Kingston, Jamaica: Press University of the West Indies, 1998), 196.
27. Viotti da Costa, *Crowns of Glory, Tears of Blood*, 207-250.
28. Gelien Matthews, *Caribbean Slave Revolts and the British Abolitionist Movement* (Baton Rouge: Louisiana State University Press, 2012) 21; Christian Høgsbjerg, "The Demerara Rebellion of 1823: Collective bargaining by slave revolt," *International Socialism* 179 (July 2023).
29. For a full discussion of the historiography, see Janet Mills, "Quamina, do you hear this?: Revisiting the Demerara Slave Rebellion, 1823," (MA thesis, Dalhousie University, Halifax, Nova Scotia, 2018).
30. David Richardson, ed., *Abolition and Its Aftermath: The Historical Context, 1790-1916* (London: Cass, 1985), 109.

31. Mary Turner, *From Chattel Slaves to Wage Slaves: The Dynamics of Labour Bargaining in the Americas* (Kingston, Jamaica: Ian Randle Publishers, 1995).
32. Joshua Bryant, *Accounts of the Insurrection of the Negro Slaves in the Colony of Demerara* (Demerara: Guiana Chronicle Office, Georgetown, 1824).
33. *Edinburgh Review*, Vol. 41, No. 81 (October 1824).
34. Gelien Matthews, *Caribbean Slave Revolts and the British Abolitionist Movement* (Baton Rouge: Louisiana State University Press, 2012), 9.
35. Ibid., 45.
36. Ibid., 78.
37. Anya Jabour, "Slave Health and Health Care in the British Caribbean: Profits, Racism and the Failure of Amelioration in Trinidad and British Guiana, 1824–1834," *Journal of Caribbean History*, vol. 28 (1994): 17.
38. Robin Blackburn, *The Making of New World Slavery: From the Baroque to the Modern 1492–1800* (London: Verso Books, 1997), 524, 542.
39. Barbara Bush, *Slave Women in Caribbean Society 1650–1838* (Kingston, Jamaica: Heinemann, 1990), 6.
40. Robert Dallas, *The History of the Maroons—From Their Origin to the Establishment of their Chief Tribe in Sierra Leone* (London: T. N. Longman and O. Rees, 1803).
41. Richard Ligon, *A True and Exact Account of the Island of Barbadoes* (London: Peter Parker and Thomas Guy, 1657).
42. Rhoda Reddock, "Women and Slavery in the Caribbean: A Feminist Perspective," *Latin American Perspectives*, vol. 12, no. 1 (1985): 64.
43. Orlando Patterson, *The Sociology of Slavery* (London: Magibbon and Kee, 1967), 67.
44. Jennifer Morgan, *Laboring Women: Reproduction and Gender in New World Slavery* (Philadelphia: University of Pennsylvania Press, 2004), 150.
45. Bush. *Slave Women in Caribbean Society*, 35–36.
46. Diana Paton, "Gender History, Global History, and Atlantic Slavery: On Racial Capitalism and Social Reproduction," *American Historical Review*, vol. 127, no. 2 (June 2022): 732.
47. bell hooks, *Ain't I a Woman: Black Women and Feminism* (London: Pluto Press, 1987).
48. Paton, "Gender History, Global History, and Atlantic Slavery," 732.
49. Ibid.
50. Robin Blackburn, *The Overthrow of Colonial Slavery, 1776–1848* (London: Verso Books, 1988), 20.
51. Jean Casimir, *The Haitians: A Decolonial History* (Chapel Hill: University of North Carolina Press, 2020), 307.

52. Barbara Bush-Slimani, "Hard Labour: Women, Childbirth and Resistance in British Caribbean Slave Societies," *History Workshop* (1993): 86.
53. Ibid., 88.
54. Hilary Beckles, *Natural Rebels: A Social History of Enslaved Black Women in Barbados* (Zed Books, 1989), 101.
55. Gabriel Debien, *Plantations et esclaves a Saint-Domingue* (Dakar: Publications de la Section d'Histoire, 1962), 130.
56. Rhoda Reddock, "Women and Slavery in the Caribbean: A Feminist perspective," *Latin American Perspectives* vol. 12 (1985): 63.
57. Orlando Patterson, *The Sociology of Slavery* (London: Magibbon and Kee, 1967), 106. "Bukra" is an offensive term for White people used by the enslaved.
58. Orlando Patterson, *Slavery and Social Death: A Comparative Study* (Cambridge: Harvard University Press, 1986) 25, 56–58.
59. Patterson, *The Sociology of Slavery*, 157.
60. Alan Watson, *Roman Slave Law* (Baltimore: Johns Hopkins University Press, 1987), 10–15, 21, 47.
61. Daniel Livesay, *Children of Uncertain Fortune: Mixed-Race Jamaicans in Britain and the Atlantic Family, 1733–1833* (Chapel Hill: University of North Carolina Press, 2018).
62. Cindi Katz, "Vagabond Capitalism and the Necessity of Social Reproduction," *Antipode* 33, no. 4 (2001): 210.
63. Bush, *Slave Women in Caribbean Society*, 46–49.
64. Hilary Beckles, "Historicizing Slavery in West Indian Feminisms," *Feminist Review* no. 59 (1998): 46.
65. Kenneth Bilby, *True-Born Maroons* (Gainesville: University Press of Florida, 2005), 150–56.
66. David Barry Gaspar, "From 'The Sense of Their Slavery,' Slave Women and Resistance in Antigua, 1632–1763," in *Black Women and Slavery in the Americas*, ed. David Barry Gaspar and Darlene Clark Hine (Bloomington: Indiana University Press, 1996), 227.
67. Anne-Marie Bruleaux et al., *Deux siecles d'esclavage en Guyane francaise, 1652–1848* (Paris: L'Harmattan, 1986), 91.
68. Bilby, *True-Born Maroons*,150–56.
69. Bush, *Slave Women in Caribbean Society*, 75.
70. Ibid., 79.
71. Bernard Moitt, "Slave Women and Resistance in the French Caribbean," in *More Than Chattel: Black Women and Slavery in the Americas*, ed. David Gaspar and Darlene Clark Hine (Indiana University Press, 1996), 241.
72. Monica Schuler, "Ethnic Slave Rebellions in the Caribbean and the Guianas," *Journal of Social History* 3 (1970): 374.

73. Turner, *Slaves and Missionaries*, 58, 153.
74. Tom Zoellner, *Island on Fire: The Revolt That Ended Slavery in the British Empire* (Cambridge: Harvard University Press, 2020).
75. Gad Heuman, "A Tale of Two Jamaican Rebellions," *Jamaican Historical Review* 19 (1996):1–8; Mary Reckord, "The Jamaican Slave Rebellion of 1831," *Past and Present*, vol. 40, no. 3 (July 1968): 108–25; Mary Turner. "The Baptist War and Abolition," *Jamaican Historical Review* 13 (1982): 1–42.
76. Turner, *Slaves and Missionaries*, 133.
77. Nicholas Draper, *The Price of Emancipation: Slave-Ownership, Compensation and British Society at the End of Slavery* (Cambridge: Cambridge University Press, 2010), 154–58; Katie Donington, "The Legacies of British Slave-Ownership," *History Workshop* (November 3, 2014).
78. Catherine Hall, "Gendering Property, Racing Capital," *History Workshop* 78/1 (September 2014).
79. Draper, *The City of London and Slavery*, 432–66.
80. Katie Donington, *The Bonds of Family: Slavery, Commerce and Culture in the British Atlantic World* (Manchester, UK: Manchester University Press, 2019), 113.
81. Ibid., 131–32.
82. Michael Taylor, *The Interest: How the British Establishment Resisted the Abolition of Slavery* (London: Bodley Head, 2020), 202–3.
83. The original legislation was for six years, but the system was abolished early.
84. Kris Manjapra, *Black Ghost of Empire: The Long Death of Slavery and the Failure of Emancipation* (London: Penguin, 2022), 105.
85. Foreign Office document FOI2017/19045, held in the National Archives, Kew, and cited in Manjapra, *Black Ghost of Empire*, 206n29.
86. John Saville, *The Consolidation of the Capitalist State, 1800–1850* (London: Pluto Press, 1994), 8.
87. Hall et al., *Legacies of British Slave Ownership, Colonial Slavery and the Formation of Victorian Britain*, 23, 33.
88. Iain MacKinnon and Andrew Mackillop, *Plantation Slavery and Landownership in the West Highlands and Islands: Legacies and Lessons* (Oban: Community Land Scotland, 2020), 3.
89. Centre for the Study of the Legacies of British Slavery, *John Gordon 4th of Cluny*, https://www.ucl.ac.uk/lbs/person/view/1301318774
90. Alison Campsie, "The £100m of slavery wealth that bought up the Highlands and Islands," *The Scotsman*, November 10, 2020.
91. Hall et al., *Legacies of British Slave Ownership*, 58, 87, 108–11.
92. Berg & Hudson, *Slavery Capitalism and the Industrial Revolution*, 27–30.

93. Hall et al., *Legacies of British Slave Ownership*, 99–102; Draper, *Possessing Slaves: Ownership, Compensation and Metropolitan Society in Britain at the Time of Emancipation 1834–40*, 89.
94. David Lambert, "The 'Glasgow King of Billingsgate': James MacQueen and an Atlantic Proslavery Network," *Slavery and Abolition*, vol. 29, no. 4 (September 2008): 389–413.
95. Pat Hudson, "Slavery, the Slave Trade and Economic Growth," in *Emancipation and the Remaking of the British Imperial World*, ed. Catherine Hall, Nicholas Draper, and Keith McClelland (Manchester, UK: Manchester University Press, 2014).
96. A. L. Moreton, *A People's History of England* (London: Lawrence and Wishart, 1974), 423.

## 7. The Organized Working Class

1. Anne Farrow, Joel Lang, and Jennifer Frank, *Complicity: How the North Promoted, Prolonged, and Profited from Slavery* (New York: Ballantine, 2008),124.
2. Ronald Bailey, "The Other Side of Slavery: Black Labor, Cotton, and Textile Industrialization in Great Britain and the United States," *Agricultural History*, vol. 68, no. 2 (1994): 46.
3. Eugene Genovese, "Marxian Interpretations of the Slave South," in *In Red and Black: Marxian Explorations in Southern and Afro-American History* (New York: Pantheon, 1968), 321, 332.
4. Edward Baptist, *The Half Has Never Been Told* (New York: Basic Books, 2015), 64, 332, 426.
5. Nancy Ogden, Catherine Perkins, and David M. Donahue, "Not a Peculiar Institution: Challenging Students' Assumptions about Slavery in U.S. History," *History Teacher*, vol. 41, no. 4 (2008): 470.
6. Friedrich Engels, *Anti-Dühring* (Moscow: Progress Publishers, 1969), 99.
7. Ibid., 211–13.
8. John Bellamy Foster and Brett Clark, "The Expropriation of Nature," *Monthly Review*, vol. 69, no. 10 (2018): 1–27; John Bellamy Foster, *Marx's Ecology: Materialism and Nature* (New York: Monthly Review Press, 2000), 165.
9. Marx, *Die Presse*, no. 293, October 25, 1861.
10. *Daily Tribune*, February 1, 1862.
11. Melvyn Bragg, "In Our Time: The Lancashire Cotton Famine," *BBC Radio 4*, May 14, 2015.
12. Dale Tomich, *New Frontiers of Slavery* (Albany, NY: SUNY Press, 2016).
13. Marx, *Capital*, vol. 1, chap. 15,sec, 5, https://www.marxists.org/archive/marx/works/1867-c1/ch15.htm#S5

14. "The Lancashire Cotton 'Famine' 1861–65," *Our History*, no. 24 (Winter 1961).
15. Karl Marx, "The Progress of Feeling in Britain," *New York Daily Tribune*, December 25, 1861.
16. James McPherson, *Battle Cry of Freedom: The American Civil War* (New York: Penguin: 1990), 521–24.
17. James Heartfield, *The British And Foreign Anti-Slavery Society, 1838–1956: A History* (New York: Oxford University Press, 2016); Douglas A. Lorimer, "The Role of Anti-Slavery Sentiment in English Reactions to the American Civil War," *Historical Journal*, vol. 19, no. 2 (1976): 405–20.
18. *Morning Post*, February 22, 1862.
19. Marx, *Die Presse*, February 2, 1862.
20. Marx, *Die Presse*, December 31, 1861.
21. Sacha Ismail, *Workers Against Slavery: The American Civil War, the First International and the British Working Class* (London: Workers Liberty, 2015), 13–14.
22. Ibid., 17.
23. C. I. Glicksberg, "Henry Adams Reports on a Trades-Union Meeting," *New England Quarterly* (December 1942): 725.
24. Inaugural Address of the International Working Men's Association (1864), https://www.marxists.org/archive/marx/works/1864/10/27.htm.
25. H. Schlüter, *Lincoln, Labor and Slavery* (New York: Socialist Literature Company, 1913).
26. Pamela Nogales, "Marx on the American Civil War: Bourgeois right and working-class politics in the age of industrial capitalism" (MA thesis, New York University, 2012), 4.
27. Karl Korsch, "The Marxism of the First International" (1923), *Marxism and Philosophy*, trans. Fred Halliday (New York: Monthly Review Press, 1970).
28. Marx, *Preface to Capital* (1867), https://www.marxists.org/archive/marx/works/1867-c1/p1.htm.
29. Marx, *Capital*, vol. 1, chap. 10, sec/ 7, https://www.marxists.org/archive/marx/works/1867-c1/ch10.htm.
30. Andrew Kliman, "Combatting White Nationalism: Lessons from Marx," audio, *Marxist-Humanist Initiative*, October 2, 2017, https://www.marxisthumanistinitiative.org/philosophy-organization/audio-combatting-white-nationalism-lessons-from-marx.html.
31. Marx and Engels, *The Communist Manifesto* (New York: International Publishers, 1948), 28.
32. Eugene Genovese, "The Slave South: An Interpretation," *Science & Society*, vol. 25, no. 4 (1961): 320–37; Charles Post, *The American Road*

to *Capitalism: Studies in Class-Structure, Economic Development and Political Conflict, 1620–1877* (Leiden, Netherlands: Brill, 2011).
33. Edward Said, *Orientalism* (New York: Vintage, 1978), 155.
34. Engels to Florence Kelley Wischnewetsky, in Zurich, https://www.marxists.org/archive/marx/works/1887/letters/87_01_27.htm.
35. Karl Marx, *Poverty of Philosophy*, chap. 2, The Metaphysics of Political Economy, Fourth Observation, https://www.marxists.org/archive/marx/works/1847/poverty-philosophy/ch02.htm#s4.
36. Karl Marx to Pavel Vasilyevich Annenkov (1846), http://hiaw.org/defcon6/works/1846/letters/46_12_28.html.
37. Henry Pachter, "The Idea of Progress in Marxism," *Social Research*, vol. 41, no. 1, 136–61, (1974).
38. The Highland Clearances was the term used for the enclosures in Scotland. The Enclosures were discussed in chapter 4.
39. Marx, "The Duchess of Sutherland and Slavery," *The People's Paper*, no. 45, March 12, 1853, https://www.marxists.org/archive/marx/works/1853/03/12.htm.
40. Thierry Drapeau, "'Look at Our Colonial Struggles': Ernest Jones and the Anti-Colonialist Challenge to Marx's Conception of History," *Critical Sociology*, vol. 45, no. 7–8 (November 1, 2019): 1195–1208.
41. Marx, *New-York Daily Tribune*, August 8, 1853, https://marxists.architexturez.net/archive/marx/works/1853/07/22.htm.
42. Thierry Drapeau, "The Roots of Karl Marx's Anti-Colonialism," *Jacobin*, April 2019.
43. Marx to Engels (January 11, 1860). quoted in Kevin B. Anderson "Revisiting Marx on Race, Capitalism, and Revolution," *Monthly Review*, Vol. 73, No. 10 (March 2022).
44. Albert Von Frank, "John Brown, James Redpath, and the Idea of Revolution," *Civil War History*, vol. 52, no. 2 (2006), 147–149.
45. J. E. Cairnes, *The Slave Power* (New York: Follett Foster, 1862).
46. Andrew Zimmerman, "From the Second American Revolution to the First International and Back Again: Marxism, the Popular Front, and the American Civil War," in Gregory P. Downs and Kate Masur (eds.), *The World the Civil War Made* (Chapel Hill: University of North Carolina Press, 2015), 313.
47. Karl Obermann, *Joseph Weydemeyer: Pioneer of American Socialism* (New York: International Publishers, 1947), 99–104, 117–123.
48. Marx to Engels (August 7, 1862), quoted in Karl Marx, Frederick Engels, Andrew Zimmerman (ed.), *The Civil War in the United States* (New York: International Publishers, 1961), 253.
49. Andrew Zimmerman, "From the Rhine to the Mississippi: Property, Democracy, and Socialism in the American Civil War," *Journal of the*

*Civil War Era*, Vol. 5, No. 1 (2015), 15–23 [Newspaper quotes from this article].

50. James Thoma, *The Negro Soldier in the Second Battle of Boonville: The Earliest Combat Soldier*, State Historical Society of Missouri, https://mogenweb.org/cooper/Military/Negro_Soldiers.pdf.
51. W.E.B. DuBois, *Black Reconstruction in America: An Essay Toward a History of the Part which Black Folk Played in the Attempt to Reconstruct Democracy in America* (New York: Harcourt, Brace and Co., 1935), chapter 4; C. L. R. James [writing as J. R. Johnson], "Negroes in the Civil War, Their Role in the Second American Revolution," *New International*, Vol. 9, No. 11 (December 1943).
52. Marx, *Capital*, vol. 1 chap. 10, sec. 5, https://www.marxists.org/archive/marx/works/1867-c1/ch10.htm.
53. Ibid., sec. 6.
54. Marx, "Wage Labour and Capital," *Neue Rheinische Zeitung* (1849), translated by Frederick Engels, 1891.
55. Robin Blackburn, *An Unfinished Revolution: Karl Marx and Abraham Lincoln* (London: Verso Books, 2011), 9–11.
56. Jairus Banaji, *Theory As History: Essays on Modes of Production and Exploitation* (Chicago: Haymarket Books, 2011), 144.
57. Surplus Value: "The surplus produced over and above what is required to survive, which is translated into profit in capitalism. Since the capitalist pays a laborer for his/her labor, the capitalist claims to own the means of production, the worker's labor power, and even the product that is thus produced. The capitalist thus buys a product (labor power, which is then turned into commodities), which s/he then sells at a profit on the market," from Dino Franco Felluga, *Critical Theory: The Key Concepts* (New York: Routledge, 2015).
58. Karl Marx, *Theories of Surplus Value*, part 2 (Moscow: Progress Publishers, 1968), 302–3.
59. Marx, Karl, *Capital*, vol. 1, chap.10, sec.2, https://www.marxists.org/archive/marx/works/1867-c1/ch10.htm.
60. Marx, *Capital*, vol. 3 part 6, Transformation of Surplus-Profit into Ground-Rent hap.c47. Genesis of Capitalist Ground-Rent, https://www.marxists.org/archive/marx/works/1894-c3/ch47.htm.
61. Thierry Drapeau, *The Atlantic Roots of Working-class Internationalism: A Historical Re-Interpretation* (University of Toronto, York, Ontario, Ph.D. Thesis, 2014), https://yorkspace.library.yorku.ca/server/api/core/bitstreams/51e9b8fe-0f7d-4c16-954a-df98f72435a2/content.
62. Marx, *Capital*, vol. 1part VIII: Primitive Accumulation, chap. 26: The Secret of Primitive Accumulation. https://www.marxists.org/archive/marx/works/1867-c1/ch26.htm

63. Charles Holm, *Black Radicals and Marxist Internationalism: From the IWMA to the Fourth International, 1864–1948* (University of Nebraska-Lincoln, MA Thesis, 2014), 46–48, https://digitalcommons.unl.edu/cgi/viewcontent.cgi?article=1071&context=historydiss.
64. Ernest Mandell, *Introduction to Capital* (London: Penguin, 1992), 35.
65. Marx, *Capital*, vol. 1, chap. 31: Genesis of the Industrial Capitalist, https://www.marxists.org/archive/marx/works/1867-c1/ch31.htm.
66. Marx, Samuel Moore (trans.), Edward B. Aveling, Friedrich Engels (eds.), *Capital; A critical analysis of capitalist production* (New York: International Publishers, 1939), 287.
67. Louis Proyect, "Andrew Zimmerman on Marx, Engels and Slavery," The Unrepentant Marxist, July 11, 2028, https://louisproyect.org/2018/07/11/andrew-zimmerman-on-marx-engels-and-slavery/.
68. *The Bee-Hive*, No. 169 (November 7, 1865).
69. Louis Proyect, "Marx, Lincoln and Project 1619," *CounterPunch* (February 14, 2020).
70. Marx, "The Civil War in the United States." *Die Presse*, November 7, 1861, quoted in Kevin Anderson, *Marx at the Margins* (Chicago: University of Chicago Press, 2010), 90.
71. Salome Lee, "Until We Are All Abolitionists: Marx on Slavery, Race, and Class," *International Marxist-Humanist* (October 22, 2011).
72. *New York Daily Tribune* (February 1, 1862).
73. Quoted in M. Sinha, "Eugene D Genovese: The mind of a Marxist conservative" (2004), *Radical History Review*. 20. https://scholarworks.umass.edu/afroam_faculty_pubs/20.
74. Genovese, "Marxian Interpretations of the Slave South," 321, 327.
75. John Bellamy Foster, "Marx and Internationalism," *Monthly Review*, vol. 52, no. 3 (July-August 2000).
76. Marx to Engels (November 20, 1865) in Marx and Engels, *Collected Works*, vol. 42, http://hiaw.org/defcon6/works/1865/letters/65_11_20.html.
77. Gad Heuman, *"The Killing Time": The Morant Bay Rebellion in Jamaica* (London: Macmillan, 1994).
78. William Oddie, *Dickens and Carlyle, the Question of Influence* (London: Centenary Press, 1972), 135–142.
79. *The Eyre Defence and Aid Fund* (London: Pelican Printing Company, 1866).
80. Thomas Carlyle, "Occasional Discourse on the Negro Question," *Fraser's Magazine for Town and Country*, vol. XL (London, February 1849).
81. E. S. Beesly, "Military Atrocities in Jamaica," *Bee-Hive*, November 25, 1865 (This and the following newspaper quotations from Priyamvada

Gopal, *Insurgent Empire: Anticolonial Resistance and British Dissent* (London: Verso Books, 2020), chap. 2.
82. The National Archives, Kew, ref. CO. 137/390, Cardwell to Eyre (June 14, 1865).[references starting CO refer to the papers of the Colonial Office].
83. "Jamaica and Its Tyrants," *Reynold's News* (December 24, 1865).
84. Peter Daniel, "The Governor Eyre Controversy," *New Blackfriars*, vol. 50, no. 591 (1969), 577–578.

## 8. Imperial Reconfiguration

1. "John Gladstone," *Centre for the Study of the British Legacies of Slavery*, https://www.ucl.ac.uk/lbs/person/view/8961.
2. Sven Beckert, *Empire of Cotton: A Global History* (New York: Alfred A. Knopf, 2015), 437.
3. Mike Davis, *Late Victorian Holocausts* (London: Verso Books, 2017).
4. Alan Lester, Kate Boehme, and Peter Mitchell, *Ruling the World: Freedom, Civilisation and Liberalism in the Nineteenth-Century British Empire* (Cambridge: Cambridge University Press, 2021), 17, 27, 152.
5. Alan Lester and Nikita Vanderbyl, "The Restructuring of the British Empire and the Colonization of Australia, 1832–8," *History Workshop Journal*, vol. 90 (Autumn 2020): 165–218.
6. Walter Rodney, *How Europe Underdeveloped Africa* (London: Bogle-L'Ouverture Publications, 1972), 105–7.
7. Lee Wengraf, *Extracting Profit: Imperialism, Neoliberalism, and the New Scramble for Africa* (Chicago: Haymarket Books, 2018), 32–39.
8. Karl Marx, *Capital*, vol. 1, chap. 31, "Genesis of the Industrial Capitalist," https://www.marxists.org/archive/marx/works/1867-c1/ch31.htm.
9. Richard Hart, *From Occupation to Independence: A History of the Peoples of the English-Speaking Caribbean Region* (London: Pluto Press, 1998), 40–44.
10. Hilary Beckles, *Great House Rules: Landless Emancipation and Workers' Protest in Barbados 1838–1938* (Kingston, Jamaica: Ian Randle, 2004), 90.
11. David Brion Davis, *The Problem of Slavery in the Age of Emancipation* (New York: Penguin, 2014), 281; Trevor Marshall, "Post-Emancipation Adjustments in Barbados, 1838 to 1876," in *Emancipation 1*, ed. Alvin Thompson (Kingston, Jamaica: University of the West Indies, 1984), 88–102.
12. Henderson Carter, *Labour Pains: Resistance and Protest in Barbados, 1838–1904* (Kingston, Jamaica: Ian Randle Publishers, 2012), chap. 3; Bentley Gibbs, "The Establishment of the Tenantry System in Barbados," in *Emancipation 2*, ed. Woodville Marshal (Kingston Jamaica: University of the West Indies, 1987), 23–46.

13. *The Creole* (October 30, 1872), University of Florida Digital Collections, https://ufdc.ufl.edu/AA00084164/01167.
14. Beckles, *Great House Rules*, 50–52.
15. Carter, *Labour Pains*, chap. 3.
16. Edward Pinder, *Letters on the Labouring Population of Barbados* (Barbadian Heritage Reprint Series, No.1, N.C.F. 1990).
17. F. R. Augier, S. C. Gordon, D. G. Hall, and M. Reckord, *The Making of the West Indies* (London: Longmans, Green and Company, 1961), 188.
18. Carter, *Labour Pains*, chap. 4.
19. Beckles, *Great House Rules*, 76.
20. *The Liberal* (September 12, 1840), quoted in Beckles, *Great House Rules*.
21. Bonham C. Richardson,"Depression riots and the calling of the 1897 West India Royal Commission," *New West Indian Guide / Nieuwe West-Indische Gids*, vol. 66, nos. 3 and 4 (1992): 169–191.
22. Carter, *Labour Pains*, chap. 7.
23. Richard Hart, *Labour Rebellions of the 1930s in the British Caribbean Region Colonies* (London: Caribbean Labour Solidarity, 2002), 9–18.
24. George Daniel, "Labor and Nationalism in the British Caribbean," *Annals of the American Academy of Political and Social Science*, vol. 310 (March 1957): 170.
25. W. Arthur Lewis, *Labour in the West Indies: The Birth of a Workers' Movement* (London: New Beacon Books, 1977), 53.
26. Beckles, "Historicizing Slavery in West Indian Feminisms," *Feminist Review*, no. 59 (1998): 49–50.
27. Hilary McDonald. Beckles, "Capitalism, Slavery and Caribbean Modernity," *Callaloo*, vol. 20, no. 4 (1997): 786.
28. Angela Davis, "Reflections on the Black Woman's Role in the Community of Slaves," *Massachusetts Review*, vol. 13, no. 1–2 (1972): 100.
29. Institutional racism is that which, covertly or overtly, resides in the policies, procedures, operations, and culture of public or private institutions—reinforcing individual prejudices and being reinforced by them in turn. See "What is institutional racism?," Institute of Race Relations, https://irr.org.uk/article/what-is-institutional-racism/.
30. Peter Fryer, *Black People in the British Empire: An Introduction* (London: Pluto Press, 1988), chap. 12.
31. Martin Nicolaus, "Theory of the Labor Aristocracy," *Monthly Review*, vol. 21, no. 11 (April 1970).
32. Marjorie Nicholson, *The TUC Overseas: The Roots of Policy* (London: Allen & Unwin, 1986).
33. Partha Sarathi Gupta, *Imperialism and the British Labour Movement, 1914–1964* (London: Palgrave, 1975), 32.

34. Yuri Prasad, Esme Choonara, Ken Olende, *Does Privilege Explain Racism?* (London: Bookmarks, 2020), 17.
35. A. Sivanandan, "From Resistance to Rebellion: Asian and Afro-Caribbean Struggles in Britain," *Race and Class*, vol. 23, nos. 2 and 3 (1981).

## Conclusion

1. Donald Winford, "Intermediate creoles and degrees of change in creole formation," in *Degrees of Restructuring in Creole Languages*, ed. Ingrid Neumann-Holzschuh and Edgar Schneider (Amsterdam: John Benjamins, 2001); Gregory Clark, "Farm Wages and Living Standards in the Industrial Revolution: England, 1670–1869," *Economic History Review*, vol. 54, no. 3 (2001): 477–505.
2. I would like to thank Danny Reilly of the National Education Union (the most important trade union for teachers in the UK) for his help with the section on education.
3. Anna Leach, Antonio Voce, and Ashley Kirk, "Black British History: The row over the school curriculum in England," *The Guardian*, July 13, 2020.
4. Farzana Shain, "Race, nation and education: An overview of British attempts to 'manage diversity' since the 1950s," *Education Inquiry*, vol. 4, no. 1 (March 2013): 63–85.
5. Bernard Coard, *How the West Indian Child Is Made Educationally Sub-Normal in the British School System* (Kingston, Jamaica: McDermott Publishing, 2021).
6. Gary Clayton Anderson, *Ethnic Cleansing and the Indian: The Crime That Should Haunt America* (Norman: University of Oklahoma Press, 2014), 3–22.
7. U.S. Census Bureau, *Race and Ethnicity in the United States: 2010 Census and 2020 Census*, https://www.census.gov/library/visualizations/interactive/race-and-ethnicity-in-the-united-state-2010-and-2020-census.html; Statistics Canada, *Indigenous Identity by Registered or Treaty Indian Status*. https://www150.statcan.gc.ca/t1/tbl1/en/tv.action?pid=9810026401.
8. Julia Boyd, "An Examination of Native Americans in Film and Rise of Native Filmmakers," *Elon Journal of Undergraduate Research in Communications*, vol. 6, no. 1 (Spring 2015): 106, https://eloncdn.blob.core.windows.net/eu3/sites/153/2017/06/10BoydEJSpring15.pdf; National Museum of the American Indian, *Do All Indians Live in Tipis?* (New York: HarperCollins, 2007).
9. UK Parliament, "The Transatlantic Slave Trade," https://heritagecollections.parliament.uk/stories/the-transatlantic-slave-trade/.
10. Henry Mayhew, *London Labour and the London Poor* (Harmondsworth: Penguin Books, 1985); Friedrich Engels, *The Condition of the Working-*

*Class in England: From Personal Observation and Authentic Sources* (London: Panther, 1972).
11. Karl Marx, "Wage Labour and Capital," *Neue Rheinische Zeitung*, April 5–8 and 11, 1849, translated by Frederick Engels (1891).
12. Henry Heller, *The Birth Of Capitalism* (London: Pluto Press, 2011), 242.
13. Andreas Malm, *Fossil Capital: The Rise of Steam Power and the Roots of Global Warming* (London:Verso 2016), 353.
14. CBS News, "ExxonMobil CEO philosophy to 'make money,'" March 7, 2013, https://www.youtube.com/watch?v=AoZI1fkiVgs.
15. Reece Jones, *Violent Borders: Refugees and the Right to Move* (London: Verso Books, 2016).
16. Kevon Rhiney and April Karen Baptiste, "Adapting to Climate Change in the Caribbean: Existential Threat or Development Crossroads?," *Caribbean Studies*, vol. 47, no. 2 (2019): 59–80.
17. Leon Sealey-Huggins, "'1.5°C to stay alive': Climate change, imperialism and justice for the Caribbean," *Third World Quarterly*, vol. 38, no.11 (2017): 2444–63.
18. John Bellamy Foster, Brett Clark, and Hannah Holleman, "Capitalism and Robbery: The Expropriation of Land, Labor, and Corporeal Life," *Monthly Review*, vol. 71, no. 7 (December 2019).
19. Patrick Greenfield, Fiona Harvey, Nina Lakhani, and Damian Carrington, "Barbados PM launches blistering attack on rich nations at Cop27 climate talks," *The Guardian*, November 7, 2022.
20. Lashmar and Smith, "He's the MP with the Downton Abbey lifestyle, but the shadow of slavery hangs over the gilded life of Richard Drax," *The Observer*, December 12, 2020.
21. "Intensified calls for British MP Drax to return plantation property," *Barbados Today*, October 16, 2021. Update on Drax Hall: At the time of printing, the government of Barbados suggested buying some of the land of Drax Hall estate from Richard Drax. This produced an outcry both in Barbados and Britain and the suggestion was withdrawn. Meanwhile, Richard Drax was no reelected as a member of Parliament in the 2024 general election. The antiracist organization in Dorset, Stand Up To Racism, is continuing to work with the Reparations movement in Barbados to campaign for the return of Drax Hall to the people of Barbados.

### Further Reading
1. https://www.marxists.org/archive/marx/
2. https://www.marxists.org/archive/marx/

# Index

Abdelkader (Emir), 163
abolitionist movements, 23, 104–6; on compensation to slave owners, 131; on free labor, 135–36; Marx on, 152; radical abolitionists, 110–13
Adams, Henry, 148
Africa: colonialism in, 169–70; slave trade in, 16
African Americans, in Union Army, 157
agriculture, 24; agricultural revolution, 77; in Britain, 108; in Carolina colony, 47; monocrop production in, 25; scientific management of, 56–58; soil depletion in, 54–56; in West Indies, 29
Aislabie, John, 69–70
Alabama, 101
Alfonso V (king, Portugal), 59
Allen, Theodore, 33–34

almshouses, 39–40
amelioration, 115–17, 121
Amsterdam (Holland), 94
Angus, Ian, 79
Anne (queen, England), 68

Annenkov, Pavel Vasilyevich, 151
Antigua, 62
Anti-Slavery Society (Society for the Mitigation and Gradual Abolition of Slavery), 104–5, 120; on U.S. Civil War, 145–46
Antwerp (Belgium), 94
Apalachees (people), 49
apprenticeships, 170
Arbuthnot, John, 76
Australia, 169

Bacon, Nathaniel, 33
Bacon's Rebellion (Virginia; 1675-76), 33

# INDEX

Banaji, Jairus, 159
Bank Charter Act (Britain, 1833), 135
banking: in Great Britain, 102; investments in slavery by, 134; in New Orleans, 101
Bank of England, 134
Baptist, Edward, 159
Baptist War (Jamaica, 1831), 115, 127–30
Barbados, 50; after abolition of slavery, 171–74; campaigns for reparations for slavery in, 25; Carolina colony settled by, 47; Christianity in, 61–62; colonial government of, 171; Drax plantation in, 53; early English settlers in, 28; labor force in, 31–32; resistance in, 174–75; slave patrols in, 84; slave revolts in, 114–15; slavery introduced in, 30, 32–33; unpaid wages in, 181–82
Barbados Rebellion (1816), 64
Barbados Slave Code (1661), 32–33, 84
Baring Brothers (firm), 135
Baring Brothers Bank, 103
Barings Bank (firm), 102
Barnwell, John, 49
Bathurst (Lord), 116
Beckert, Sven, 159
Beckford, William, 124
Beckles, Hilary, 115, 176
Beesly, Edward, 148
Belgrove, William, 56
Berkeley, William, 33
bills of exchange, 134
Birmingham (England), 113

Birmingham Ladies Society for the Relief of Negro Slaves, 113
Black Act (Britain, 1723), 79–80
Blackburn, Robin, 121–22, 124, 159
Black Caribs, 51
Black Regiment (Jamaica), 128
Blasphemous and Seditious Libels Act (Britain, 1819), 112
Blathwayt, William, 60–61
Bogle, Paul, 164
Boston: as colony, 44; police in, 85; in triangular trade, 46
brass, 98
Brazil: British investment in, 97; Dutch colonies in, 30; slavery in, 94; slavery used in sugar production in, 109
Brenner, Robert, 159
Bright, John, 152, 165
Bristol (England), 94
Bristol Fire Insurance Office, 94
Britain, see Great Britain
British Empire, 13–14; education about, 182–83; enclosures in, 72; North American colonies in, 41–42
British West Indies, 19; after abolition of slavery, 24, 167–68; compensation to slave owners in, 130–38; Labour Rebellions and trade unions in, 175–76; slave revolts in, 115; slavery abolished in, 21; Treaty of Paris (1763) on, 51; unpaid wages in, 182
Brodnock, Erika, 103
Brougham (Lord), 146
Brougham, Henry, 132
Brown, John, 154, 156

Brown Brothers (bank; New York), 101
Bruleaux, Anne-Marie, 126
Bush, Barbara, 19, 122, 127
Bussa's War (Barbados, 1816), 114–15
Butler, Smedley, 86
Buxton, Thomas Fowell, 116

Cabot brothers, 141
Cain, Louis, 27
calico (fabric), 38
Canning, George, 116
capitalism: continuous expansion required for, 107; green capitalism, 192; industrial, origins of, 91–92; Marx on origins of, 72, 73
Captain Swing movement (Britain, 1830), 129
Cardigan (Lord), 166
Caribbean colonies: in British Empire, 41; earliest slave trade in, 28–30
Caribbean Community (CARICOM), on reparations, 25–26
Caribbean Community Climate Change Centre, 191
Caribbean islands, climate change in, 190–93
Carib War (1772-73), 51
Carlyle, Thomas, 165, 178
Carolina colony, 47–52
Casimir, Jean, 124
Centre for the Study of the Legacies of British Slavery, 130
charity (philanthropy), 38–40
Charles I (king, England), 31, 41
Charles II (king, England), 36, 47
Charleston (South Carolina), 84
Chartism, 153
Chattel House (Barbados), 172
chattel slavery, *see* slavery
children: in Barbados, 173–74; enslaved, 124–25
China, 168, 169
Christianity, 59–65
Church of England, 9–10, 59–61, 65
City of London (financial services), 81, 82, 107
Civil War (United States, 1861-65), 15, 107; attitudes of British working class on, 139–40; British responses to, 143–50; Marx on, 156, 161, 162
Clapham Sect, 104, 136
Clarkson, Thomas, 104–5, 131, 136
Clausewitz, Karl von, 106
climate change, 25, 190–93
coal, 77–78; steam engines use of, 96, 99; used in production of brass, 98
Coal and Iron Police (Pennsylvania), 85
Cobbett, William, 112
Cobre Company (Cuba), 99
Codrington, Christopher, 53–54
Collins (Dr.), 19
colonialism, 153, 154, 163; in Africa, 169–70
Colonial Union of Coloured Classes (Barbados), 174–75
Colquhoun, Patrick, 82–85
Colston, Edward, 37, 185
Comissiong, David, 25–26, 193
Committee of West Indian Merchants, 82

INDEX

Company of Proprietors of the Royal Copper Mines of Cobre (Cuba), 99
compensation to slave owners, 130–38
Confederate States of America: British support for, 145–47; Missouri's support for, 155–56
Consolidated Association of the Planters of Louisiana (CAPL), 101
Consolidated Slave Act (Jamaica, 1788), 126
Cooke, Bill, 56–57
copper, 98–99
Corn Laws (Britain), 108; repeal of, 109
Cort, Henry, 97–98
Cort process, 97–98
Coster, John, 98
Coster, Thomas, 98
cotton industry, 96–97, 140–43; after abolition of slavery, 139; in Britain, 144–45; slavery essential for, 100, 108
Cromwell, Oliver, 31
Cuba: British investment in, 97; deforestation of, 54–55; slave patrols in, 83–84; slavery used in mining in, 99; slavery used in sugar production in, 109

Dallas, Robert, 122
Davis, Angela, 176–77
Dawkins-Pennant, George Hay, 89
Defoe, Daniel, 69
deforestation, 54–55, 190
Demerara-Essequibo (Guyana), Demerara Rebellion (1823) in, 115, 117–21

Denmark, 13
*Desire* (ship), 43
Dominica, 50–51
Drapeau, Thierry, 160
Draper, Richard, 10
Drax, Henry, 53, 54, 56, 58
Drax, James (father; 1609-62), 28, 30, 32
Drax, James (son; 1639-63), 53
Drax, John Sawbridge Erle, 74–75
Drax, Sir Richard, 193
Drax family, 193
Drogheda, Battle of, 31
drumming, 65
Du Bois, W. E. B., 157
Dunbar, 127
Dunkirk, Battle of, 13
Dutch colonies, in Brazil, 30
Dutch East India Company, 37

Eamer, Sir John, 81
East India Company, 71, 108, 168
Edmundson, William, 61, 62
education: of enslaved people, 64–65, 173; racism maintained by, 182–83
Emancipation Proclamation (U.S., 1863), 157
Enclosure Acts (Britain, 1750 to 1860), 73, 76
Enclosures (England), 24, 66, 70–78, 99
Engels Frederick, 187; on deforestation of Cuba, 54–55; on philanthropy, 39; on slavery, 140, 150–51; on soil exhaustion, 142; on U.S. Civil War, 144, 149, 156, 161
England, *see* Great Britain

English East India Company, 37–38
enslaved persons: unpaid wages owed to, 181–82; use of term, 27
epidemics, 52
Equiano, Olaudah, 110–11
Erie Canal (New York), 142
Eurocentrism, 162
Eyre, Edward, 164–66

financial services industry, 88, 102, 103, 135
First Maroon War (1728-40), 127
Fleetwood, William, 60
Florida, 101
Floyd, George, 10
Foache, Stanislas, 124
Forbes, William, 98, 99
fossil fuels, 96, 100, 190
Fowler, Corinne, 74
France: Caribbean colonies of, 50; North American colonies of, 48; Treaty of Paris (1763) on, 51
free labor, 135–36, 168–70
free trade, 109, 168–70
fur trade, 42
futures market, 103

Gallay, Alan, 48
Garifuna (people), 52, 184
Garwood, Jesse, 85–86
Geffrye, Sir Robert, 28, 34–35, 39; statue of, 40
genocide, 184
Genovese, Eugene, 150, 162–63
George I (king, England), 68, 69
George IV (king, England), 131–32
Gifford, Anthony, 10
Gladstone, Sir John, 167; Amelioration proposed by, 116; on Demerara Rebellion, 118, 120–21; on U.S. Civil War, 145
global warming, 16, 190–93
Glorious Revolution (England), 36
Gordon, George William, 164
Gordon, John, 133
Governing of Negroes, An Act for the (Barbados, 1688), 84
Grant, Bernie, 10
Gray, George, 63
Great Britain: abolition of slavery in, 109; compensation to slave owners in, 130–33; Enclosures in, 72–78; origins of policing in, 84; responses to U.S. Civil War in, 143–50; Royal Proclamation of 1763 by, 47; South Sea Bubble in, 67–70; sugar in diet of, 90; sugar refineries in, 94; Windrush scandal in, 179–80
green capitalism, 192
Greene, Lorenzo, 45–46
greenhouse gas emissions, 191
Greg, Samuel, 97
Grenada, 51
Grigg, Nanny, 64
Guardian Royal Exchange (Royal Exchange Insurance), 102
Guy, Sir Thomas, 69

Haiti: revolution in, 113; women denied vote in, 176
Hall, Catherine, 10
Hall, Prince, 10
Hardy, Thomas, 110–12
Harwood, Richard, 54
health: sugar consumption and, 16, 90–91; sugar production and, 94

Heyrick, Elizabeth, 113
Hibbert, George, 81–82, 131
Hibbert, Margaret, 97
Highland Clearances, 133
Highland Clearances (Scotland), 24
Hill, Roger, 185
Hinton, Richard, 154
Hoare, Benjamin, 69
Hoare, Henry, 69
Hoare's Bank (Britain), 69
Hodgson, Thomas, 97
Home Guards (Union Army), 155–57
Hume, David, 33
Hunt, James, 178
hurricanes, 191
Hyde Park (London, 1866), 86

Ideology, of capitalist class, 22
Importation Act (Repeal of the Corn Laws; Great Britain, 1846), 109
indentured labor, 31–32; in New England, 43
India, 71; as central to British Empire, 167; cotton and textile production in, 108–9; English East India Company and Dutch East India Company in, 37–38; famines in, 168; Marx on, 153–54
Indian Mutiny (1857–59), 163
Indigenous people: in Caribbean colonies, 29; genocide of, 184; Marx and Engels on, 163–64; in North American colonies, 42, 47–52; in United States, 185
industrial capitalism: origins of, 91–92; slave-labor in development of, 100, 103; steam engines for, 95
industrialization, 100
Industrial Revolution: financed by slavery, 88; state used to support, 23; sugar exports in financing of, 21
Industrial Workers of the World (IWW), 162
Inikori, Joseph, 92
institutionalized racism, 177–78, 189
insurance industry, 88, 102
International Workingmen's Association (IWA), 148–49, 152
Ireland, 85, 86–87, 163
iron smelting, 97–98
Islam, 65

Jabour, Anya, 121
Jack (enslaved worker), 118, 120
Jackson, Claiborne Fox, 155–56
Jackson, William, 147–48
Jamaica: Baptist War in, 115, 127–30; Barbados Slave Code in, 33; Consolidated Slave Act in, 126; Morant Bay Rebellion in, 86, 140, 164–66; Pennant's plantations in, 89–90; slave-based economy of, 19; sugar cultivation in, 55; unpaid wages in, 182
James II (king, England), 35, 36
James (Duke of York), 38
James, C. L. R., 159
*Jesus of Lübeck* (ship), 16
Johnson, Walter, 159
Jones, Ernest, 152, 153

Kalinago (people), 50–52

Katz, Cindi, 125–26
Kelton, Paul, 29
Kennedy, John F., 10
King Phillip's War (Metacom's War; 1675-76), 42
Kirk, Ashley, 183
Klein, Herbert, 44
Kleinwort Benson (investment bank), 138
Korsch, Karl, 149

Labour Rebellions (British West Indies), 175
Lamartinière, Marie-Jeanne, 127
Latimer Massacre (1897), 85
Leach, Anna, 183
Lenhard, Johannes, 103
Lewis, Arthur, 176
life expectancy of slaves, 18
Ligon, Richard, 122
Lincoln, Abraham, 156; Emancipation Proclamation issued by, 157; Marx's letter to, 149, 152, 161–62
Linebaugh, Peter, 83
literacy, 63–64
Little Ice Age, 29
Littleton, Edward, 18
Lloyds of London (firm), 102
Locke, John, 33
London (England): River Police and Metropolitan Police in, 83–87; sugar refineries in, 94; West India Dock in, 66–67, 80–83
London Assurance Company, 102
London Corresponding Society, 22, 110–12
London Insurance (firm), 102

London West India Committee, 106
Louisiana Purchase (1802), 102, 135
Luddites, 129

Macaulay, Zachary, 137
Mackillop, Andrew, 133
MacKinnon, Iain, 133–34
MacQueen, James, 134
Malm, Andreas, 190
Manchester (England): antislavery rally in, 147–48; Peterloo Massacre in, 112
Manchester Society for Constitutional Information, 110
Mandel, Ernest, 160–61
Manning, Brian, 79
Marine Police Office (London), 82–83
Markland, James Heywood, 60
Maroons (people), 113, 114; women as, 126–27
Marx, Karl, 57; on British cotton industry, 145; on colonialism, 170; on enclosures, 74, 78; on India, 153–54; in International Workingmen's Association, 148–49; letter to Lincoln by, 161–62; on Morant Bay Rebellion, 164; on origins of capitalism, 72, 73, 91–92; on primitive accumulation, 93; on slaveholders, 143; on slavery, 140, 150–53, 156–61; on soil exhaustion, 142; on U.S. Civil War, 144, 146–47, 149–50, 156, 161; on wages, 187–88
Marxism, on political economy of slavery, 150–64

INDEX 241

Mary Stuart (Countess of Bute; England), 36
Massachusetts Bay colony, 41; rum produced in, 45; in triangular trade, 46–47
Master and Servant Act (Barbados, 1838), 171, 174
Matthews, Gelien, 119–20
Maxwell, William, 74
Mayhew, Henry, 187
Metacom's War (King Phillip's War; 1675-76), 42
Metropolitan Police (London), 83, 85
Mexico, 13; secession of Texas from, 71, 86
Middle Passage, 36
Miles, Philip John, 94–95
Miles, William, 94
Miles Bank, 94
Mintz, Sidney, 90
Missouri, 155–56
Moore, Audley (Queen Mother Moore), 10
Moore, James, 49
Morant Bay Rebellion (Jamaica, 1865), 86, 140, 164–66
Morton, A. L., 136–37
Mottley, Mia, 192–93

Native Americans: enslavement of, 48; *see also* Indigenous people
Native Baptists, 128
Nef, John, 77–78
neocolonialism, 192
Nevis, 62
New England, 41; cotton clothing made in, 141–42; slavery in, 42–44; in triangular trade, 44–45

New Orleans (Louisiana), 101
Newport colony, 44
Newton, Sir Isaac, 69, 70
Newton, John, 57
New Zealand, 169
Nicholas V (pope), 59
Nonconformists (Protestant group), 117, 129
North Carolina, 84
North Wales Quarrymen's Union, 89

obesity, 16, 90–91
oil, 96
Olivier, Sydney, 179
opium, 168, 169
Opium Wars, 168
Owen, Ken, 54

Paine, Thomas, 110
Pares, Thomas, 97
Paris, Treaty of (1763; ending Seven Years' War), 51
Paris, Treaty of (1783), 52
Patnaik, Utsa, 77
Patterson, Orlando, 123, 125
Peace Preservation Act (Ireland, 1814), 85
Peate, Richard, 34
Peel, Sir Robert, 83, 85
Pennant, George Sholto Gordon Douglas (Second Baron Penrhyn), 89
Pennant, Richard, 89
Pennsylvania State Police, 85–86
Penrhyn Castle (Wales), 89–90
Penrhyn slate quarry (Wales), 89, 90
People's Charter (Britain; 1838), 153

Pequot War (1636-38), 42
Peterloo Massacre (Manchester, 1819), 112
Peters, George, 131
philanthropy (charity), 38–40
Philippine Constabulary, 85–86
Phillips, Ulrich, 43
Pierce, William, 43
Pile, A. J., 175
Pinder, Edward, 173
plantations: in Barbados, after abolition of slavery, 170, 173–74; management of, 53–54; religion on, 62; scientific management of, 56–58; slavery on, 94; soil conservation in, 54–56; soil exhaustion in, 142
Plymouth Colony (Massachusetts), 41
poisonings, 127
police, 83–85, 171
political economy, 20; of slavery, Marxism on, 150–64
Poor Law Amendment Act (Britain, 1834), 137
Portugal, slavery in colonies of, 8
Post, Charles, 150
Powell, Enoch, 183
Prescod, Samuel Jackman, 174–75
Prescod, Trevor, 193
primitive accumulation, 93
Protestantism, 59, 62, 63
Proudhon, Pierre-Joseph, 151
Puritans, 42, 43

Quakers, 62–63
Quamina (enslaved worker), 118, 120
Queen Anne's War (1702-13), 49

race, class and, 177–80
racism, 178; in British West Indies, 176; in class struggle, 22; institutionalized, 177–78; legacy of, 189; maintained by education, 182–83
Reddock, Rhoda, 122–25
Redpath, James, 154
Reeder, John, 97–98
Reform Act of 1832 (Britain), 21, 130
relative income measure, 26
reparations, 9–10, 182; Caribbean Community demands for, 25–26; for Indigenous people, 185; movement for, 184
Rhode Island colony, 43, 140–41; rum produced in, 45; in triangular trade, 46
River Police (London), 67, 83–87
Roatán, 52
Robertson, Robert, 63–64
Rodney, Walter, 169
Rothschild & Co. (bank), 132–33
Royal African Company, 28, 35–37; in triangular trade, 45, 47
Royal Exchange Insurance (Guardian Royal Exchange), 102
Royal Irish Constabulary, 85
Royal Mail Steam Packet Company, 134
Royal Navy, 14, 98; in slave trade, 38
Royal Proclamation of 1763 (Britain), 47
rum, in triangular trade, 45
Ruskin, John, 165, 166
Russell (Lord), 145

INDEX

Said, Edward, 150
Saint Vincent, 50–52
Salem (Massachusetts), 44, 46
Santiago Company (Cuba), 99
Savannah (people), 48
scientific management, 16
Scotland, 133
Scott, Sir Walter, 95–96
Seditious Meetings Prevention Act (Britain, 1819), 112
Seven Years' War (Britain and France), 51
Sharpe, Sam, 128
Sheffield Cutlers, 22
shipbuilding, 44
Sigel, Franz, 157
Slave Emancipation Act (Britain, 1833), 135
slave rebellions, 102, 106, 113–15; Barbados Rebellion, 64; Black Regiment, 127–30; Demerara Rebellion, 117–21; First Maroon War, 127; Morant Bay Rebellion, 164–66; women in, 126
slavery: abolished in Great Britain, 109; abolitionist movements against, 104–6; amelioration of conditions of, 116–17; Barbados Slave Code on, 32–33; Christianity and, 59–65; compensation to slave owners, 130–38; condemned as Crime Against Humanity, 25; cotton industry tied to, 97; demands for reparations for, 9–10; in early Barbados, 30, 32; history of abolition of, 13; Industrial Revolution financed by, 88; life expectancy of slaves, 18; management techniques for, 56–57; Marxism on, 150–64; in New England colonies, 42–44; opposed by working class organizations, 22; in origins of capitalism, 92, 94; origins of police tied to, 83–84; renamed apprenticeship, 170; reparations for, 182; in triangular trade, 45–47; of women, 121–27
slave trade, 18; abolition of, 104, 105, 112; in early Caribbean colonies, 28–30; financing of, 100–103; investments in, 102–3; in North American colonies, 44–47; Royal African Company in, 35–37; South Sea Company in, 67–70; United Kingdom website on, 186
Slave Trade Act (Britain, 1807), 104
Smith, Adam, 91
Smith, John, 120
social class, race and, 177–80
Society for Constitutional Information, 110
Society for the Mitigation and Gradual Abolition of Slavery (Anti-Slavery Society), 104–5, 120; on U.S. Civil War, 145
Society for the Mitigation and Gradual Abolition of Slavery Throughout the British Dominions, 116
Society for the Propagation of the Gospel in Foreign Parts, 59–60, 63, 65
Society of West Indian Planters and Merchants, 131
Sons of Africa, 110–11

South Carolina, 33; slave patrols in, 84
South Sea Bubble (1720), 67–70
South Sea Company, 67–70
Spain: deforestation of Cuba by, 54–55; North American colonies of, 48; sale of enslaved Africans from Britain to, 68; slavery in colonies of, 28
Spence, Thomas, 110
steam engines, 24, 95, 96, 98–99
Steeds, Mark, 185
Stephen, James, 170
strikes, in Barbados, 174
sugar: commerce in, 92–93; health and, 16, 90–91, 94; Industrial Revolution financed by exports of, 21; refining of, 94–95; tariff protections removed for, 109; transported by Royal African Company, 36
Sugar Act (Britain, 1764), 46
Sugar Duties Act (Britain, 1846), 109, 172
sugar trade, 14
surplus value, 159
Sutherland, Duchess of, 74

Taiping Rebellion (China, 1850-64), 163
taxation: in Barbados, 171; to finance compensation to slave owners, 133; on sugar trade, 14
Temin, Peter, 69
tenant farmers, 78, 171–72
Ten Years' War (1868-78), 99
Texas, 71
Texas Rangers, 86
textile industry, 93, 97, 108–9
Thelwall, John, 111–12

Thompson, E. P., 75, 79
Tillerson, Rex, 190
Tobago, 51
Toleration Act (Britain, 1812), 117
Tolpuddle Martyrs, 135
Tooke, John Horne, 111–12
Townsend, Joseph, 58
trade unions, 136; in British West Indies, 175–76; in cotton industry, 95, 96; racism in, 179
Trade with Africa Act (Britain,1697), 37
Transport and General Workers' Union (Wales), 90
Trenchard, John, 69
Trent Affair, 144
triangular trade, 45–47
Trollope, Anthony, 178
Turner, Mary, 119
Turner, Nat, 115
Tuscaroras (people), 49
Tyler, Imogen, 72

Union and Emancipation Society, 148
United Farm Workers of America (UFWA), 86
United Kingdom, 13; abolition of slavery in, 105–6; demands for reparations from, 9–10; *see also* Great Britain
United Nations, 25, 191–92
United States, 13; Civil War in, 107, 139–40, 143–50, 161; Indigenous people in, 184–85; Louisiana Purchase by, 102, 135; origins of policing in, 84, 85; as part of British Empire, 14
Utrecht, Treaty of (1713-14), 68

# INDEX

Vagrancy Act (Britain, 1824), 137
Vaughan, William, 81
Victoria (queen, England), 10
Virginia: Bacon's Rebellion in, 33; Nat Turner's rebellion in (1831), 115; slave patrols in, 84
Virginia Slave Code (1705), 33
Voce, Antonio, 183
Voth, Hans-Joachim, 69

wages, 187–88
Wales, 89
Walpole, Robert, 70, 79–80
Wapping Police Office (London), 83
Watt, James, 24, 95, 98
Wedderburn, Robert, 110
West India Dock (London), 67, 80–83, 107
West India Dock Company, 81
West Indies: after abolition of slavery, 167–68; agriculture in, 29; slavery in, 43–44; in triangular trade, 45
Westmoreland County Coal Strike (Pennsylvania, 1910-11), 85
Westo (people), 48
Weydemeyer, Joseph, 155, 156
Wharton, Duke of, 80
White people: introduction of term, 33; Marx on, 161–62; in settler colonies, 177–78
White supremacy, 33–34, 177
Whitney. Eli, 141
Wilberforce, Samuel, 145

Wilberforce, William, 112, 136; as abolitionist, 131, 137, 186; led campaign against British slave trade, 104; monument to, 183
William III (king, England), 60
William III (William of Orange; king, England), 36, 37
William IV (king, England), 131
Williams, Eric, 159; on abolition of slavery, 105; on capitalism and slavery, 11, 88; on mass movements, 104
Williamson, Samuel H., 27
Windrush scandal (Britain, 2018), 179–80
Windward Maroons (people), 126–27
Winthrop, John, 41–43
women: as antislavery activists, 113; in Barbados, 173; Davis on, 176–77; enslaved, 121–27; enslaved, sexual abuse of, 19; in postcolonial British West Indies, 176; as slave owners, 130
working class: in Britain, 139–40; in Britain, on U.S. Civil War, 147–48; definition of, 27; slavery opposed by, 21–22

Yamasee (people), 48
Yamasee War (1715-17), 50

Zahedieh, Nuala, 98
Zulu War (1879), 164